ROOTS OF RABBINIC JUDAISM

ROOTS OF RABBINIC JUDAISM

An Intellectual History, from Ezekiel to Daniel

GABRIELE BOCCACCINI

WILLIAM B. EERDMANS PUBLISHING COMPANY
GRAND RAPIDS, MICHIGAN / CAMBRIDGE, U.K.

© 2002 Wm. B. Eerdmans Publishing Co.
All rights reserved

Wm. B. Eerdmans Publishing Co.
255 Jefferson Ave. S.E., Grand Rapids, Michigan 49503 /
P.O. Box 163, Cambridge CB3 9PU U.K.

Printed in the United States of America

07 06 05 04 03 02 7 6 5 4 3 2 1

Library of Congress Cataloging-in-Publication Data

Boccaccini, Gabriele, 1958-
Roots of Rabbinic Judaism: an intellectual history, from Ezekiel to Daniel /
Gabriele Boccaccini.
p. cm.
Includes bibliographical references and index.
ISBN 0-8028-4361-1 (pbk.: alk. paper)
1. Judaism — History — Post-exilic period, 586 B.C.–210 A.D.
2. Priests, Jewish — History. I. Title.

BM176.B52 2002
296'.09'014 — dc21
2001051076

www.eerdmans.com

For Aloma

CONTENTS

ABBREVIATIONS

AB	Anchor Bible
ABD	*Anchor Bible Dictionary,* ed. David Noel Freedman
AGJU	Arbeiten zur Geschichte des antiken Judentums und des Urchristentums
AHR	*American Historical Review*
AJSR	*Association for Jewish Studies Review*
AnBib	Analecta biblica
APOT	*Apocrypha and Pseudepigrapha of the Old Testament,* ed. R. H. Charles
ASE	*Annali di storia dell'esegesi*
BA	*Biblical Archaeologist*
BAR	*Biblical Archaeology Review*
BEATAJ	Beiträge zur Erforschung des Alten Testaments und des antiken Judentum
BETL	Bibliotheca ephemeridum theologicarum lovaniensium
Bib	*Biblica*
BJS	Brown Judaic Studies
BRev	*Bible Review*
BZAW	Beihefte zur Zeitschrift für die alttestamentliche Wissenschaft
CBQ	*Catholic Biblical Quarterly*
CBQMS	CBQ Monograph Series
CRINT	Compendia rerum iudaicarum ad Novum Testamentum
DJD	Discoveries in the Judaean Desert
DSBP	*Dizionario di spiritualitá biblico-patristica,* ed. Salvatore A. Panimolle
EJ	*Encyclopaedia Judaica* (New York: Macmillan, 1971)
ErIsr	*Eretz Israel*

ExpTim	*Expository Times*
FOTL	The Forms of the Old Testament Literature
GCFI	*Giornale critico della filosofia italiana*
HDR	Harvard Dissertations in Religion
Hen	*Henoch*
Herm	Hermeneia
HeyJ	*Heythrop Journal*
HSM	Harvard Semitic Monographs
HTR	*Harvard Theological Review*
HTS	Harvard Theological Studies
HUCA	*Hebrew Union College Annual*
IEJ	*Israel Exploration Journal*
IHN	*Intellectual History Newsletter*
ITC	International Theological Commentary
JBL	*Journal of Biblical Literature*
JHI	*Journal of the History of Ideas*
JHP	*Journal of the History of Philosophy*
JJS	*Journal of Jewish Studies*
JMH	*Journal of Modern History*
JNES	*Journal of Near Eastern Studies*
JP	*Journal of Philosophy*
JSJ	*Journal for the Study of Judaism*
JSJSup	Journal for the Study of Judaism Supplement
JSOTSup	Journal for the Study of the Old Testament Supplement
JSPSup	Journal for the Study of the Pseudepigrapha Supplement
JTS	*Journal of Theological Studies*
MVHR	*Mississippi Valley Historical Review*
OBT	Overtures to Biblical Theology
OTL	Old Testament Library
OTP	*Old Testament Pseudepigrapha,* ed. James H. Charlesworth
OtSt	Oudtestamentische Studiën
PAAJR	*Proceedings of the American Academy for Jewish Research*
PAPS	*Proceedings of the American Philosophical Society*
PHR	*Pacific Historical Review*
RB	*Revue biblique*
RCSF	*Rivista critica di storia della filosofia*
RevQ	*Revue de Qumran*
RHR	*Revue de l'histoire des religions*
RivB	*Rivista biblica italiana*
RSB	*Ricerche storico-bibliche*
RSO	*Rivista degli studi orientali*
RSR	*Recherches de science religieuse*
RTL	*Revue théologique de Louvain*

SBLDS	Society of Biblical Literature Dissertation Series
SBLMS	Society of Biblical Literature Monograph Series
SBT	Studies in Biblical Theology
SJLA	Studies in Judaism in Late Antiquity
SNTSMS	Society for New Testament Studies Monograph Series
STDJ	Studies on the Texts of the Desert of Judah
SUNT	Studien zur Umwelt des Neuen Testaments
TBC	Torch Bible Commentaries
TThS	Trier theologische Studien
USQR	*Union Seminary Quarterly Review*
VT	*Vetus Testamentum*
VTSup	Supplements to VT
WMANT	Wissenschaftliche Monographien zum Alten und Neuen Testament
WUNT	Wissenschaftliche Untersuchungen zum Neuen Testament

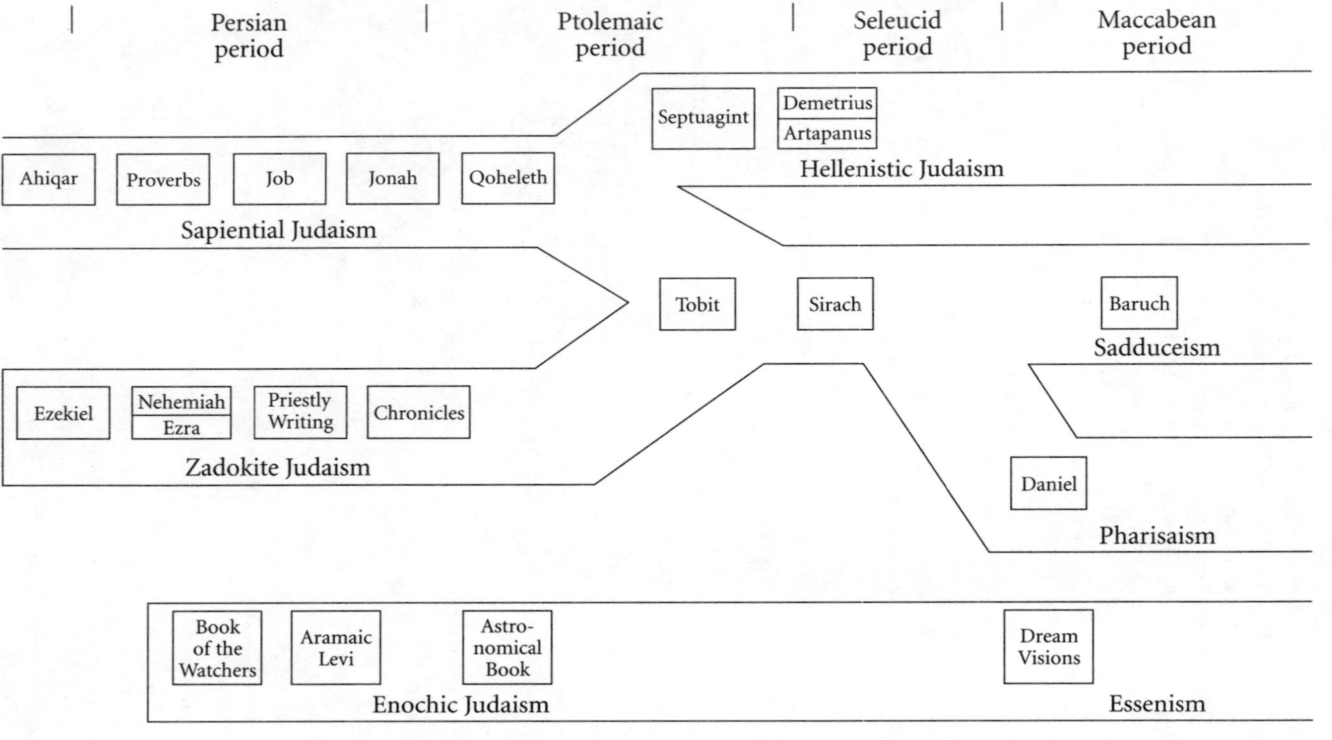

A Map of Ancient Judaism (6th cent. to 2nd cent. B.C.E.)

PREFACE

From Formative Judaism to Rabbinic Origins and Roots

The idea that already during the Second Temple period Rabbinic Judaism was normative or mainstream Judaism belongs to the history of scholarly research.[1] Specialists in Judaism of late antiquity now deem such an idea as anachronistic and rather agree that "the rabbinic literature is not the timeless and universal summary of Jewish belief that it was once taken to be."[2] Rabbinic Judaism was discontinuous with both Scripture, as it "represented a sustained and organized development and interpretation of the biblical traditions," and the Second Temple period, as "the shift from Second Temple Judaism to rabbinic Judaism [was] not a mere chronological transition but a substantive change."[3]

Far from being the trustees of the accepted tradition of Israel, the sages were the leaders of a bold reform movement that developed in the aftermath of the destruction of the Jerusalem temple and took its shape in

1. See Joachim Jeremias, *Jerusalem in the Time of Jesus: An Investigation into Economic and Social Conditions during the New Testament Period* (Philadelphia: Fortress, 1969); George Foot Moore, *Judaism in the First Centuries of the Christian Era: The Age of the Tannaim,* 3 vols. (Cambridge, Mass.: Harvard University Press, 1927-1930); Joseph S. Bonsirven, *Palestinian Judaism in the Time of Jesus Christ* (New York: Holt, Rinehart and Winston, 1964).

2. Mark Adam Elliott, *The Survivors of Israel: A Reconsideration of the Theology of Pre-Christian Judaism* (Grand Rapids: Wm. B. Eerdmans, 2000), 4.

3. Lawrence H. Schiffman, *From Text to Tradition: A History of Second Temple and Rabbinic Judaism* (Hoboken: Ktav, 1991), 1; and Shaye J. D. Cohen, *From the Maccabees to the Mishnah,* Library of Early Christianity 7 (Philadelphia: Westminster, 1987), 210.

the first centuries of the Common Era. "Through their distinctive literature and patterns of religion [the sages] gave Judaism a new form of expression. . . . The destruction of the Temple thus marked not only an end but also a beginning."[4]

At its inception, the rabbinic movement, with its theology and halakhah, was just one of several varieties of Judaism of the time, competing with, and being influenced by, other theological and halakhic systems. With their major competitors (namely, Christians and Hellenistic Jews) the sages engaged a life-or-death fight for supremacy and survival that would shape their own identity and ultimately decide the destiny of Israel. "Many of the Judaic worlds of Second Temple Judea and the Hellenistic Diaspora persisted for quite some time into the post–70 CE period and influenced rabbinic Judaism dramatically. . . . Rabbinic Judaism did not even begin to dominate the religious imagination and life patterns of large groups of Jews until the 3rd century CE at the earliest. And it did not finally succeed until well after 650 CE."[5] In fact, only during Islamic times was Rabbinic Judaism able to claim a clear victory within the entire Jewish people and become the norm, although neither totally exclusive nor unchallenged, of Jewish life.

The rise of Rabbinic Judaism as a reform movement out of the diverse world of Second Temple Judaism strikingly parallels that of its Christian sibling. The centuries from the Maccabean Revolt to the Jewish War were neither the end point of an already established monolithic Judaism before Jesus ("late Judaism"), nor the starting point of a linear process of evolution naturally leading to the rabbinic stage ("early Judaism"). Those centuries were the transitional and diverse age ("middle Judaism") of many competing Judaisms, in which both Christianity and Rabbinic Judaism had their "origins" in common "roots" in postexilic Jewish thought.[6] After the destruction of the Jerusalem temple, their ways gradu-

4. Shaye J. D. Cohen, "Roman Domination: The Jewish Revolt and the Destruction of the Second Temple," in Hershel Shanks, ed., *Ancient Israel: A Short History from Abraham to the Roman Destruction of the Temple*, rev. ed. (Washington: Biblical Archaeological Society, 1999), 265-98; cf. Cohen, "The Significance of Yavneh: Pharisees, Rabbis, and the End of Jewish Sectarianism," *HUCA* 55 (1984): 27-53.

5. Martin S. Jaffee, *Early Judaism* (Upper Saddle River, N.J.: Prentice-Hall: 1997), 18.

6. Gabriele Boccaccini, *Middle Judaism: Jewish Thought, 300 B.C.E to 200 C.E.* (Minneapolis: Fortress, 1991); cf. Hershel Shanks, ed., *Christianity and Rabbinic Juda-*

ally parted; "formative" Judaism and "formative" Christianity shared a destiny of struggle and competition before "the Judaism of the rabbis and the Christianity of the church fathers . . . emerged as . . . primary Western religions."[7]

These recent scholarly premises, which all stress the novelty of Rabbinic Judaism from Second Temple Judaism, have not eliminated the problem of the prehistory of the movement; they have only made it more intriguing. The elements of continuity are no less apparent than those of discontinuity. As Lawrence H. Schiffman argues, "Rabbinic Judaism represented the fruition of ideas already part of the earlier approaches, and provided an eventual rallying point around which a consensus emerged. . . . The Judaism of the rabbis of the Mishnah and Talmuds was deeply rooted in that of their predecessors."[8]

That some of the tenets of the rabbinic system predate the actual emergence of the movement is quite obvious. For example, the idea of covenant is as ancient as Scripture, and so are many foundational elements of what would become known as the rabbinic halakhah, while the notions of end of times and afterlife retribution go back at least to the Maccabean period.

That some elements of the rabbinic system are ancient, however, does not mean that the entire system is as ancient as the earliest of its constituent parts. A Christian basilica cannot be dated before Constantine's time because its actual columns, if not the entirety of its structural elements, were taken from a preexisting Roman building. Obviously, a system of thought, like a Christian basilica, cannot be earlier than the latest of its constituent parts. And we know that such important elements of Rabbinic Judaism as the preexistence of the Torah or the Sinaitic origin of the oral

ism: A Parallel History of Their Origins and Early Development (Washington: Biblical Archaeology Society, 1992); Alan F. Segal, *Rebecca's Children: Judaism and Christianity in the Roman World* (Cambridge Mass.: Harvard University Press, 1986); Jacob Neusner, *Judaism in the Beginning of Christianity* (Philadelphia: Fortress, 1984).

7. Schiffman, *From Text to Tradition,* 2; cf. Stephen G. Wilson, *Related Strangers: Jews and Christians, 70-170* (Minneapolis: Fortress, 1995); Jack T. Sanders, *Schismatics, Sectarians, Dissidents, Deviants: The First One Hundred Years of Jewish-Christian Relations* (Valley Forge: Trinity, 1993); James D. G. Dunn, *The Partings of the Ways between Christianity and Judaism and Their Significance for the Character of Christianity* (Philadelphia: Trinity, 1991).

8. Schiffman, *From Text to Tradition,* 4.

Torah are post-70 developments.[9] Furthermore, even when all the elements of a system of thought are proved to be available, it is only their assembly in a coherent whole that marks the birth of a new subject. This rule is valid in the history of architectural structures, as well as in the history of systems of thought. In vain would one search Second Temple Judaism for rabbinic documents or rabbinic institutions or evidence of rabbinic thought and halakhah — a hopeless task like finding a Christian basilica before Constantine. At the end of the 2nd century C.E., the Mishnah is the first evidence of the rabbinic system in its making and the founding document of all later rabbinic systems.[10]

Like Christianity, Rabbinic Judaism was not born overnight in a vacuum of ideas. This does not mean that there were rabbis and rabbinic institutions before Rabbinic Judaism, and Jesus-believers and Christian institutions before Christianity. Both Christians and the sages built their system of thought upon the foundations that other Judaisms had laid before them. The issue of antecedents and forerunners must be reexamined afresh, out of the founding myths each group developed to validate their existence and authority.

In a recent book, *Beyond the Essene Hypothesis,* I have expressed the view that the earliest "roots" of Christianity are to be traced in ancient Enochic Judaism, while its more immediate "origins" are to be found within the non-Qumran wing of the Essene movement, which was a post-Maccabean variant of the Enochic system.[11] Both historiographic and systemic analysis of Second Temple sources suggest that an analogous diachronic line of thought links Rabbinic Judaism back to Zadokite Judaism through the mediation of the Pharisaic movement. The very structure of the rabbinic canon also points to this conclusion; at the core of the Hebrew Bible are exclusively the documents written, edited, or collected by

9. See Gabriele Boccaccini, "The Preexistence of the Torah: A Commonplace in Second Temple Judaism, or a Later Rabbinic Development?" *Hen* 17 (1995): 329-50; E. P. Sanders, "Did the Pharisees Have Oral Law?" *Jewish Law from Jesus to the Mishnah* (Philadelphia: Trinity, 1990), 97-130; Mayer I. Gruber, "The Mishnah as Oral Torah: A Reconsideration," *JSJ 15* (1984): 112-22.

10. Lawrence H. Schiffman, "Mishnah: The New Scripture," *From Text to Tradition,* 177-200; cf. Jacob Neusner, *Judaism: The Evidence of the Mishnah* (Chicago: University of Chicago Press, 1981).

11. Gabriele Boccaccini, *Beyond the Essene Hypothesis: The Parting of the Ways between Qumran and Enochic Judaism* (Grand Rapids: Wm. B. Eerdmans, 1998).

the Jerusalem priesthood in the early Second Temple period, up to and including the book of Daniel, which signals, within the Zadokite system, a radical turning point toward the emergence of the Pharisaic system. The "roots" of Rabbinic Judaism are to be traced in the belief-system developed by the Second Temple priesthood under the leadership of the house of Zadok, while its more immediate "origins" are to be found within the Pharisaic tradition, which was a post-Maccabean variant of the Zadokite system.

The present volume explores those earliest "roots" of the rabbinic system of thought in the period from the Babylonian exile to the Maccabean Revolt, or from Ezekiel to Daniel. It was in this period that the scriptural idea of covenant developed to include the idea of afterlife retribution and the Mosaic Torah acquired cosmic dimensions thanks to its connection with the heavenly wisdom.

In a following publication I will deal with what more properly is to be defined as the period of rabbinic "origins," from the Maccabean Revolt to the establishment of the patriarchate, or from Daniel to the Mishnah. It was in this period that the ideas of covenant and afterlife retribution were supplemented by the ideas of the preexistence of the Torah and of the oral Torah. Only when these elements arose and were connected harmoniously in a coherent system of thought did Rabbinic Judaism emerge and enter its "formative" period.

My warmest thanks go to my publisher, Wm. B. Eerdmans, for their competence and enthusiasm in making this project possible, to the Department of Near Eastern Studies and the Frankel Center for Judaic Studies of the University of Michigan for giving me the perfect environment for teaching and research, to the distinguished colleagues of the Enoch Seminar and the "Italian Evenings" at the SBL for graciously sharing their wisdom and expertise, and above all, to my family and friends for their continuous support. Without trust, friendship and love, my research would never have been accomplished.

January 2001 GABRIELE BOCCACCINI

The Intellectual Quest of Rabbinic Origins and Roots

1. Back to Sinai: The Founding Myth of Rabbinic Judaism

The search backwards from "formative" Judaism to rabbinic "origins" and "roots" is a contemporary scholarly quest. Had one asked the ancient sages of Israel, the question would not have made much sense.

The opening of the treatise *'Abot* solemnly declares that "Moses received Torah at Sinai and committed it to Joshua, Joshua to elders, and elders to prophets. . . ." At the beginning, there were collective bodies of learned people and teachers — the elders, the prophets, and after them "the men of the great synagogue." Toward the end of this period of collective and anonymous teaching, Simeon the Righteous and Antigonus are singled out as, respectively, "one of the last survivors among the men of the great synagogue" and the disciple who received his teaching. Then came five pairs of sages, until Hillel and Shammai, to whom both the founding authorities of the Mishnah — the patriarchs and the sages — are connected. From Moses and Joshua, therefore, the Torah has been passed on from one generation to the next by a continuous chain of tradition, which links the Mosaic revelation to the authorities cited in the Mishnah itself and to their followers.[1]

The ordained and well-constructed structure of the opening chapters of *'Abot* betrays their function — to explain the Mishnah and to validate

1. On *'Abot,* see Frédéric Manns, *Pour lire la Mishna* (Jerusalem: Franciscan, 1984); Jacob Neusner, *Torah from Our Sages: Pirke Avot* (Chappaqua: Rossel, 1984).

its authority by giving its genealogy straight back to Sinai. The upshot is that Rabbinic Judaism is the normative form of Judaism since Moses' time. Its institutions have stood unchanged, parallel to all the other changing institutions of Israel (monarchy, priesthood), in the form of a single unbroken chain of teachers and disciples, and have not been affected by any of the dramatic changes (political, social, or religious) that marked the history of the Jewish people, especially during the Second Temple period.

For the sages, there is perfect synchrony between biblical and rabbinic origins. Rabbinic Judaism is as ancient as the Mosaic revelation; furthermore, it is the Mosaic Torah.

In their assumption of antiquity the sages found from the beginning an unlikely ally — the Christians. Far from being the object of denominational debate, the idea of the one Judaism became the balancing point of a difficult coexistence. From different points of departure and with different aims, both Rabbinic Judaism and Christianity needed the assumption of Judaism as an unchanging, unchanged, and unchangeable system — the Christians in order to confine Judaism within the boundaries of an "old" covenant, the sages in order to identify themselves with the only Judaism.[2]

For oppressed Jews, the paradigm served to emphasize their enduring fidelity to an ancient and unaltered tradition and polemically to sanction the complete otherness of Christianity (as well as any other "deviation") compared to the one Judaism. The so-called Christian fulfillment was nothing but estrangement, if not treachery and betrayal.

Paradoxically, in the opinion of triumphant Christians the same paradigm served to highlight the newness and uniqueness of Jesus of Nazareth, whose claim of fulfillment was seen as grafted onto an older religion at the end of its role as a "precursor." The so-called Jewish fidelity was nothing but an apathetic, demoded attitude, if not a guilty manifestation of stubbornness and disbelief.

The continuous fortune of Josephus (and of his Christian and Jewish doubles, Hegesippus and Josippon) kept alive the memory of ancient Jewish diversity up to the Middle Ages.[3] References to the Jewish sects are scat-

2. For a comparative analysis of the Christian and Jewish interpretations of Second Temple Judaism over the centuries, see Gabriele Boccaccini, *Portraits of Middle Judaism in Scholarship and Arts: A Multimedia Catalog from Flavius Josephus to 1991* (Turin: Zamorani, 1992).

3. The works of Flavius Josephus were known in the Middle Ages mainly through

tered in medieval Jewish and Christian chronicles; some authors, such as Epiphanius and Philastrius, Ibn Daud and Maimonides, occasionally even made them the center of some interest.[4] Yet, the "Jewish sects" caught no theological attention. The decisive dramatic conflict between the Synagogue and the Church, each so well defined in its respective role, certainly had no need for other, minor characters — in fact, they were quickly forgotten. The complex conflicts among rival groups in middle Judaism were turned into the lasting confrontation between two static and atemporal identities — the Christians of every time and every place against the Jews of every time and every place. Not accidentally, the most comprehensive treatment of ancient Jewish diversity would be offered in the Middle Ages outside both the Christian and the rabbinic tradition by the Karaite Abu Yusuf Yaqub al-Qirqisani (Kitab al-Anwar) at the beginning of the 10th century.[5]

The sages and the Christians also shared an interest in relating their Judaism directly to Scripture and to censuring any idea of a gradual development or theological evolution "from the Old Testament to the New Testament," or "from the Bible to the Mishnah." They pursued the same goal in a different way, the Christians emphasizing continuity between their tradition and Scripture in terms of prophecy/fulfillment, and the sages stressing the identity of their traditions with the Mosaic revelation. They both dismissed the importance of Second Temple Judaism as a time of theological insignificance.

---

the Latin translation by Rufinus (4th century). Two adaptations were even more popular: among the Christians, Hegesippus (4th century), and among the Jews, Josippon (10th century). See Vincenzo Ussani, ed., *Hegesippi qui dicitur historiae libri V*, 2 vols. (Vienna: Hoelder-Pichler-Tempsky, 1932-1960); and *Sepher Josiphon* (Jerusalem: Hominer, 1967).

4. See Adolf Neubauer, *Mediaeval Jewish Chronicles,* 2 vols. (1887-1895, repr. Amsterdam: Philo, 1970); August Potthast, *Wegweiser durch die Geschichtswerke des Europäischen Mittelalters bis 1500,* 2nd ed., 2 vols. (1896, repr. Graz: Akademische, 1954). On Epiphanius *(Panarion),* see Frank Williams, *The Panarion of Epiphanius of Salamis,* 2 vols., Nag Hammadi and Manichean Studies 35 (Leiden: Brill, 1987-1994). On Philastrius *(Liber de haeresibus),* see *Diversarum hereseon liber* (Turnhout: Brepols, 1991). On Ibn Daud *(Sefer ha-qabbalah),* see Gerson D. Cohen, ed., *Abraham ibn Daud, Sefer ha-qabbalah* (Philadelphia: Jewish Publication Society of America, 1967). On Maimonides *(Kitab es-Siraj),* see Yosef Kafah, *Mishnah ʿim perush Moshe ben Maimon,* 3 vols. (Jerusalem: Mosad ha-Rav, 1963-67).

5. Yaqub al-Qirqisani, *On Jewish Sects and Christianity* (Frankfurt: Lang, 1984).

Although the Christian *historia sacra* claimed its very beginning with the preexistent Christ and preempted the history of Israel as the history of the "Jewish Church," nevertheless it needed to contrast the times when the prophecies were issued and when they were fulfilled. According to the Christian view of history (to which Augustine and then Otto of Freising gave philosophical dignity), the events of Jewish history and religion after the closure of the Old Testament had no importance except as the historical setting preordained by God for Jesus' revelation.[6] A dark age served well to stage the miraculous coming of the true light from heaven. Second Temple Judaism was an intermission of stagnation and silence before Christ came to earth and the establishment of the Christian Church superseded a single uniform Judaism.

Although the rabbinic *historia sacra* claimed continuity between the sages and Sinai, nevertheless it also needed a break in order to avoid any compromise or interference by rival institutions, which would have challenged the exclusive authority of the sages. The relationship between Moses and Joshua cuts off Aaron and his descendants, thus allowing the chain of rabbinic tradition to bypass the hereditary line of Jewish priesthood, that is, the central institution of Second Temple Judaism. The incidental inclusion of the Zadokite high priest Simon the Righteous even sharpens the contrast. He received Torah not as a high priest but as one of the last survivors of the men of the great synagogue, and committed Torah not to his son along with the priesthood, but to a disciple, Antigonus. The result was the creation of an alternative and autonomous genealogy that is inclusive of the ancient religious institutions of Israel (prophecy, priesthood), yet remains autonomous and untouched by historical events and nonrabbinic influence. Continuity was reached in terms of survival of the Sinaitic tradition vis-à-vis and in spite of the complex historical social and intellectual developments of Judaism in the Second Temple period.

The agreement of Christian and Jewish traditions over against the ancient origins of Rabbinic Judaism has made the emancipation of critical scholarship from the theological model of the one Judaism remark-

6. On Augustine of Hippo *(De civitate dei)*, see Robert W. Dyson, *The City of God against the Pagans* (Cambridge: Cambridge University Press, 1998). On Otto of Freising *(Historia de duabus civitatibus)*, see Charles Christopher Mierow, *The Two Cities: A Chronicle of Universal History to the Year 1146 A.D.* (New York: Columbia University Press, 1928).

ably slow and hesitant. When in the second half of the 17th century Baruch Spinoza in his *Tractatus theologico-politicus* openly questioned the Mosaic origins of Scripture as well as the reliability of the rabbinic chain of tradition back to Sinai, his work faced the same hostility and outrage by his contemporaries, both Christians and Jews.[7] Even when it became impossible not to bow to the fact that the Torah was "Mosaic" only in the sense of being a mosaic of traditions, the idea of a single Judaism proved to be stronger than any historical criticism. However obscure and mythical the origins of Scripture might have been, the synchrony between the oral and the written Torah was not challenged. It seemed sound to hold that by the time of Ezra at the latest the rabbinic tradition existed and had become normative, at least among the sages of Israel. The very idea of a search for "rabbinic origins" was ruled out. Textual criticism and archaeology — it was believed — would have certainly not failed to provide the earliest evidence of rabbinic traditions and institutions. It would take a long time before modern scholars dared challenge such an established paradigm.

However, the rise of critical scholarship soon produced a first, important turn. Until the 17th century, Christian theologians and preachers had used postbiblical Jewish literature and history only occasionally, for missionary ends against the Jews.[8] Now the same sources were studied for apologetical reasons in order to confirm the "credibility" of the New Testament.[9] As a result of the new critical interest in history and philology, Christian theology began to admit that, to a certain extent, postbiblical Ju-

7. See Benedictus de Spinoza, *Tractatus Theologico-Politicus,* trans. Samuel Shirley (Indianapolis: Hackett, 1998).

8. Raimundus Martini, *Pugio Fidei adversus Mauros et Judaeos,* 3 vols., ca. 1270-1280; Porchetus de Salvaticis, *Victoria adversus impios Hebraeos,* 1303; Petrus Galatinus, *De archanis catholicae veritatis, contra obstinatissimam Iudaeorum nostrae tempestatis perfidiam* (Ortona, 1518).

9. Christopher Cartwright, *Mellificium Hebraicum,* 5 vols. (London, 1649); John Lightfoot, *Horae Hebraicae et Talmudicae,* 6 vols. (Cambridge: J. Field, 1658-1674); Nathaniel Lardner, *The Credibility of the Gospel History; or, The Facts Occasionally Mentioned in the New Testament, Confirmed by Passages of Ancient Authors Who Were Contemporary with Our Saviour or His Apostles, or Lived near Their Time* (London: Gray, 1727); Christian Schoettgen, *Horae Hebraicae et Talmudicae in Universum Novum Testamentum* (Dresden: Christoph Hekel, 1733); Blasio Ugolino, *Thesaurus Antiquitatum Sacrarum,* 34 vols. (Venice, 1744-1769).

daism served to prepare for the coming of Jesus. God's providence acted in the Second Temple period to create the right conditions for the acceptance of the Christian message. The age "from Malachi to Jesus" then emerged as a distinct historical period: it was the necessary "connection" between the Old and the New Testament. In 1716, a retired English ecclesiastic, Humphrey Prideaux, turned a neglected appendix of biblical history into an autonomous and successful genre, which "may serve as an epilogue to the Old Testament in the same manner as . . . a prologue to the New." Reprinted dozens of times, translated into French, German, and Italian, Prideaux's work would rule the scene for more than one century; his notion of "intertestamental history" has not passed away yet.[10]

The interest of Christian scholarship in the religious life of the Jews for the period when Jesus was born increased in the 19th century; *neutestamentliche Zeitgeschichte* became an established field of research.[11] This scholarly interest did not result, however, in a more appreciative approach to Judaism. On the contrary, the spread of anti-Semitic attitudes, which came to dominate European culture particularly after the second half of the 19th century, added to the legacy of medieval religious anti-Judaism to make most Christian scholars even harsher in their contempt of Second Temple Judaism. What was previously seen as a time of stagnation came more and more to be regarded as a time of religious decadence. After the Babylonian exile and the decline of prophecy, Judaism regressed from its biblical premises to become "in the age of Jesus" the legalistic and

10. Humphrey Prideaux, *The Old and New Testament Connected in the History of the Jews, and Neighbouring Nations; from the Declension of the Kingdoms of Israel and Judah to the Time of Christ,* 2 vols. (London: Knaplock & Tonson, 1716-18); cf. Samuel Cradock, *The History of the Old Testament Methodiz'd: to Which Is Annexed a Short History of the Jewish Affairs, from the End of the Old Testament to the Birth of Our Saviour* (London: T. Simmons, 1683); Laurence Howel, *A Compleat History of the Holy Bible, in Which Are Inserted the Occurrences That Happened during the Space of about Four Hundred Years, from the Days of the Prophet Malachi to the Birth of Our Blessed Saviour,* 3 vols. (London: J. Nutt, 1716).

11. Étienne Rimond, *Recherches sur les opinions religieuses des Juifs à la venue du Messie* (Geneva, 1830); Aurelio Bianchi-Giovini, *Storia degli ebrei e delle loro sette e dottrine religiose durante il secondo tempio* (Milan, 1844); Joseph Langen, *Das Judenthum in Palästina zur Zeit Christi* (Freiburg, 1866); Adolf Hausrath, *Neutestamentliche Zeitgeschichte,* 3 vols. (Heidelberg: F. Bassermann, 1868-1874); 2nd ed., 4 vols. (1873-77).

sanctimonious religion against which the Christ had to fight and over which his followers now were still committed to claim superiority. The term *Spätjudentum* ("late Judaism") appeared the most appropriate — chronologically and morally — to denote this period.[12]

Even in the face of such derogatory attacks, the reaction of Jewish scholars, or actively pro-Jewish scholars like George Foot Moore, was significantly ambiguous; while defending the validity of the one Judaism, they showed little interest in defending the religious value of the Second Temple period. Against the *neutestamentliche Zeitgeschichte*, the *jüdische Wissenschaft* concentrated on the cultural importance of this period in the long, glorious, and not yet concluded history of the Jewish people. The rise and influence of Zionism added a political touch to this otherwise theologically insignificant age: after all, the Second Temple period was the last glorious time of Jewish independence and self-government in the land of Israel — the time of the Second Jewish Commonwealth.[13]

The Second World War and the Holocaust shook even the most insulated consciences. In France, Jules Isaac denounced the Christian teaching of contempt, which preached the religious "end" of Judaism. His appeal was heard by the conference of Seelisburg in 1947 and by the Vatican Council in 1965; the two events mark the formal debut of contemporary Jewish-Christian dialogue at the grassroots and the official level, respectively.[14] The

12. Emil Schürer, *Lehrbuch des Neutestamentlichen Zeitgeschichte* (Leipzig: J. C. Hinrichs, 1874); 2nd ed., *Geschichte des jüdischen Volkes im Zeitalter Jesu*, 3 vols. (1886-1890; 3rd ed., 1898-1901; 3rd-4th ed., 1901-9; 4th ed., 1911); Wilhelm Baldensperger, *Das spätere Judenthum als Vorstufe des Christenthums* (Giessen, 1900); Alfred Bertholet, *Das religionsgeschichte Problem des Spätjudentums* (Tübingen, 1909); Wilhelm Bousset, *Die religion des Judentums im neutestamentlichen Zeitalter* (Berlin: Reuther & Reichard, 1903; 2nd ed., 1906); 3rd ed., *Die Religion des Judentums im späthellenistichen Zeitalter*, ed. Hugo Gressmann (Tübingen: Mohr, 1926).

13. Heinrich H. Graetz, *Geschichte der Juden von den ältesten Zeiten bis auf die Gegenwart*, 11 vols. (Leipzig: Leiner, 1870-1897); *History of the Jews*, 6 vols. (Philadelphia: Jewish Publication Society of America, 1891-98); Simon Dubnow, *Weltgeschichte des jüdischen Volkes*, 10 vols. (Berlin: Jüdischer Verlag, 1925-1930); *History of the Jews* (South Brunswick: T. Yoseloff, 1967-1973); Solomon Zeitlin, *The History of the Second Jewish Commonwealth: Prolegomenon* (Philadelphia: Dropsie College, 1933).

14. See Jules Isaac, *Jesus and Israel* (New York: Holt, Rinehart and Winston, 1971); *The Teaching of Contempt: Christian Roots of Anti-Semitism* (New York: Holt, Rinehart and Winston, 1964). On the history of contemporary Jewish-Christian dialogue, see John Rousmaniere, *A Bridge to Dialogue: The Story of Jewish-Christian Relations* (New

discovery of the Dead Sea Scrolls was timely, opening up broad, unanticipated horizons of research and fostering a renewed interest in ancient Jewish literature other than rabbinic. This did not mean the immediate collapse of the single-Judaism model. Postwar scholarship retreated to less controversial notions of intertestamental or New Testament history; the "new Schürer" revised critically the work of previous generations.[15] The most derogatory traits having now being removed, the time was ripe for a reappraisal of Second Temple Judaism as a dynamic age of Jewish diversity and creativity and the common cradle of both Christianity and Rabbinic Judaism. The Jewish monolith began to show its first cracks.[16]

2. From Judaism to Judaisms: Four Scholarly Models

The 1970s are the turning point in the study of rabbinic origins. Full confidence in the continuity of the tradition between the Bible and the Mishnah was still expressed by scholars like Louis Finkelstein, Alexander Guttmann, and Jacob Weingreen. "Some passages in rabbinic literature . . . probably date back to the Babylonian exile or even earlier. . . . The Syna-

York: Paulist, 1991); Leon Klenicki and Geoffrey Wigoder, eds., *A Dictionary of the Jewish-Christian Dialogue,* rev. ed. (New York: Paulist, 1995).

15. Charles F. Pfeiffer, *Between the Testaments* (Grand Rapids: Baker, 1959); D. S. Russell, *Between the Testaments* (Philadelphia: Muhlenberg, 1960); Bo Reicke, *The New Testament Era* (Philadelphia: Fortress, 1968); F. F. Bruce, *New Testament History* (London: Nelson, 1969); Eduard Lohse, *Umwelt des Neuen Testament* (Göttingen: Vandenhoeck & Ruprecht, 1971); Emil Schürer, *The History of the Jewish People in the Age of Jesus Christ,* rev. Geza Vermes and Fergus Millar, 3 vols. (Edinburgh: T. & T. Clark, 1973-1987).

16. See Erwin R. Goodenough, *Jewish Symbols in the Greco-Roman Period,* 13 vols. (New York: Pantheon, 1953-1968); Morton Smith, "Palestinian Judaism in the First Century," in *Israel: Its Role in Civilization,* ed. Moshe Davis (1956, repr. New York: Arno, 1970), 67-81; James W. Parkes, *The Foundations of Judaism and Christianity* (Chicago: Quadrangle, 1960); Beryl D. Cohon, *Men at the Crossroads between Jerusalem and Rome, Synagogue and Church: The Lives, Times, and Doctrines of the Founders of Talmudic Judaism and New Testament Christianity* (South Brunswick: T. Yoseloff, 1970). For a pioneering emphasis on Jewish diversity, see Isaac M. Wise, *History of the Hebrews' Second Commonwealth with Special Reference to Its Literature, Culture, and the Origin of Rabbinism and Christianity* (Cincinnati: Bloch, 1880); and George H. Box, "The Jewish Environment of Early Christianity," *ExpTim* 42 (1916): 1-25.

gogue service came into being before the Babylonian Exile. . . . As early as the beginning of the fourth century B.C.E. the Pharisaic movement was in full vigor as an effort to establish the authority of the lay scholars."[17]

But the 1970s are also the decade in which two revolutionary contributions on Pharisaism were published — Ellis Rivkin's *A Hidden Revolution* and Jacob Neusner's *From Politics to Piety.*[18] Rivkin and Neusner placed a different emphasis on the role of the Pharisees and so gave a different reconstruction of rabbinic origins, but they both agreed on one point: Rabbinic Judaism was a reform movement that became normative at a relatively late stage in Jewish history, in postbiblical times. Be this stage either the Maccabean War or the destruction of the Second Temple, the synchrony between biblical and rabbinic origins was definitively broken, and so the notion of a single Judaism.

The term *Frühjudentum* ("early Judaism") established itself in the 1970s and early 1980s as an attempt to voice this new understanding of Second Temple Judaism not as a time of stagnation or regression but as a creative and dynamic age of new beginning. James H. Charlesworth went straight to the point: "As 'Early Christianity' signifies the origins of Christianity, so 'Early Judaism' denoted the beginning of synagogal (modern) Judaism."[19] The breakdown with the polemical concerns that originated the single-Judaism model could not be expressed more effectively: what once was "late" was now labeled "early."

The last 20 years of scholarship have wiped out any residual confidence about the immutability of Rabbinic Judaism and its normativeness in the Second Temple period. The unbroken normative tradition from

17. Louis Finkelstein, *Pharisaism in the Making: Selected Essays* (New York: Ktav, 1972), v-vii; cf. Alexander Guttmann, *Rabbinic Judaism in the Making: A Chapter in the History of the Halakhah from Ezra to Judah I* (Detroit: Wayne State University Press, 1970); Jacob Weingreen, *From Bible to Mishna: The Continuity of Tradition* (Manchester: Manchester University Press, 1976).

18. Ellis Rivkin, *A Hidden Revolution: The Pharisees' Search for the Kingdom Within* (Nashville: Abingdon, 1978); and Jacob Neusner, *From Politics to Piety: The Emergence of Pharisaic Judaism* (New York: Ktav, 1979).

19. James H. Charlesworth, *The Old Testament Pseudepigrapha and the New Testament,* SNTSMS 54 (Cambridge: Cambridge University Press, 1985), 59; cf. Johann Maier and Josef Schreiner, eds., *Literatur und Religion des Frühjudentums* (Würzburg: Echter, 1973); Robert A. Kraft and George W. E. Nickelsburg, eds., *Early Judaism and Its Modern Interpreters* (Atlanta: Scholars, 1986).

Moses to the Mishnah has been unveiled for what it is — nothing more than an ideological construct without any historical foundation, no less artificial than the Christian *historia sacra.* From the common recognition of the novelty of Rabbinic Judaism and diversity of Judaisms in the Second Temple period, four different scholarly approaches have emerged about what Judaism is and what its origins are — four models that will be illustrated here through the works of those scholars who have come better to represent them, namely, E. P. Sanders, Lawrence H. Schiffman, Shaye Cohen and Martin Jaffee, and Jacob Neusner.

(a) According to E. P. Sanders, any discourse about Jewish diversity and historical changes regards the accidents, not the essence, of Judaism.[20] Sanders strongly rejects "the assumption that Judaism was *divided* into parties,"[21] that is, that there may have been not one Judaic system but many. Underneath the diversity of Second Temple Judaism he recovers the profound unity of "common Judaism" as "that of the ordinary priests and the ordinary people. . . what was *common* in two senses: agreed on among the parties, agreed on by the populace as a whole."[22] The result of Sanders's "common-denominator theology" is the conceptualization of the essence of Judaism as "covenantal nomism."[23]

In Sanders's perspective, there is a profound difference between Christian and rabbinic origins. "Common Judaism" comprises Jesus, not his movement, as Paul's system is not simply diverse but incompatible with the ideological boundaries of Judaism. The emergence of Christianity with Paul represents the birth of a new essence other than "covenantal nomism." On the contrary, the emergence of the rabbinic stage does not signal a breakthrough but the continuation of "common Judaism" under different historical forms and circumstances. Accidents may change, but in its essence Judaism has no history: over the centuries, beyond the plurality of its diverse historical manifestations, Judaism was, is, and remains "covenantal nomism."

20. See E. P. Sanders, *Paul and Palestinian Judaism* (Philadelphia: Fortress, 1977); *Jesus and Judaism* (Philadelphia: Fortress, 1985); *Jewish Law from Jesus to the Mishnah* (Philadelphia: Trinity, 1990); *Judaism: Practice and Belief, 63 BCE–66 CE* (Philadelphia: Trinity, 1992).

21. Sanders, *Judaism,* 11.

22. Sanders, *Judaism,* 11-12.

23. Sanders, *Paul and Palestinian Judaism.*

(b) Lawrence H. Schiffman parts from Sanders as he unreservedly accepts the dynamism and pluralism of Judaism and the existence of different groups: "Judaism is not a monolithic phenomenon."[24] Schiffman also, however, supports the idea of an intellectual unity of Judaism over the centuries. The claim is that the different groups "shared sufficient common ground as to be classified as one, albeit variegated, religious tradition."[25] Judaism is the result of a continuous process of evolution; its unity is demonstrated not by the permanence of an unchanged "essence" but by the gradual and consistent evolution and synthesis of its diverse ideological systems into a mainstream tradition. In other words, while Sanders stresses that the essence of Judaism remains unchanged in spite of its history, Schiffman claims that the essence of Judaism is its history.

The evolutionary model is by far more flexible than Sanders's common-denominator theology. Evolution gave room to diversity, discontinuity, and dead possibilities before mainstream Judaism found its natural course: "continuity can only be achieved in a tradition which adapts and develops."[26] The historian's task is to "see the various approaches to Judaism as standing in a dynamic and interactive relationship to one another" and to recognize "what each period and approach bequeathed to that which came after. . . . Rather than subdividing and compartmentalizing the phenomenon we call Judaism, we prefer to understand the complex historical processes which led the whole, composite and dynamic as it was, to develop in the directions that it did."[27] Out of the Judaisms of the Second Temple period, "the rise of the rabbinic form of Judaism . . . was no accident. The Judaism that emerged at the end of the Talmud era had been chosen by a kind of natural selection process in the spheres of history and religion."[28]

Schiffman's evolutionary model offers a less conflicting framework to study the parallel birth of Christianity and Rabbinic Judaism. Christianity also was part of Judaism, until the latter reached the rabbinic stage of its evolution. Having missed the chance to develop within mainstream Juda-

24. Lawrence H. Schiffman, *From Text to Tradition,* 2; cf. *Texts and Traditions: A Source Reader for the Study of Second Temple and Rabbinic Judaism* (Hoboken: Ktav, 1998).

25. Schiffman, *From Text to Tradition,* book jacket.

26. Schiffman, *From Text to Tradition,* 3.

27. Schiffman, *From Text to Tradition,* 4-5.

28. Schiffman, *From Text to Tradition,* 15.

ism, Christianity faced the alternative either to die or to develop, as it did, thanks mostly to Paul, as a separate religion.

(c) Shaye J. D. Cohen and Martin S. Jaffee offer a very interesting variant of the evolutionary model. With Schiffman, Jaffee agrees that "Judaism is misunderstood by viewing it as a single body of doctrine and practice originating pure and whole in a flash of revelation."[29] Yet, Jaffee is skeptical that the unity of Judaism can be found on an abstract intellectual level. He rejects Schiffman's approach itself as teleological and ultimately apologetical: neither is Judaism "a straight evolutionary line culminating inevitably in a victorious rabbinic Judaism."[30] In its stead, Jaffee sees "patterns of disharmony and points of intellectual and social stress, a picture of flux and experiment, rather than one of continuity and broadly recognized authority."[31] Cohen agrees: "Judaism changed dramatically during the Persian, Hellenistic, Maccabean, Roman, and rabbinic periods. . . . In addition, at any given moment Jews practiced their religion in manifold different ways."[32]

Neither Jaffee nor Cohen denies, however, that the historian's primary task is "to see the unity within the diversity."[33] This common ground is provided not by an intellectual unity as Sanders and Schiffman seek, but by the ethnic bond that links the Jewish people to its religious expressions. "Like the bumblebee which continues to fly, unaware that the laws of aerodynamics declare its flight to be impossible, the Jews of antiquity saw themselves as citizens of one nation and one religion, unaware of, or oblivious to, the fact that they were separated from each other by their diverse languages, practices, ideologies, and political loyalties."[34] Judaism therefore is neither its unchangeable essence, nor its ever-changing intellectual evolution; Judaism is the history of its people. Judaism is "the religious behavior of all people who call themselves and are known to others as Jews, Israelites, and Hebrews," or "a religious world inhabited by people who regard themselves as physical descendants of the Israelites."[35] Judaism is its Jewishness.

29. Martin S. Jaffee, *Early Judaism,* 245.

30. Jaffee, 246.

31. Jaffee, 246.

32. Shaye J. D. Cohen, *From the Maccabees to the Mishnah,* 24.

33. Cohen, *From the Maccabees to the Mishnah,* 26.

34. Cohen, *From the Maccabees to the Mishnah,* 26.

35. Cohen, *From the Maccabees to the Mishnah,* 135; and Jaffee, 19.

The search for rabbinic origins is then the search for the early manifestations of the ethnic bond between the Jewish people and its religion (Jaffee's "early Judaism"), or as Cohen has effectively titled his latest major contribution, the "beginnings of Jewishness."[36]

Like Schiffman's intellectual model, Cohen and Jaffee's historical model has the advantage of accommodating both Christian and rabbinic origins, and offering an explanation of their separating. For Schiffman, Christianity was discarded by the process of intellectual evolution itself, after serving as an antithesis till the emergence of a superior synthesis. Cohen and Jaffee instead describe Christianity as a variety of Judaism that ceased to be such when it broke its bond with the Jewish people: "Early Christianity ceased to be a Jewish sect when it ceased to observe Jewish practices. It abolished circumcision and became a religious movement overwhelmingly gentile in composition and character."[37] Jewishness was in fact an original, yet only temporary, feature of Christianity. Once again, Paul is the prime suspect. By claiming that "ethnic distinctions between Jew and Greek were meaningless," Paul "made the vertical and horizontal axes of Jewish symbolic thought [the Messiah and the Torah] collapse into one another."[38] On the contrary, the sages "achieved a balance between its vertical and horizontal axes that seems to have been rare in other worlds of early Judaism."[39] Outside the Jewish people there is no Judaism; all Judaisms, in order to be defined as such, must share the feature of being ethnically Jewish. Neither for preserving the Jewish "essence" uncontaminated, nor for reaching the most perfect synthesis of Judaic thought, but for keeping the ethnic bond, "the rabbis were the 'winners'of ancient Jewish history."[40]

(d) Jacob Neusner's approach is characterized by his renunciation of defining any essence or unity, intellectual or historical, of Judaism. "The issue, how to define Judaism, is now settled: we do not. We define Judaisms. . . . There never was, in real, social terms, that single Judaism,

36. Shaye J. D. Cohen, *The Beginnings of Jewishness: Boundaries, Varieties, Uncertainties* (Berkeley: University of California, 1999).

37. Cohen, *From the Maccabees to the Mishnah,* 168.

38. Jaffee, 152, 154.

39. Jaffee, 121.

40. Cohen, *From the Maccabees to the Mishnah,* 18.

there were only the infinite and diverse Judaic systems, as various social entities gave expression to their way of life, worldview, and theory of the social entity they formed."[41]

There is no Judaism but, in today's world as well as in the past, only Judaisms — a set of parallel systems in competition. The fundamental characteristic of Judaism is its fragmentary nature, that is, the constant coexistence of a plurality of groups, movements, and traditions of thought. Such discontinuity and fragmentation cannot be overlooked and brought back to continuity and unity, to an atemporal essence, or to the boundaries of a single incremental tradition. Each Judaism must be studied historically in its own terms and not as part of a metaphysical whole. "Whether we deal with a long period of time, such as a millennium, or a brief period of just a few centuries, the picture is the same. . . . Judaisms flourished side by side. Or they took place in succession to one another. Or they came into being out of all relationship with one another."[42]

As the history of Judaism is the history of Judaisms, the model greatly simplifies the relationship between Christianity and Rabbinic Judaism as that between two autonomous systems of thought that just happened to emerge synchronically and flourished "side by side." Neusner's approach cuts short as a theological problem the question whether or not, and until when, Rabbinic Judaism and Christianity belonged to the same whole and concentrates instead on the diversity of their systems of thought in relation to one another.

Neusner's approach has already left its clear imprint on Judaic studies ("from Judaism to Judaisms") and the indication of a much promising method of studying rabbinic origins and roots as a comparison of systems of thought that "took place in succession to one another."[43]

41. Jacob Neusner, *The Judaism the Rabbis Take for Granted* (Atlanta: Scholars, 1994), 12, 18.

42. Jacob Neusner, William Scott Green, and Ernest S. Frerichs, eds., *Judaisms and Their Messiahs at the Turn of the Christian Era* (Cambridge: Cambridge University Press, 1987), xii.

43. Jacob Neusner, *The Four Stages of Rabbinic Judaism* (London: Routledge, 1998); cf. Neusner, ed., *Judaism in Late Antiquity,* 4 vols. (Leiden: Brill, 1995).

3. The Rise of Intellectual History

In order to understand fully the implications of these four competing approaches to the history of Judaism, we must look at the broader picture of the contemporary debate about the methods of writing history of philosophical or religious phenomena.[44]

In the trajectory of Western civilization, it was first the philosopher (not the historian) who began studying the history of thought as a branch of philosophical enterprise. And it was first the theologian (not the historian) who began studying the history of religion as a branch of theological enterprise. Theologians' and philosophers' histories have contributed significantly to our civilization; they stand among the greatest accomplishments of human genius. It was not curiosity about what people thought or believed, however, that prompted the study of intellectual phenomena; it was not in fact as history that the past of philosophy and religion aroused interest. Coherently with their own agenda, philosophers and theologians looked at ancient authors with the goal of finding support for or defending (what they held to be) the Truth, the religious or philosophical Orthodoxy to which they were bound, and rejecting (what they held to be) the (many) Errors, the religious or philosophical Heresies or Sects. They looked at the diversity of philosophical or religious systems as "a museum of eccentricities of the human mind,"[45] disrupting the atemporal unity of philosophy and religion. As such, the study of philosophy and religion was set apart from cultural and social history, which was maintained to be properly the only domain of the historian. Any attempt at crossing the boundaries was felt as a threat and an illegitimate intrusion. The Truth stands beyond any temporal limitation; only the Errors have a history.

It would take centuries before the fields of religion and philosophy were opened to purely historical investigation and intellectual history was allowed to determine for itself how the ordinary rules of historical criticism should be applied to philosophical and religious phenomena. Historical criticism was born in the 17th century from the same intellectual movement as the philosophy of Descartes. The Cartesian methodological

44. A comprehensive bibliography on the subject is provided at the end of the volume.

45. Émile Bréhier, "Introduction," *The History of Philosophy,* 1: *The Hellenic Age* (Chicago: University of Chicago Press, 1963), 1-33 (quotation 13).

doubt tested the reliability of traditions and accepted interpretations of their interposition between the past and its modern interpreters. Baruch Spinoza's *Tractatus theologico-politicus* (1670) is one of the first and highest expressions of the new critical approach.

Spinoza attacked philosophers and theologians for imposing on ancient texts their own ideas. "They have expressed boundless wonder at Scripture's profound mysteries, yet I do not see that they have taught anything more than the speculations of Aristotelians or Platonists, and they have made Scripture conform to these as to avoid appearing to be the followers of heathens. . . . Most of them assume as a basic principle for the understanding of Scripture and for extracting its true meaning that it is throughout truthful and divine — a conclusion which ought to be the end result of study and strict examination."[46]

Instead of subordinating the historical truth to rules previously laid down, Spinoza advocated a method that "allows no other principles or data for the interpretation of Scripture and study of its contents except those that can be gathered only from Scripture itself and from a historical study of Scripture. . . . It is not permissible for us to manipulate Scripture's meaning to accord with our reason's dictates and our preconceived opinions."[47]

Spinoza's method opened the study of religion and philosophy to historical inquiry and laid the foundations for a history of religion and a history of philosophy free from subjection to theology and philosophy. With historical criticism leaning toward diversity and fragmentation in the presentation of the past manifestation of the human mind, and Immanuel Kant showing in his *Critique of the Pure Reason* (1781) how reason itself allows the possibility of a plurality of divergent metaphysical theories, the question arose as to how the fact that philosophy has a history is compatible with its being true. Can there be a unity behind diversity?

Kant maintained that behind the diversity of philosophical systems are the a priori possibilities of thought, as they are given us by reason. Philosophical systems may diverge, yet there is philosophy only where there is rational thought. Historical inquiry is necessary to identify the period and civilization in which philosophical systems are born and the different intentions of people who use them, but philosophy in itself is only accidentally connected with historical conditions.

46. Spinoza, *Tractatus Theologico-Politicus*, 5.
47. Spinoza, *Tractatus Theologico-Politicus*, 89, 92.

The emergence, in the 18th century, of the idea of progress led to the assertion that there was a unity in the evolution of all manifestations of the human spirit. Such an idea of progress made appear too narrow and obsolete an approach to the history of philosophy as a history of ideas solely produced by the natural laws of the mind in isolation from conditions of period and civilization.

George Wilhelm Friedrich Hegel offered a different solution to the problem of the unity of philosophy with a dynamic perspective that made philosophy the ultimate result of historical evolution, which multiplies choices before selecting the predominant. "The history of philosophy makes clear, in the different philosophies which appeared, that there is only a single philosophy at different stages of development, and also, that the particular principles on which a system rests are only divisions of one and the same whole. The newest philosophy to evolve is the result of all preceding philosophies and must contain the principles of all of them; for this reason, it is the most unfolded, the richest, and the most concrete one."[48] As a result, the bond between philosophy and its history was strongly emphasized and the history of philosophy was celebrated as an essential part of the philosophical process. The Hegelian approach gave an unprecedented dignity to history but allowed no autonomy to the history of philosophy apart from its teleological frame, and even more strongly than in the past barred the historian's way to the philosopher's domain. It seemed that history had no alternative than losing its autonomy in order to see recognized its dignity, or losing its dignity in order to see recognized its autonomy.

The roots of intellectual history as a historical discipline autonomous from theology and philosophy, yet legitimate in its interpreting the religious and philosophical phenomena of the past, are to be traced back to the philosophical debate in the first half of the 20th century between Hegelians and anti-Hegelians about the relationship between philosophy and its history. The theoretical issue was whether history belongs to the essence of philosophy or is simply one of the accidents of philosophy. The debate would challenge consolidated paradigms and lay the foundations of contemporary intellectual history.

In the first half of the 20th century, the Hegelian concept of unity of history and philosophy led some of his followers (notably the Italian

48. G. W. E. Hegel, *Encyklopädie der philosophischen Wissenschaften* (Heidelberg: Osswald, 1817), no. 13.

Benedetto Croce) to develop the idea of the identity of history and philosophy. "The history of philosophy is philosophy, philosophy that is fully self-conscious and therefore aware of the way in which has evolved and was formed philosophy that, by thinking over, assesses and defines the stages of its history."[49] More strongly than ever, any legitimacy was denied to "philological history" and to "the historian, empty of philosophy." According to Croce, the history of thought is only the philosopher's business. "The philosopher . . . in the very act of philosophizing is a historian, the only true historian of human thought."[50]

In Europe, the catalysts of the opposition to Hegel were the French philosophers and historians of philosophy, like Léon Robin and Émile Bréhier. They looked at history and philosophy as two distinct and autonomous forms of knowledge and struggled to keep philosophy uncontaminated and pure, far from any historical accident. Their view of the relation between philosophy and history sharply contrasted with that of the Hegelians. "The history of philosophy is a history of ideas — ideas that get systematized into doctrines. . . . The history of philosophy . . . is philosophy, but philosophy philosophizing over its past efforts and contemplating itself in the eternity of its mutable existence."[51]

Without the task of discovering the immutable ideas — the continuity of the spiritual life — history alone is nothing but "the curiosity of the pedant," and the historical approach "the approach to a cemetery, to a field of ruins."[52]

Within such a framework, it was possible, however, to recognize the autonomy of history, while proclaiming the untouchable superiority of philosophy. As Bréhier used to say: "Truly, the philosopher has a history, philosophy has not."[53] The object of the history of philosophy, therefore,

49. Benedetto Croce, *Il carattere della filosofia moderna* (Bari: Laterza, 1941), 57.

50. Croce, 60.

51. Léon Robin et al., "Sur la notion d'histoire de la philosophie," *Bulletin de la Société française de la philosophie* 36 (1936): 103-406 (quotation, 107); "L'histoire et la légende de la philosophie," *Revue philosophique de la France et de l'Étranger* 120 (1935): 161-75 (quotation, 175).

52. Robin, *Revue philosophique de la France et de l'Étranger* 120 (1935): 174; and Léon Brunshvicg, in Robin et al., *Bulletin de la Société française de la philosophie* 36 (1936): 120.

53. Émile Bréhier, *La philosophie et son passé* (Paris: Presses universitaires de France, 1940), 74.

is not "philosophy" but "the philosophers" in all the diversity of their social and intellectual manifestations. "There are no longer either 'sects' as in the Renaissance, or systems as in Cousin, or 'collective mentalities' which the historian aims to reach. There are individuals, in all the varied richness of their intelligence."[54] Such a humanistic shift had profound consequences.

First, the Hegelian view of the historical unity of philosophy was rejected as "a postulate which can only be accepted with the philosophy of which it is a part."[55] The history of philosophy cannot be replaced by a philosophy of history, based on the apriorism that "history is oriented toward a doctrine which it contains potentially."[56] Where the Hegelians saw unity and continuity, Bréhier stressed diversity and discontinuity: "a ceaseless and continuous progress is quite contrary to historical reality. . . . The truth is that the course of intellectual life is, so to speak, extremely tortuous."[57]

Second, granted that historians cannot accomplish the superior philosophical task of searching the unity of philosophy — a task that goes beyond the possibilities of their method — yet they have the right to apply without any restrictions the rules of historical criticism to the plurality of intellectual phenomena. Philosophy must welcome unreservedly the autonomous and creative contribution of history in the interpretation of intellectual events and texts, and shall not refuse to acknowledge its legitimacy. "The battle of Marengo is a historical fact. But the philosophy of Descartes is a historical fact too. . . . The historian of Descartes's thought has to use the same methodology as the historian of the battle of Marengo."[58]

Bréhier's conclusion was a strong call against the Hegelian method as the only means to pursue an authentic history of philosophy that would not confuse history and philosophy, plurality and unity, accidents and essence. "In spite of the brilliance of Hegel's gifts as an historian of philosophy, in spite of the fact that many of his views still command admiration to-day, in spite even of his great personal learning, the history of philoso-

54. Bréhier, "Introduction," 26.
55. Bréhier, "Introduction," 23.
56. Bréhier, "Introduction," 32.
57. Bréhier, "Introduction," 30.
58. Bréhier, *La philosophie et son passé,* 34-35.

phy could only advance if it freed itself from a master of such formidable genius."[59]

In the United States, in the first half of the 20th century, the debate of Hegelians vs. anti-Hegelians was as topical and controversial as in Europe. In 1938, Sterling P. Lamprecht and John Herman Randall clashed on the issue at the Symposium on "Historiography of Philosophy" given at a meeting of the American Philosophical Association.[60] The American landscape, however, was enriched by the presence of two important and influential protagonists: the so-called American intellectual history and the History of Ideas.

When in 1903 James Harvey Robinson offered a course at Columbia University entitled "The History of the Intellectual Class in Europe," the event marked the recognition of a new and very successful field of history. American intellectual history took two fundamental steps. First, it made the history of thought a branch of history. For the first time an approach to the history of philosophy was initiated and accomplished by scholars, trained as historians, who continued to be historians and considered themselves as such, not philosophers. "The intellectual historian's approach . . . is different from that of the philosopher. . . . What primarily interests him is not the values of ideas in the ultimate scheme of things . . . but their development and relation to each other in time, how and why they appear and spread at a particular time, and their effects on concrete historical situations."[61] Second, American intellectual history promoted a strong interdisciplinary approach by claiming that the history of philosophy ought not to be separated from the other ("nonphilosophical") manifestations of human thought. "Ideally, at least, the history of thought embraces not only theology, philosophy, the natural and social sciences, but also belles-lettres, the fine arts, and popular literature of all sorts."[62]

59. Émile Bréhier, "The Formation of Our History of Philosophy," in *Philosophy and History*, ed. Raymond Klibansky and Herbert J. Paton (1936, repr. New York: Harper & Row, 1963), 159-172 (quotation, 171).

60. See Sterling P. Lamprecht, "Historiography of Philosophy," *JP* 36 (1939): 449-60; John Herman Randall, "On Understanding the History of Philosophy," *JP* 36 (1939): 460-74.

61. Franklin L. Baumer, "Intellectual History and Its Problems," *JMH* 21 (1949): 191-203 (quotation, 191-92).

62. Baumer, 191.

In spite of their purely historical and interdisciplinary approach, American intellectual historians retained the philosophical, Hegelian ideal of the search for "the climate of opinion or the *Zeitgeist* of particular periods of history" — for what they called the evolving unity of "the American mind" as they saw it emerging and growing autonomously from "the European mind."[63]

The publication in 1936 of Arthur O. Lovejoy's *The Great Chain of Being* marks the beginning of yet another influential trend in the history of philosophy that soon would find its expression in the *Journal of the History of Ideas.*[64] A philosopher turned historian, Lovejoy shared the same interdisciplinary, critical, and nonconformist approach as the American intellectual historians. In the first issue of the new journal, Lovejoy would reiterate that "the processes of the human mind . . . do not run in enclosed channels corresponding to the officially established divisions of university faculties."[65] The freedom from traditional boundaries is highlighted as one of the major points in the agenda of the new movement. "It is hoped that the journal will serve — among other things — as a useful medium for the publication of researches which traverse the customary boundary-lines."[66]

In his view of the history of philosophy, Lovejoy strongly rejected any kind of synthetic analysis and the consequent categories created by philosophers and historians of philosophy: "These large movements and tendencies . . . conventionally labeled -isms, are not as a rule the ultimate objects of the interest of the historian of ideas; they are merely the initial materials."[67] In Lovejoy's view, the ideas from which philosophical systems are formed are inert materials of mental edifices which can be demolished and whose primary elements (the "unit-ideas") have been used again and again, just as they are, in other constructions. "There are . . . many unit-ideas . . . which have long life-histories of their own, are to be found at work in the most various regions of the history of human thinking and feeling, and upon which the intellectual and affective reactions of men —

63. Baumer, 192.

64. Arthur O. Lovejoy, *The Great Chain of Being: The Study of the History of an Idea* (Cambridge, Mass.: Harvard University Press, 1936). Lovejoy launched the *Journal of the History of Ideas* in 1940.

65. Arthur O. Lovejoy, "Reflections on the History of Ideas," *JHI* 1 (1940): 3-23 (quotation, 4).

66. Lovejoy, *JHI* 1 (1940): 7.

67. Lovejoy, *The Great Chain of Being,* 182.

individuals and masses — have been highly diverse. . . . Until these units are first discriminated, until each of them which has played any large role in history is separately pursued through all the regions into which it has entered and in which it has exercised influence, any manifestation of it in a single region of intellectual history, or in an individual writer or writing, will, as a rule, be imperfectly understood — and will sometimes go unrecognized altogether."[68]

By rejecting any Hegelian search for *Zeitgeist* or any collective mentalities and shifting the emphasis from the philosophical systems to their constituent parts, Lovejoy offered a refreshing counterbalance to the organicistic and nationalistic approach that so distinctively characterized the beginnings of American intellectual history. However, Lovejoy also retained a philosophical assumption in the concept that human thought is made of pure, unchangeable elements (the "unit-ideas") to such an extent that he used to describe his methodology as being "somewhat analogous to that of analytic chemistry."[69]

After World War II, all these different anti-Hegelian trends, European and American, would finally come together, and as a result of their converging efforts intellectual history would emerge as an autonomous branch of historical enterprise.

In the United States, the followers of Lovejoy, under the leadership of George Boas, concentrated their historical attention on the more comprehensive analysis of intellectual phenomena and their relationship with social phenomena.[70] American intellectual history also was defining itself more and more as "intellectual history," abandoning the neo-Hegelian and metaphysical reference to the historical unity and uniqueness of the "American mind." The articles of John Higham and John C. Greene can be taken as representative of the new climate of the 1950s.[71]

Intellectual history is now clearly defined as "a branch of history" whose scope is limited by its own method and not by philosophical apriorisms. "Intellectual history differs from other varieties [of history]

68. Arthur O. Lovejoy, "The Historiography of Ideas," *PAPS* 78 (1938): 529-43.

69. Lovejoy, *The Great Chain of Being,* 179.

70. See George Boas, ed., *Studies in Intellectual History* (Baltimore: Johns Hopkins University Press, 1953).

71. John Higham, "Intellectual History and Its Neighbors," *JHI* 15 (1954): 339-47; John C. Greene, "Objectives and Methods in Intellectual History," *MVHR* 44/1 (1957): 58-74.

simply because it has a distinctive subject-matter. It concentrates on experiences occurring inside men's heads. . . . Intellectual history is unlimited in scope, but it should respect the historian's method."[72] The debate about the predominance of internal or external causes in the development of intellectual phenomena is solved in the recognition that both aspects must be considered and that the emphasis on external analysis must not resolve into one organicistic approach that denies diversity. "The [historical] process involves both analysis and synthesis. . . . It becomes apparent . . . that there was not just *one* pattern of thought in the epoch, but that there were several, some dominant, the others subdominant, incipient, or vestigial."[73] As for the search for collective and national identities, the call is to avoid any form of "chauvinism and . . . parochialism": "America for the Americans; Europe for the Europeans. This Monroe Doctrine in intellectual history is entirely untenable. . . . American thought is but an aspect of Western thought. . . . In short, the American intellectual historian must be first and foremost an intellectual historian and only secondarily an American historian."[74]

In Europe, Bréhier's call for emancipation from the Hegelian method was met by a new generation of historians led by Marc Bloch and Lucien Febvre.[75] The French *nouvelle histoire* not only vindicated its autonomy from any philosophy of history, but also claimed to have the dignity and right of submitting any manifestation of humankind, social and intellectual, to historical inquiry without any concern for philosophical essences. Tired of waiting for the philosopher to decide the degree of autonomy and dignity of history, the French historians cut the umbilical cord and took their destiny into their own hands.

But it was in Italy (not accidentally, since Italy had been the stronghold of Hegelianism) that the settling of old scores between Hegelians and anti-Hegelians had to be accomplished on the philosophical level. It was a real battle, fought on the pages of the *Rivista di filosofia,* the *Rivista critica di storia della filosofia,* and the *Giornale critico della filosofia italiana,* with

72. Higham, 340.

73. Greene, 60.

74. Greene, 72, 68, 71.

75. Marc L. B. Bloch, *Apologie pour l'histoire; ou, Métier d'historien* (Paris: A. Colin, 1949); trans. Peter Putnam, *The Historian's Craft* (New York: Knopf, 1953); Lucien P. V. Febvre, *Combats pour l'histoire* (Paris: A. Colin, 1953).

dozens of important philosophical contributions. A new generation of philosophers, led by Eugenio Garin, attacked and demolished, in article after article, the philosophical premises of the Hegelian unity of history and philosophy.[76] In a pivotal article published in 1959, Garin summarized the results of the revolution in three major points.[77]

First, any philosophical apriorism in the history of philosophy must be rejected. The relationship between philosophy and history must be reversed: "not the history of philosophy after philosophy, but philosophy after the history of philosophy."[78] The historian of philosophy has no philosophy but the rules of the historical method.

Second, intellectual history cannot be separated from social and political history. "It cannot be taken for granted that the antecedents of a philosopher are in the philosophy. . . . Internal analysis of the development of philosophy is completely sterile and irrelevant if the dialectic is meant as pure movement of ideas that are generated by ideas. . . . History cannot be done if not in a perspective that studies ideas and their histories, and the unfolding of systems and how issues urge and vary — against their human roots — their rhythms within the people's conscience, in the actualities of the people's real life."[79]

Third, the concept of unity of philosophy has no foundation, either on the historical or on the philosophical level. "In philosophy we cannot seriously talk, at any time, of an ultimate philosophy, one and true: as many and diverse philosophies, each excluding the other, all claim to be the ultimate and only true one."[80] Consequently, historians of philosophy have to learn to think and talk in plural terms: the object of the history of philosophy is neither "philosophy," as the Hegelians claimed, nor the "philosophers" only, as Bréhier suggested, but "the philosophies" in the complexity of their relations with individual and social life. "The multiplicity of philosophical systems is as ancient as philosophy. . . . Since in every moment of the [historical] process the actual present is diverse and polycentric, the ideas that express the aspirations [of the present], and the systems that give

76. Eugenio Garin, *La filosofia come sapere storico* (Bari: Laterza, 1959); cf. Arrigo Pacchi, *Definizione e problemi della storia della filosofia* (Milan: UNICOPLI, 1985).

77. Eugenio Garin, "Osservazioni preliminari a una storia della filosofia," *GCFI* 38 (1959): 1-55.

78. Garin, *GCFI* 38 (1959): 4.

79. Garin, *GCFI* 38 (1959): 39, 42, 49.

80. Garin, *GCFI* 38 (1959): 9.

structure to the cultural articulations [of the present], cannot help being diverse, in conflict with one another or in peaceful coexistence. There is not in one epoch only one idea, but many ideas and systems."[81] The motto "from philosophy to philosophies" would become the mark of Garin's revolution.

Thanks to the convergent efforts of European and American philosophers and historians, intellectual history established itself in the 1950s as an autonomous and dignified branch of historical enterprise. Ever since, the debate about the method and the philosophical foundations of the history of philosophy has continued and continues today, as intensely and creatively as ever, in particular due to the influence and challenge of postmodernist theories.[82] The "linguistic turn" has questioned the validity of intellectual history as well as of any historical reconstruction of the past, stressing that the historical method is itself an a priori.[83] As the contemporaneous debate greatly enhances the philosophical dimension of the historical work, it is even more remarkable that intellectual historians have chosen to engage in the discussion primarily as historians, and no longer, as it was mostly the case before the 1950s, as philosophers competing with rival philosophies.[84] The emancipation of intellectual history from philosophy stands today as a consolidated achievement of Western civilization.

81. Garin, *GCFI* 38 (1959): 21-23.

82. See Georg G. Iggers, *Historiography in the Twentieth Century: From Scientific Objectivity to the Postmodern Challenge* (Hanover: Wesleyan University Press, 1997); Peter Augustine Lawler, *Postmodernism Rightly Understood: The Return to Realism in American Thought* (Lanham: Rowman & Littlefield, 1999).

83. See Dominick LaCapra, *Rethinking Intellectual History* (Ithaca: Cornell University Press, 1983); LaCapra and Steven L. Kaplan, eds., *Modern European Intellectual History: Reappraisals and New Perspectives* (Ithaca: Cornell University Press, 1982); Martin Jay, *Force Fields: Between Intellectual History and Cultural Critique* (London: Routledge, 1993).

84. John E. Toews, "Intellectual History after the Linguistic Turn: The Autonomy of Meaning and the Irreducibility of Experience," *AHR* 92 (1987): 879-907; David A. Hollinger, "The Return of the Prodigal: The Persistence of Historical Knowing," *AHR* 94 (1989): 610-21; Donald R. Kelley, *The History of Ideas: Canon and Variations* (Rochester: University of Rochester Press, 1990); Murray G. Murphey, *Philosophical Foundations of Historical Knowledge* (Albany: State University of New York Press, 1994).

4. An Intellectual History of Judaism

It is striking to note how closely the contemporary debate about the history of Judaism has repeated, 50 years later, the same forms and models that animated worldwide in the first half of the 20th century the debate about the rise of intellectual history. Sanders's search for Jewish essence behind the accidents of history, Schiffman's evolutionary and teleological model, as well as Jaffee's and Cohen's emphasis on the selective and unifying power of the "Jewish mind" demonstrate that the quest for the unity of Judaism touches upon a very sensitive point in contemporary Jewish identity — no less sensitive than the quest for the unity of philosophy was in modern philosophy.

The similarity of solutions may be striking, yet not surprising. The emancipation of the history of religion from theology is a by-product of the same cultural changes that have caused the emancipation of the history of thought from philosophy. The process was irreversible, and the outcome simply inevitable; the delay must be attributed only to the natural tendency of established theological models to last longer and vanish less rapidly than philosophical models. Even the lack of a methodological debate comparable to the controversies that accompanied in the 1950s the rise of intellectual history must not be viewed with surprise. Everything that theoretically had to be said has been already said — methodologically speaking, there is not much to be added.

As an intellectual historian educated in Florence at the school of Eugenio Garin, I have great sympathy with the general principles of his methodology, and great respect and admiration for the one who has first consistently applied these principles to the study of ancient Jewish thought, the doyen of Italian scholarship in Second Temple Judaism and my former teacher at the University of Turin, Paolo Sacchi.[85] Sacchi's historiographical work, with its emphasis on the relationship between "spiritual experiences" and "historical events,"[86] offers a remarkable example of intellectual history, which is fully respectful of the diversity of an-

85. Paolo Sacchi, *The History of the Second Temple Period,* JSOTSup 285 (Sheffield: Sheffield Academic, 2000); *Storia del Secondo Tempio: Israele tra vi secolo* A.C. *e i secolo* D.C. (Turin: Società Editrice Internazionale, 1994); *Storia del mondo giudaico* (Turin: Società Editrice Internazionale, 1976).

86. Sacchi, *The History of the Second Temple Period,* 27.

cient Jewish thought, as well as of the complex intellectual and social interactions among different "currents" or movements.

A student of intellectual history cannot help having a deep interest and curiosity in the contemporary international debate about the history of Judaism, and in Neusner's work in particular. Neusner's revolution "from Judaism to Judaisms" is comparable to Garin's revolution "from philosophy to philosophies." The principles of Neusner's method are the ones that more closely meet the requirements of contemporary intellectual history, and the most convenient starting point for further discussions about the theoretical foundations of an intellectual history of Judaism. Yet, Neusner's approach also has its own flaws, in particular its patent inability to engage in a constructive dialogue with other approaches and its disturbing tendency to freeze and isolate each variety of Judaism from the others in almost impermeable systems.

My work on "middle Judaism" is an attempt to study Judaisms, in themselves and in the complexity of their diachronic developments and synchronic relations, according to the methodological principles of intellectual history I derived mostly, but not exclusively, from the Italian school.[87] I believe that our understanding of ancient Jewish thought can only benefit from a more constant and consistent application of the criteria commonly used by intellectual historians in the study of the development of competing philosophical systems. Middle Judaism is the common matrix within and from which two world religions took their form, Christianity and Rabbinism. It is also the bridge where the East met the West, laying the foundations of Western civilization. My goal is to elaborate an intellectual history of ancient Jewish thought, methodologically commensurable and compatible with the parallel history of ancient Greco-Roman thought, so that the contribution of both traditions and the diversity and richness of their respective components may be highlighted and compared.

I have devoted books and articles to this methodological task.[88] Here I

87. Gabriele Boccaccini, *Middle Judaism.*

88. Boccaccini, *Middle Judaism; Portraits of Middle Judaism;* "History of Judaism: Its Periods in Antiquity," in *Judaism in Late Antiquity,* ed. Jacob Neusner, 4 vols. (Leiden: Brill, 1995), 2: 285-308; "Middle Judaism and Its Contemporary Interpreters (1986-1992): Methodological Foundations for the Study of Judaisms, 300 BCE to 200 CE," *Hen* 15 (1993): 207-33; "Middle Judaism and Its Contemporary Interpreters (1993-1997): What Makes any Judaism a Judaism?" *Hen* 20 (1998): 349-56.

would like only to address briefly three major issues which are crucial for a correct definition of the problem of rabbinic roots and origins.

A. *From Canons to Judaisms; or, From the Study of Parallels and Literary Genres to the Identification of "Communities of Texts"*

The major obstacle to the study of ancient Jewish thought is ironically not the lack of documentation but the way in which sources have come down to us, grouped into denominationally determined corpora, or canons (the Hebrew Bible or Old Testament, the New Testament, the Apocrypha and Pseudepigrapha, the Dead Sea Scrolls, etc.). In our Christian-influenced civilization, such denominational division has given birth to a denominationally divided scholarship with clear boundaries between Christian and Judaic studies, canonical and noncanonical studies. To a large extent, each corpus still lives its own separate, self-sufficient existence, with its own specialists, journals, bibliographies, and audience. The canonical status of a document, more than any intrinsic historical value, is still the best warranty of success: it secures a high frequency of editions and commentaries, the presence in the programs of universities and seminaries, and a predictable and consolidated degree of popularity among readers.

Contemporary critical scholarship is no longer bound by canonical or denominational divisions. There is now a growing awareness also in the general public that Christian and Jewish sources cannot be studied apart from one another, or canonical documents in isolation from the noncanonical. Yet, so serious a problem as the existence of canons cannot be solved by simply balancing the specific weight of each corpus and giving an introduction, distinct research tools, or even the dignity of a theology to each and every collection. Canons and corpora make sense only in relation to the epoch and ideology in which they were born, and tell us the fascinating history of how ancient texts were collected, selected, and handed down to us, and how religious groups found identity and legitimacy in the process. Canons and corpora, however, are misleading in their interposition between the sources (their author, their age, their worldview) and modern interpreters. What is the point of studying and teaching sources within a framework that creates a posteriori affinities while separating originally related texts? A denominational criterion for collecting sources is not a criterion for understanding their original content.

The problem will not be solved until the focus of attention is shifted from the corpora to the documents themselves. Documents need to be freed from the cages of their anachronistic corpora and rearranged, according to purely historical criteria, into collections that more closely correspond to the texts' original function as ideological expressions of competing forms of ancient Judaism. In so doing, the interpreter should not be afraid of, or surprised by, finding forgotten connections or unexpected distances, new hierarchies or unsettling marginalities, supporting roles elevated to protagonists and protagonists reduced to supporting roles. A hard and fascinating task is before us: hundreds of texts — one of the most impressive amounts of literature coming to us from antiquity — still need to be classified, document by document, as ideological records of competing forms of Judaism.

The task of regrouping documents according to their original ideological relations is based neither on the amount of parallels nor on their sharing the same literary genre.

Four centuries of search for parallels have made evident the many transcanonical links among documents, and eventually the necessity of placing early Christianity within Judaism. This methodological approach first emerged in the 17th century, when Christian scholars began to use Jewish postbiblical literature to gain a better understanding of the New Testament, and flourished in the following centuries.[89] By the middle of the 20th century, however, it became clear that the method was drifting into an inconclusive "parallelomania." Samuel Sandmel defined it as "that extravagance among scholars which first overdoes the supposed similarity in passages and then proceeds to describe source and derivation as if implying literary connection flowing in an inevitable or predetermined direction."[90]

89. For the earliest examples of such a scholarly tradition, see above n. 9. The climax was reached in the first half of the 19th century with the publication of Hermann L. Strack and Paul Billerbeck, *Kommentar zum Neuen Testament aus Talmud und Midrasch*, 6 vols. (Munich: Beck, 1922-1961); and the launching of Gerhard Kittel and Gerhard Friedrich, eds., *Theologisches Wörterbuch zum Neuen Testament,* 10 vols. (Stuttgart: Kohlhammer, 1933-1973); trans. Geoffrey W. Bromiley, *Theological Dictionary of the New Testament* (Grand Rapids: Wm. B. Eerdmans, 1964-1974).

90. Samuel Sandmel, "Parallelomania," *JBL* 81 (1962): 1-13.

While parallels are misleading in establishing ideological similarities and dissimilarities among documents, they testify to the complexity of interaction and confrontation among parallel systems of thought. Hunting ideas means entering the fascinating and capricious universe of synchronic relations, cultural influences, and dependencies from a common heritage. As Lovejoy used to say: "Ideas are the most migratory things in the world."[91] Ideas are the raw ingredients that are borrowed, exported, adapted, recycled within different systems of thought, cooked according to the most diverse recipes.

Ideas are not systems of thought. The same ideas or traditions often happen to play completely different roles in different documents. Conversely, ideologically related documents can use different ideas and traditions to express the continuity of the same ideological system. This has been well stated by E. P. Sanders: "One may consider the analogy of two buildings. Bricks which are identical in shape, color, and weight could well be used to construct two different buildings which are totally unlike each other."[92] Ideas and traditions are not Judaisms, but constituent elements of Judaisms.

From the identification and study of parallel ideas and traditions, scholars turned to the identification and study of larger units — the literary genres. The result has been the creation of new collections of ancient texts parallel to the traditional corpora. We have now a vast scholarly literature that focuses on transcanonical groups of apocalyptic texts, wisdom texts, mystical texts, halakhic texts, etc.[93] Many documents have been given a universally recognized double citizenship that has created new and dynamic links among them: the same collection of apocalyptic literature includes the pseudepigraphic 1 Enoch, the Old Testament Daniel, and the New Testament Revelation, while the pseudepigraphon Ahiqar, the Old Testament Qoheleth, and the apocryphon Sirach belong to the same collection of wisdom literature.

The grouping and study of ancient texts according to their literary genre has contributed significantly to our understanding of the role these

91. Lovejoy, *JHI* 1 (1940): 4.

92. Sanders, *Paul and Palestinian Judaism,* 13.

93. The work of John J. Collins on apocalypticism is an example and a model of study of an ancient Jewish literary genre. See *The Apocalyptic Imagination: An Introduction to Jewish Apocalyptic Literature,* 2nd ed. (Grand Rapids: Wm. B. Eerdmans, 1998).

literary genres and their respective worldviews played in ancient Judaism, and has shown that the traditional canons are not the only way in which the literature can be grouped. Furthermore, the recognition of a literary connection has often been the first step in the rediscovery of ideological affinities among documents. However, classifying and analyzing the history and worldview of literary genres is not the same as identifying systems of thought. What John J. Collins says about apocalypticism, that "neither was it peculiar to a particular sect or the product of a single movement,"[94] applies to every literary genre (mysticism, wisdom, halakhah, etc.). The fact that two documents share the same worldview does not mean that they belong to the same form of Judaism. Conversely, documents belonging to the same form of Judaism expressed the same system of thought by using different literary genres. Literary genres are not Judaisms, but worldviews that shaped, influenced, or were used by different varieties of Judaisms.

Neither the abundance of parallels nor the sharing of the same literary genre (or worldview) is therefore enough to determine an ideological connection among documents. Only a holistic comparison of systems of thought can do so.

Systemic analysis is an interdisciplinary enterprise, aiming at a comprehensive assessment of the ideological relations among ancient sources.[95] By borrowing criteria commonly used in the study of intellectual history (or history of philosophy), systemic analysis offers a reliable methodology both to deconstruct the traditional corpora and reconstruct the original relations among documents. By taking into consideration the complexity of literary, sociological, historical, and ideological factors, it establishes a continuum among groups of related writings, thus identifying a variety of synchronic "chains of documents" or "communities of texts" that correspond to different varieties of ancient Judaism.

Systemic analysis is limited by the quantity of surviving documents, by their state of preservation, and by the historical probability or accident of their survival. The identification of a chain of documents does not nec-

94. John J. Collins, *Apocalypticism in the Dead Sea Scrolls* (London: Routledge, 1997), 8.

95. See my work on middle Judaism, above n. 88. Cf. Jacob Neusner, *Wrong Ways and Right Ways in the Study of Formative Judaism: Critical Method and Literature, History, and the History of Religion,* BJS 145 (Atlanta: Scholars, 1988), 44-55; *The Systemic Analysis of Judaism,* BJS 137 (Atlanta: Scholars, 1988).

essarily mean that all texts are directly linked to one another but that the documents belong to the same trajectory of thought. Missing links and chronological gaps make impossible a complete mapping of ancient Judaisms and their documents. However, the study of ancient Jewish literature can only benefit from this process of regrouping ancient sources. A significant advance will be made once the original "communities of texts" are reconstructed and take permanently in contemporary scholarship the place that is now illegitimately occupied by the anachronistic corpora. A scholarly controlled collection, although imperfect and incomplete, is far more reliable than any denominational canon for a reconstruction of ancient Jewish thought. Where a text belongs does not depend on theological, unchangeable assumptions but on scholarly consensus; it is and will always remain an open question, susceptible of further inquiry.

B. *Unity vs. Diversity; or, What Makes Any Judaisms a Judaism?*

The emphasis that the subject of our research is primarily Judaisms does not remove the problem of defining "Judaism." As Philip R. Davies argues: "the replacement of the concept of 'Judaism' by the concept of 'Judaisms' solves one problem only to create another, perhaps even more fundamental one — namely what it was that made any 'Judaism' a Judaism. . . . The plural 'Judaisms' requires some definition of 'Judaism' in the singular, in order itself to have any meaning."[96] In other words: Which elements make it possible to characterize a system of practice and belief as a Judaism?

Both E. P. Sanders and Schiffman offer an a priori unity, which Garin would call "a philosophy before the history of philosophy." Sanders's books are a mine of knowledge for those who want to learn more about the changing accidents of Jewish religion and society from one of the most distinguished contemporary interpreters of Judaism. However, the common-denominator approach in which Sanders has so much confidence cancels differences and creates an essence ("covenantal nomism") that historically never existed.[97] Schiffman is definitively correct when he points

96. Philip R. Davies, "Scenes from the Early History of Judaism," in *The Triumph of Elohim: From Yahwisms to Judaisms,* ed. Diana Vikander Edelman (Grand Rapids: Wm. B. Eerdmans, 1995), 145-82 (quotation, 147, 151).

out that we cannot "isolate each Judaism from the others, not only from those that existed at the same time, but also from those that came before."[98] However, forcing the diversity of Judaism into a single line of evolution is a Hegelian enterprise, aimed to present one's own tradition, philosophy, or religion as the providential synthesis of historical processes.

By linking Judaism to Jewishness, Cohen's and Jaffee's model seems to suggest a more descriptive and less aprioristic answer to what belongs or does not belong to Judaism. Historically Judaism was born within the Jewish people and is the product of the "Jewish mind." However, from the point of view of intellectual history, it is hard to understand why the loss of ethnicity should make a Judaism cease to be a Judaism. The identification between Judaism and the Jewish people was the conscious choice of some ancient Judaisms and one of the reasons for the strength and lasting success of Rabbinic Judaism. But history offers many and diverse examples of relationships between religion and ethnicity in Judaism. An intellectual history of Judaism is not one and the same with an intellectual history of the Jewish people. Historically, we have Judaisms without Jewishness and Jewishness without Judaism. The two fields of research, although interwoven, should be kept separated.

Christianity is a case in point. The Christians' religious world offers an example of a Judaic world that, in its own view as well as in the eyes of Jews, is not part of Judaism. Neither the Christians nor the Jews regard the religious world of the Christians as continuous with Judaism. But a reciprocal excommunication cannot cancel the truth of their common origin, nor has it the authority to sanction before the tribunal of history that a Judaism is no longer a Judaism. The Christian and the rabbinic system of thought are certainly distinct and very different from one another. The debate over which of them is the authentic development of Judaism (that is, the "true Israel") belongs to denominational polemics. "Had Judaism been monolithic," writes Sacchi, "then Christianity could only have inherited from Judaism or broken away from it. But, if Judaism contained various different and at times opposite tendencies within itself, then our comprehension of the Christian phenomenon changes."[99] Christianity was as le-

97. Sanders, *Judaism,* ix.
98. Schiffman, *From Text to Tradition,* 4.
99. Sacchi, *The History of the Second Temple Period,* 15.

gitimate an outgrowth from ancient Jewish intellectual premises as any other form of Judaism, including Rabbinic Judaism.

Rabbinic Judaism was no less innovative than Christianity. The sages stressed the centrality of the Torah by claiming its pre-existence and expanding its boundaries to include the oral Torah, and strengthened the bond between ethnicity and Judaism into an unprecedented identification. In so doing, the sages sacrificed part of the rich intellectual heritage of ancient Judaism, exactly as the Christians did.

Christianity was no less conservative than Rabbinic Judaism. The Christians built on the theological foundations that the Enochic tradition had laid for many centuries before Jesus, around the principle of the superhuman origin of evil. The result was a parallel development of the ancient Jewish religion according to a trajectory different from that of Rabbinic Judaism, a trajectory in which ultimately the Torah was subordinated to the Messiah and ethnicity was no longer considered a prerequisite for membership. In so doing, the Christians undoubtedly sacrificed part of the rich intellectual heritage of ancient Judaism, but this was what the sages also did.

What gradually failed in both Christianity and Rabbinic Judaism was the common consciousness and recognition of being part of the same religion. The gradual and reciprocal weakening of such consciousness marked the parting of their ways and the emergence of two distinct branches of Judaism. In their own ways, the Christian and rabbinic siblings continued to honor the same unrejected tradition and their common elders, while they taunted each other with having betrayed the family. The more the Jews lost interest in Christianity and Christianity became a predominantly gentile movement, the more the gentile Christians lost their love of and interest in the Jewish people, to the extent of causing the emergence of harsh anti-Jewish attitudes. The religious debate against Rabbinic Judaism ruined Christians' consciousness of the Jewish cultural and ethnic roots of their own religion.

The clear sociological discontinuity between Christians and Jews, however, is not as apparent on the intellectual level, where continuity between Christianity and Judaism prevails over discontinuity: the religious bond to ancient Judaism was never rejected. Why should an unfortunate history of estrangement and hostility bar the historian of religion from including also the Christian world in any discussion of the worlds of Judaism?

I have held for some time that a distinction between the terms "Jewishness" and "Jewish," on the one hand, and "Judaism and "Judaic," on the other hand, would be particularly useful and refreshing. These terms in modern English are actually synonyms, but in a technical vocabulary, "Jewishness" and "Jewish" should refer to the people, history, and culture of ethnic Jews, while "Judaism" and "Judaic" should be used as a referent to the monotheistic religion of YHWH.

Such a terminological distinction would allow each and every scholar to pursue his or her own legitimate research interest. It is one thing to trace the history of Jewish cultural self-identity, the history of "Jewishness," or of what is "Jewish" — a history that does not include Christianity, except at its very early stage and in a very few of its later species. It is a quite different thing to trace the history of the religion of YHWH, the history of "Judaism," or of what is "Judaic" — a history that does include Christianity in all the variety of its species. We could finally come to agree that while Christianity is no longer a Jewish phenomenon from the cultural and ethnic point of view, ideologically it has never ceased to be a Judaism. No longer "Jewish," Christianity is still entirely "Judaic."

The necessary unity of Judaism and Jewishness and the consequent exclusion from Judaism of everything that is not Jewish have more to do with the contemporary quest for Jewish identity than with historical inquiry. The confidence in the selective power of the "Jewish mind" also is a philosophy before the history of the philosophy.

Neusner's definition of Judaism as any religious system that "appeals as an important part of its authoritative literature or canon to the Hebrew Scriptures of ancient Israel, or Old Testament," is correct in that it tries to be descriptive and not aprioristic.[100] Yet, it appears inadequate to embrace the complexity of Judaic systems from their inception. The very idea that at the beginning was the canon transfers back to history an ideological criterion. Not all Judaisms appealed to the same canon of Scriptures, and canons appeared relatively late in the history of Judaisms. The relationship between canons and Judaisms is the opposite of what Neusner's definition assumes: historically, canons are the product not the foundation of Judaisms.

More appropriate is to describe Judaism historically as the set of monotheistic belief systems associated with the deity named YHWH, as

100. Jacob Neusner, *Studying Classical Judaism: A Primer* (Louisville: Westminster John Knox, 1991), 59.

the recent book, *The Triumph of Elohim,* edited by Diana V. Edelman, also suggests.[101]

The history of Judaism — a genus composed of many species and developing in a plurality of branches — can in fact be effectively described as a genealogical tree. The roots of Judaism are in the ancient polytheistic religion of Israel. Since the beginning, the genus Judaism was made of various synchronic species, or Judaisms — movements in competition, diachronically influencing each other by means of dialogue or opposition, having their own distinct identity yet sharing a common sense of membership to the same religious community. Since the beginning, we do not have one system of thought but rather many parallel systems. Some of these had a short history; some flourished and developed side by side for centuries. No Judaism ever existed in isolation. Social history dictated the agenda and set the priorities each species had to cope with. Intellectual diversity challenged the inner development of each system of thought, suggesting experiences of merging and synthesis, creating the premises for the birth of new species, and offering a continuous opportunity for borrowing and dialogue.

Sometimes the competition among species happened to increase so much as to destroy any sense of mutual recognition. Although each claimed to be faithful to the same ancient tradition, one was no longer available to recognize the legitimacy of the other. Sometimes the struggle grew so deep and bitter as to produce bad feelings of estrangement and betrayal, even overt acts of hostility. The common sense of membership failed and some species grew apart from the others, losing in some cases even the memory of their shared origins. The parting of their ways generated distinct (and no less pluralistic) branches of Judaism. Samaritanism, Christianity, and Rabbinism are only the first branches generated by the trunk of the Judaic genealogical tree. The history of each branch reproduces on a small scale that of the entire genus. New species were born within each branch and branches parted into further branches, fueling the mechanism of borrowing, dialogue, and competition that has characterized the history of Judaism since its inception and that still characterizes the life of Judaism in the extraordinary diversity of its manifestations.

Christianity and Rabbinism in particular have been extremely prolific in both species and branches, and remarkably effective in their capability of influencing each other through the ups and downs of their restless rela-

101. Diana V. Edelman, "Introduction," *The Triumph of Elohim,* 15-25.

tions. A history of Judaism that cuts off either branch, or any other branch, loses an essential element to the internal evolution of each of its components and for the future development of the entire genus. Anti-Judaism and anti-Semitism have obviously played a major role in the shaping of both Jewish and Christian identities.[102] However, Christians and Jews have never completely lost the capability of listening appreciatively to each other and being positively affected by each other.[103]

After more than 2500 years, the life-blood of the Judaic tree does not show any sign of exhaustion, but is capable today of producing yet newer species at a rate that has few parallels in history. Neither do the ongoing dialogue and competition among species and branches know any rest, but are capable today of such amazing developments as the exciting season of contemporary Jewish-Christian dialogue that is reshaping the identity of two long-estranged branches.

C. *How Does a Judaic System Connect with the Previous Ones? or, How Does Rabbinic Judaism Connect with Second Temple Judaisms?*

The problem of the relationship between Rabbinic Judaism and Second Temple Judaisms has received many theological answers, aimed to validate the continuity of the tradition and therefore its legitimacy. The problem is not less fascinating from the historical point of view.

In a recent book, Neusner speaks of "four stages of Rabbinic Judaism," the first two being pre-Mishnaic — Scripture and Second Temple Judaism. Scripture marks theoretically "the first stage" of Rabbinic Judaism; without Scripture we would not have had Rabbinic Judaism. "Take the principal propositions of Scripture read in sequence and systematically, meaning, as exemplary, from Genesis through Kings. Consider the story of the exile from Eden and the counterpart exile of Israel from the Land. Sages did not invent that paradigm. Scripture's framers did. Translate into prop-

102. See Dan Cohn-Sherbok, *The Crucified Jew: Twenty Centuries of Christian Anti-Semitism* (Grand Rapids: Wm. B. Eerdmans; Philadelphia: American Interfaith Institute, 1997).

103. Alan Edelstein, *An Unacknowledged Harmony: Philo-Semitism and the Survival of European Jewry* (Westport: Greenwood, 1982).

ositional form the prophetic messages of admonition, rebuke, and consolation, the promise that as punishment follows sin, so consolation will come in consequence of repentance. Sages did not fabricate those categories and make up the rules that govern the sequence of events. The prophets said them all."[104]

More complex is Neusner's assessment of the importance of the second stage, Second Temple Judaism. The sages acknowledge the founding role of Scripture for their system of thought, but "accord no recognition to any document from the Pentateuch and the Scripture of which it is part to the Mishnah."[105]

Neusner recognizes that Second Temple Judaism was a period of great creativity that had a tremendous yet ill-defined role in rabbinic origins, much more than the sages were prepared to admit. "Between the closure of Scripture and the commencement of the earliest layers of articulated thought in the Mishnah, a vast labor of reflection yielded propositions of fundamental and enduring consequence. . . . The undocumented period comes to us in the signals of premises taken for granted by the law of the Mishnah and related compilations but not incorporated, or only partially incorporated, by the norms of the Pentateuch itself."[106]

Neusner, however, is unable to connect the rabbinic system to any known Second Temple Judaisms. "We do not know when in social reality Rabbinic Judaism reached its earliest tangible formulation. . . . We have not a single piece of writing to tell us where, when, and by whom such reflection was undertaken."[107] As a result, Neusner relies only on a comparison between the two corpora of Scripture and rabbinic literature. This "long and critical moment has to be reconstructed by our own logical analysis . . . by examining the relationship between two cognate religious documents, the Pentateuch and the corpus of halakhah — normative law — set forth by the Mishnah and related compilations. . . . What we do is work backward from the generative premises of the halakhah of the Mishnah and the Tosefta to Scripture to see whether and how . . . the rabbinical sages worked forward from Scripture to the Mishnah."[108]

104. Neusner, *The Four Stages of Rabbinic Judaism*, 23.
105. Neusner, *The Four Stages of Rabbinic Judaism*, 28.
106. Neusner, *The Four Stages of Rabbinic Judaism*, 28, 30.
107. Neusner, *The Four Stages of Rabbinic Judaism*, 5, 28.
108. Neusner, *The Four Stages of Rabbinic Judaism*, xi, 28.

In short, Neusner recognizes that the premises on which Rabbinic Judaism built its system of thought are not from Scripture only but also come from the creative period between Scripture and the Mishnah, yet he abandons any attempt to situate rabbinic origins in the realities of society and politics or in the existing literature of Second Temple Judaism.

Such a minimalist and skeptical approach to rabbinic origins and roots would not be shared by specialists in Second Temple Judaism. Neusner is reacting against the tendency in scholarship to enroll all Second Temple Judaisms into one single rank of precursors and antecedents and present Rabbinic Judaism as the ultimate synthesis of centuries of intellectual inquiry. But can we conclude that none of Second Temple Judaisms is meaningful for rabbinic origins, and bypass all existing evidence, only because the sages did not recognize as authoritative any document between the Bible and the Mishnah? By embracing their ideological perspective, are we not abdicating too quickly and too easily our responsibility as historians to verify the historical reliability of their assumptions?

We know that the sages had the strongest interest in eradicating even the memory of any connection of their Judaism with previous Judaisms, which, in their eyes, would have contaminated the autonomy of their tradition. Between themselves and Scripture they created an artificial bridge — a chain of sages. Led by the belief that the truest origins of their movement lay not in history but in the miracle of God's eternal will, they projected themselves into the past and modeled the past on themselves. What better way to validate their own tradition than making themselves the trustees of the tradition since the earliest times!

Our problem is that our modern, post-Enlightenment sensitivity simply cannot accept a theological or philosophical paradigm, however legitimate and respectable, to be affirmed by imposing itself on history and changing retrospectively the course of events. Now that historical criticism has made the bridge provided by the rabbinic tradition collapse as an ideological construct, theologians are urged to replace it with something else, which, while respectful of history, will show the unity of Judaism behind its diversity — be such unity an atemporal essence, an evolutionary system, or the product of the Jewish mind.

The search for the unity of Judaism is a theological and philosophical problem — a meaningful aspect of the contemporary search for Jewish identity. The task of the historian of Judaism is different. "The good historian resembles the ogre of the fairy-tale: where he scents the human flesh, he knows that his prey is there."[109] Bloch's witty remark reminds us that the historical task is never a matter of "logical analysis" only. It is a dirty job: it makes one meddle in other people's affairs, as intellectual phenomena are linked to social factors and social groups — flesh-and-blood people. The historian acknowledges that answers are not contained in the questions and effects in the causes. There is in history an indefinite space for freedom and surprise, where human genius and blind fate (the theologian would add, the divine revelation) exercise their power above any deterministic constraint. Yet, thoughts and ideas cannot be understood historically apart from the social setting in which they were born and apart from the people who produced them. In Garin's words, the intellectual historian's task is "to be aware of the plurality of philosophies, understand the many voices, put them in context, identify their relations with the social groups in which they emerged, assess what they meant for these groups, how they acted if they acted, how they change, and how they decline — human thoughts, how they were created by people, how they changed people."[110]

Searching the origins and roots of Rabbinic Judaism, historians have no alternative but excavating the realities of Second Temple Judaism for any clues of the chain of events and intellectual phenomena that bridged the gap from Scripture to the sages. What they will find are neither the mythical institutions of Rabbinic Judaism nor elusive oral traditions, but flesh-and-blood people and the struggle of real social groups. Within such a variety of social groups and intellectual systems, the historian will assess which of them step-by-step contributed to the foundations of the rabbinic system.

That no document between the Bible and the Mishnah was recognized by the sages as authoritative and no social group (except the Pharisees) was singled out as forerunners does not mean that all documents produced in Second Temple Judaism are insignificant for rabbinic origins and no social group other than the sages had a role.[111] History is full of actual paternities disclaimed and forgotten for the sake of ideology and replaced by ideological pedigrees aimed to highlight a philosophical or religious truth underneath the historical processes. The ancient sages of Israel

109. Bloch, *Apologie pour l'histoire,* 35.

110. Garin, *GCFI* 38 (1959): 41.

111. Gabriele Boccaccini, "Esiste una letteratura farisaica del secondo tempio?" *RSB* 11/2 (1999): 23-41.

would have been scandalized to admit that at the roots of their own tradition were priests and not rabbis and that they owed so much to some of the apocryphal literature they rejected from their canon — no less scandalized than the first Christians to admit that their belief system was at its inception little more than a sophisticated variant of Enochic thought.

Historiographical and systemic analysis of extant sources suggests that there was in fact a line of continuity between some pre-Rabbinic Judaisms and Rabbinic Judaism, exactly as there was a line of continuity between some pre-Christian Judaisms and early Christianity. Like Christianity and any other intellectual or religious phenomena in history, Rabbinic Judaism emerged not in a flash of revelation but as a modification or variant of previous systems of thought that, in turn, developed from earlier systems, and as a modification or variant of social groups that, in turn, developed from previous groups.

The rise of critical scholarship and the emancipation of intellectual history from established theological paradigms have been long perceived as a deliberate attack on religious beliefs. Sometimes that might have been the case. Ultimately, they are the result of intellectual honesty and curiosity — the restless thirst for knowledge that urges each generation to challenge the restraints of the old wisdom. Our Western civilization, in Dante's words, praises this pursuit as humankind's highest mission and accomplishment. "Ye were not made to live like unto brutes, but for pursuit of virtue and of knowledge" (*Inferno* XXVI.119-20).[112]

Theologians and intellectual historians may still struggle today to find a nonconflicting balance between their disciplines. They agree, however, that the historical concern for providing the facts (including the unfolding of intellectual phenomena) and the theological concern for providing the meaning (essence, or unity) of those facts are autonomous and independent enterprises, each to be pursued in accordance to its own rules *(iuxta sua propria principia)*. By describing the continuous evolution and modification of religious systems of thought in their original context, intellectual history reconstructs legitimately, outside of any philosophical and theological apriorism, the historical unfolding of what theology will legitimately keep seeing, in its deepest meaning, as the miraculous and providential manifestation of a divine apriorism.

112. Dante Alighieri, *The Divine Comedy*, trans. Henry Wadsworth Longfellow (Boston: Ticknor and Fields, 1867), 1:163.

CHAPTER ONE

The Rise of Zadokite Judaism

1. The Struggle for Priestly Supremacy

After the Babylonian exile and the end of the Davidic monarchy, the leadership of the Jewish people was provided by the Zadokites. They claimed descent from Zadok, according to the ancient Jewish historiography a priest and companion of David (2 Sam 8:17), who supported Solomon as the legitimate heir and anointed him king (1 Kgs 1:32-46). For around 350 years, the high priesthood in Jerusalem was held by individuals who asserted themselves, and were recognized by their subjects, as members of a single family line. From the construction of the Second Temple to the eve of the Maccabean Revolt, Flavius Josephus gives a list of 14 names: Joshua, Joiakim, Eliashib, Joiada, Jehohanan, Jaddua, Onias I, Simon I, Eleazar, Manasseh, Onias II, Simon II, Onias III, and Joshua (Jason).[1] Whether the list is accurate and complete, and whether the continuity of blood was never broken, are matters of scholarly debate, yet there are no doubts about the historicity of Zadokite supremacy.[2] The Zadokites were the first

1. Erroneously, Josephus adds to the list of Zadokite high priests also Menelaus, the usurper (*Ant* 12:238-39; 15:41; 19:298; 20:235), who was not from the house of Zadok but from that of "Bilgah" (2 Macc 3:4 [Old Latin and Armenian]). See below, Ch. 4.

2. James C. VanderKam, "Jewish High Priests of the Persian Period: Is the List Complete?" in *Priesthood and Cult in Ancient Israel,* ed. Gary A. Anderson and Saul M. Olyan, JSOTSup 125 (Sheffield: JSOT, 1991), 67-91; Menahem Mor, "The High Priests in Judah in the Persian Period," *Bet Miqra* 23 (1977): 57-67 (Hebrew); Frank Moore Cross, "A Reconstruction of the Judean Restoration," *JBL* 94 (1975): 4-18.

and most successful dynasty of high priests in the history of the Second Temple, and the dominant institution in pre-Maccabean Judaism.

The earliest document in which we can read a claim for Zadokite supremacy is Ezekiel 40–48, from the time of the Babylonian exile. The text is clearly polemical and innovative. It neither expresses a nostalgic view nor describes an actual situation; it is a political and religious agenda for the future restoration of Israel. The aim is to lay the foundations of a new order that in the eyes of its proponents has to be profoundly different from that of preexilic Judaism.[3]

Ezekiel 40–48 assumes and displaces the Deuteronomistic view that "the sons of Levi," originally a warlike Israelite clan without any particular priestly function (Gen 34:25-31; 49:5-7), were the hereditary priesthood of the First Temple, "for YHWH your God has chosen [Levi] out of all your tribes, to stand and minister in the name of YHWH, him and his sons for all time" (Deut 18:5; cf. 17:9; 21:5; 31:9).

Ezekiel 40–48 agrees that in order to be a priest one must be a descendant of Levi and that all the sons of Levi, and they alone among the tribes of Israel, are consecrated to the service in the temple. However, Ezekiel 40–48 argues that a sinful behavior has disqualified the majority of Levites from serving as priests. "The Levites who went far from me, going astray from me after their idols when Israel went astray, shall bear their punishment. . . . They shall not come near to me, to serve me as priest, nor come near any of my sacred offerings, the things that are most sacred; but they shall bear their shame, and the consequences of the abominations they have committed" (Ezek 44:10-14). Only one particular Levitical family, the "sons of Zadok," is singled out for their faithfulness. They "kept my charge [and] did not go astray when the people of Israel went astray, as the [other] Levites did" (Ezek 48:11; cf. 44:15). Hence, the sons of Zadok alone shall have the rights to the office, privileges, and perquisites of priesthood in the future temple of Jerusalem (Ezek 40:45-46; 43:19; 44:15-16). The other Levitical families shall not lose entirely their responsibilities toward the temple; their punishment is to be degraded to a second-class temple personnel, the levites, under the sons of Zadok, the priests.

The second major concern of Ezekiel's agenda is to change and restrict

3. Iain M. Duguid, *Ezekiel and the Leaders of Israel,* VTSup 56 (Leiden: Brill, 1994); Jon D. Levenson, *Theology of the Program of Restoration of Ezekiel 40–48,* HSM 10 (Missoula: Scholars, 1976).

the cultic position of the king. Some ancient texts (notably, the so-called enthronement psalms, such as Ps 20 or 110) and the parallels from kingship elsewhere in the ancient Near East suggest that during the monarchic age the Davidic king must have played a much more prominent role in the cult than Jewish sources from the exilic and postexilic periods are prepared to admit.[4] The king offered sacrifices (2 Sam 6:13, 17; 1 Kgs 3:4), blessed the people (2 Sam 6:18; 1 Kgs 8:14), wore the priestly ephod (2 Sam 6:14) and most importantly, nominated the priests, who were reckoned among the king's officials (2 Sam 8:16-18; 20:23-26; 1 Kgs 4:1-6). None of the preexilic sources seems to be scandalized by the king acting as a priest; the "Mosaic" rules that would make these actions unlawful had not been issued yet.

Ezekiel 40–48 challenges the tradition and opposes this combining of kingship and priesthood. The struggle is for complete autonomy. At the foundation of the power of the sons of Zadok is God's decision, not the king's; they alone are the chosen to perform the sacred duties. Yet, Ezekiel 40–48 does not dare reduce the king purely to the level of laity and still gives him some cultic privileges and functions, such as the right of special access to the temple (Ezek 44:2-3; 46:1-10) and the obligation to furnish offerings for the expiation (45:16-25), a task that later would be reserved for the priests (Lev 9:7; 10:17; 16:33 [P]). While no longer a priest himself, the king maintains a unique role of "patron of the cult."[5]

The circumspect approach by Ezekiel 40–48 to the office of the king was not a nostalgic tribute to an institution of the past that might or might not be restored, but a calculated act of realpolitik. When the Ezekielian program of future restoration was articulated, the Davidic king was still in charge.

Although the later Jewish tradition would blame Nebuchadnezzar for the end of the Jewish monarchy (2 Chr 36), the Babylonians had less interest in destroying the house of David than in domesticating it as a tool to keep peace and stability in the region. Accordingly, when in 597 B.C.E. they deposed the Judean king Jehoiachin, son of the rebellious Jehoiakim, and took him among the Jewish notables who were brought as hostages to Bab-

4. A. R. Johnson, *Sacral Kingship in Ancient Israel*, 2nd ed. (Cardiff: University of Wales Press, 1967).

5. Kenneth E. Pomykala, *The Davidic Dynasty Tradition in Early Judaism: Its History and Significance for Messianism* (Atlanta: Scholars, 1995), 30.

ylon, they also "made Mattaniah, Jehoiachin's uncle, king in his place and changed his name to Zedekiah," as a token of vassalage (2 Kgs 24:17). At the beginning, it was Jehoiachin, not the puppet-king Zedekiah, on whom the exiles placed their hopes of revenge; and it was Zedekiah, not the exiled Jehoiachin, on whom the Babylonians placed their hope of stability for the vassal kingdom of Judah. That Ezekiel's first vision is dated to "the fifth year of the exile of King Jehoiachin" (Ezek 1:2) is clear evidence that the exiles viewed Jehoiachin, not Zedekiah, as the legitimate king. Many in Judah shared the same view; among them, "the prophet Hananiah son of Azzur, from Gibeon, spoke. . . in the house of YHWH. . . . Within two years . . . I will. . . bring back to this place king Jeconiah [= Jehoiachin] son of Jehoiakim of Judah, and all the exiles from Judah who went to Babylon, says YHWH, for I will break the yoke of the king of Babylon" (Jer 28:1-4). While preaching submission to Nebuchadnezzar (Jer 27), Jeremiah had to dismiss and ridicule any hope related to Jehoiachin (22:24-30; 28:5-16).

Had Zedekiah proved to be a loyal vassal to the Babylonians, the fate of Jehoiachin would have been sealed. But in 588-586 "Zedekiah rebelled against the king of Babylon" (2 Kgs 24:20b) with tragic consequences for himself, his direct descendants, and his people. After a two-year siege, Jerusalem fell, the walls were broken down, the temple was burned, and many Israelites were killed or exiled (2 Kgs 25:1-11). The Babylonians treated Zedekiah as a traitor; he was blinded, bound in fetters, and carried to Babylon to die in prison (2 Kgs 25:7; Jer 52:11).

Administratively, the dethronement and punishment of Zedekiah marked the end of the vassal kingdom of Judah, but not the end of the Davidic dynasty and of its political role — a fact that the Deuteronomistic historiography did not fail to emphasize (2 Kgs 25:27-30; Jer 52:31-34).[6] In

6. Nadav Na'aman, "Royal Vassals or Governors? On the Status of Shashbazzar and Zerubbabel in the Persian Empire," *Hen* 22 (2000): 35-44. The continuity of the Davidic monarchy through the Babylonian exile to the early Persian period has been emphasized by Jacob Liver, "The Return from Babylon: Its Time and Scope," *ErIsr* 5 (1958): 114-19 (Hebrew); Paolo Sacchi, "L'esilio e la fine della monarchia davidica," *Hen* 11 (1989): 131-48; *The History of the Second Temple Period,* 46-68; Herbert Niehr, "Religio-Historical Aspects of the 'Early Post-Exilic' Period," in *The Crisis of Israelite Religion: Transformation of Religious Tradition in Exilic and Post-Exilic Times,* ed. Bob Becking and Marjo C. A. Korpel, OtSt 42 (Leiden: Brill, 1999), 228-44; André Lemaire, "Zorobabel et la Judée à la lumière de l'épigraphie (fin du VIe S. av J.-C.)," *RB* 103 (1996): 48-57; Francesco Bianchi, "Zorobabele re di Giuda," *Hen* 3 (1991): 133-50.

an amazing reversal of fortune and roles, Jehoiachin was now the Babylonian's natural candidate for securing peace and stability in the region, provided that he was willing to separate his destiny from that of the exiles. After all, he had never been personally involved in any act of rebellion. In 597, it was his father Jehoiakim who led the revolt, not Jehoiachin who "gave himself up to the king of Babylon" (2 Kgs 24:12). The same very compelling reasons that kept Jehoiachin out of the rebellion of Zedekiah guaranteed his loyalty in similar future circumstances: had any of his relatives in Judah been successful in an uprising against the Babylonians, Jehoiachin would have definitively lost his royal status and the right to succession for his sons.

This time, the Babylonians acted very cautiously; they had already bidden on the wrong horse. Both the killing of Zedekiah's sons and the appointment of the non-Davidic Gedaliah as a special envoy are consistent with the new course of Babylonian policy. Judah was annexed to the empire as a province and Jehoiachin remained a prisoner, yet the Babylonian archives show that he was granted the title of "king of the land of Judah" and his five sons that of "sons of the king of Judah," and food was provided to them and a small court of 13 people.[7]

The royal dignity attributed to Jehoiachin was not merely "honorific."[8] The recognition by the Babylonian authorities that he and his sons could legitimately bear the title of *nasi* (vassal king) even after the vassal kingdom of Judah ceased to exist was in itself a political-administrative act with profound implications. On the one hand, it served to legitimize the Babylonian rule in the eyes of the loyalists in Judah and in Babylon, as the Davidic king was honored as such by the new administration. On the other hand, it served to delegitimize any attempt at restoring the Davidic monarchy in Judah, as an act of rebellion not only against the Babylonian rule but also against Jehoiachin, the legitimate Judean king who lived in Babylon. The still volatile political situation explains the caution of the Babylonians. Members of the Davidic family who remained in Judah proved to be a continuous source of trouble; "Ishmael son of Nethaniah. . . of the royal family" led the bloody conspiracy that cut short Gedaliah's life (2 Kgs 25:22-

7. Ran Zadok, *The Jews in Babylonia during the Chaldean and Achaemenian Periods according to the Babylonian Sources* (Haifa: University of Haifa Press, 1979), 38-39.

8. *Pace* Na'aman, *Hen* 22 (2000): 38.

26; Jer 40:13–41:18). Only when the situation finally became more stable was King Jehoiachin of Judah "released from prison" after 37 years of captivity and granted a position corresponding to his royal status, as he was allowed to sit at the table of the new Babylonian king Evil-merodach (Awel-Marduk). Throughout the Babylonian and early Persian periods, Jehoiachin and his successors Sheshbazzar and Zerubbabel continued to act and be recognized as kings of Judah.

The exiled priests who are behind the tradition of Ezekiel had many good reasons to be upset at King Jehoiachin. He was their king, the one on whom they had placed so much hope, but now, in order to survive, he had disavowed his companions. In the midst of misfortune, he acquiesced to the interests of the Babylonian monarchy. From their vantage point, the Davidic king, with his prophets and Levitical priests, was a quisling who had deserted them and sided with the enemy. In fact, they did not hide their growing antimonarchic attitudes (Ezek 22:6; 45:8-9). The defection of Jehoiachin after the revolt of Zedekiah was a serious blow. However, they did not give up their hopes and soon found in the house of Zadok their most congenial leadership.

The Zadokites were the direct descendants of Seraiah, who had been the "chief priest" under King Zedekiah, and with him had been deported and then executed as one of the leaders of the revolt (2 Kgs 25:18). Seraiah's son "Jehozadak went into exile" (1 Chr 6:15[Heb. 5:41]). The future of the house of Zadok in Babylon looked quite gloomy. As the son of a convicted conspirator, Jehozadak had no prospects for rehabilitation under the Babylonians. The support his family gave to Zedekiah also barred him from any present or future role at Jehoiachin's side, as far as Jehoiachin himself was concerned. The only part which the house of Zadok could reasonably play up to their prestige and past glories was as the heroes of the anti-Babylonian (now increasingly antimonarchic) party. Taking advantage of discontent and dissatisfaction among the exiles, the house of Zadok took a step that would have monumental consequences for the future of Judaism. They made clear that they were no longer available to recognize the Davidic king's right to exclusive leadership, in particular his right to appoint the chief priest — an office that they now claimed for themselves as a divine right. Yet, in spite of their anger and ambitions, the Zadokites could not easily ignore the *nasi* and his claims to the future order of Israel. Ezekiel 40–48, with its advisedly detailed regulations, opted for a policy of containment.

2. The Return from the Babylonian Exile

When the Persians defeated the Babylonians, the Zadokites' dreams of power came true, but only through a series of complex and even fortuitous circumstances. Ancient sources barely shed light on the obscure events that led to the building of the Second Temple under Darius I (522-486 B.C.E.), to the reforms of Nehemiah under Artaxerxes I (464-424) and Darius II (423-404), and possibly to the subsequent mission of Ezra under Artaxerxes II (404-359), if Ezra is indeed a historical person and not merely a fictional priestly double of Nehemiah.[9]

The Ezekielian restoration program was never carried out in its entirety, as it had to compete with alternative views and had to adapt to political unpredictability. It was a complex and painful process, which required constant and vigilant attention from the Babylonian diaspora. The autonomous traditions associated with Nehemiah and Ezra respectively, the Priestly writing (P), and Chronicles are the major literary accomplishments of Zadokite Judaism in the early Second Temple period and allow us, if not to understand historical details, at least to follow the gradual establishment of the Zadokite power, step by step.[10]

The tradition of Ezra (1 Esd 2:1-15; 6:17-20 = Ezra 1:1-11; 5:13-16; cf. Josephus *Ant* 11:1-11) betrays that the old order survived the Babylonian exile. The "edict of Cyrus," dated to "the first year" of his kingdom (538; cf. 1 Esd 2:1 = Ezra 1:1), established a policy of the Persian government of re-

9. See Lester L. Grabbe, *Ezra-Nehemiah* (London: Routledge, 1998).

10. The biblical text of Ezra-Nehemiah in its present form may be very late. Flavius Josephus does not know it. Consistent with the earliest Jewish tradition (see Sirach and 2 Maccabees), he is also unaware of any synchrony or association between the two reformers. Josephus locates both of them at the time of Artaxerxes I as in Ezra-Nehemiah, but in his account Nehemiah came to Jerusalem only after the death of Ezra. The editorial effort of Ezra-Nehemiah to integrate and harmonize the two characters is awkward and secondary. Originally, the traditions of Nehemiah and Ezra must have existed independently from one another. While there is no surviving evidence of the tradition of Nehemiah besides the excerpts in Ezra-Nehemiah and the summary of Josephus (*Ant* 11:159-83), we may get a better idea of what the tradition of Ezra looked like before being unified to that of Nehemiah, from the Greek 1 Esdras and its synopsis in *Ant* 11:120-58, which supplements the missing ending with the story of the celebration of the festival of booths and the narrative of the death of Ezra. See Sacchi, *The History of the Second Temple Period,* 130-35; Grabbe, *Ezra-Nehemiah.*

turning hostage kings to their homelands and restoring the sanctuaries of their gods. Among the hostage kings that Cyrus met in Babylon there was also the Davidic king, Sheshbazzar, the son of Jehoiachin, who had inherited from his father the title of *nasi* ("vassal king") of Judah (Ezra 1:8; 5:14; 1 Esd 2:12; 6:20).[11] He also probably "brought tribute [to Cyrus] and kissed [his] feet in Babylon," as the other kings did — a detail that the softened and heavily edited version of Jewish historiography omits.

In its present form, the edict of Cyrus as preserved in Hebrew (Ezra 1:1-4) or Aramaic (6:1-5) by the tradition of Ezra is essentially a forgery or, more likely, a sort of free adaptation elucidating the implications of Cyrus's general decree for the Jewish people. Much more reliable is the letter of Tattenai, the satrap of Ebir-nari (Ezra 5:7-17), which significantly confirms the role of Sheshbazzar at the time of Cyrus.[12] To Sheshbazzar the Persian king returned "the vessels of the house of YHWH that Nebuchadnezzar had carried away from Jerusalem and placed in the house of his gods" (Ezra 1:7), and allowed him to go back to Jerusalem, as "governor" of the province of Judah (5:14).

Scholars of the Persian Empire concur that "at its inception the new Achaemenid administration of Babylon sought to retain the same economic, political, and social conditions that had prevailed under the Babylonian kingship."[13] It was Sheshbazzar, and he alone, who "laid the foundations of the house of God in Jerusalem" (Ezra 5:16; 1 Esd 6:20; *Ant* 11:93). For hereditary right as well as in the eyes of the new Persian authority, the Davidic king, not the Zadokite priest, was in charge of the Judean cult.

11. Sheshbazzar is usually identified with Shenazzar, the son of "Jeconiah [= Jehoiachin] the captive" (1 Chr 3:17-18). See Sacchi, *The History of the Second Temple Period,* 60; James D. Purvis (rev. Eric M. Meyers), "Exile and Return: From the Babylonian Destruction to the Reconstruction of the Jewish State," in *Ancient Israel: From Abraham to the Roman Destruction of the Temple,* ed. Hershel Shanks, rev. ed. (Washington: Biblical Archaeological Society, 1999), 218. Other scholars suggest that Sheshbazzar was the Babylonian name of Shenazzar's brother Shealtiel, the father of Zerubbabel. See Na'aman, *Hen* 22 (2000): 37.

12. See Grabbe, *Ezra-Nehemiah,* 126-32.

13. Kenneth G. Hoglund, *Achaemenid Imperial Administration in Syria-Palestine and the Missions of Ezra and Nehemiah,* SBLDS 125 (Atlanta: Scholars, 1992), 5. See also A. T. Olmstead, *History of the Persian Empire* (Chicago: University of Chicago Press, 1948), 70-85.

While sources mention a project of reconstruction of ruined buildings under Cyrus (Isa 44:28), the emphasis is clearly on continuity rather than discontinuity with the preexilic religious institutions. Only a limited portion of the Jewish population had been actually deported as hostages: the upper class and the leadership of society, that is, members of the royal family, priests, military personnel, and craftsmen — a total of 4600 people according to Jer 52:28-30. The inconspicuous and unskilled, yet the most numerous portion of the Jewish people ("the poorest people of the land . . . vinedressers and tillers of the soil," 2 Kgs 24:14; 25:12), were left behind; possibly as many as 90-95 percent of the population remained in Judah.[14]

Where there are people, there is religious life, and where there is religious life, there are priests and sanctuaries. As the famous incident recorded in Jer 41:4-5 attests, the cult to YHWH in its preexilic form had not been discontinued, and sacrifices were offered to YHWH in Judah during the time of the Babylonian exile. Zechariah also testifies that "for seventy years" the people in Judah "fasted and mourned" in memory of the destruction of the temple (Zech 7:1-7). The Babylonians did not carry out any form of religious persecution, nor did they impose any religious loyalty. "Although the Babylonians were savage in battle, they took no delight in useless destruction and wholesale slaughter. The remnant of Judah was not exterminated or scientifically tortured to death. Nobody desecrated the graves in Jerusalem; nobody prevented the believers from bringing meal offerings and frankincense to the burned-down house of YHWH and from weeping on its ruins."[15]

The cultic structures of Judah needed to be renewed, not rebuilt from scratch. In Jerusalem, or more likely in Mizpah — the town that during the Babylonian exile took over from Jerusalem the role of Judah's administrative center (2 Kgs 25:23) — there was already a royal sanctuary, and in Judah and Samaria there were groups of Levitical priests faithful to the Davidic king.[16]

14. See Purvis, 201-29.

15. Written in the aftermath of World War II, Elias J. Bickerman's words could not help being reminiscent of the experience of the Holocaust. See Bickerman, "The Historical Foundations of Postbiblical Judaism," in *The Jews: Their History, Culture, and Religion,* ed. Louis Finkelstein (Philadelphia: Jewish Publication Society of America, 1949), 71; repr. in Bickerman, *From Ezra to the Last of the Maccabees: Foundations of Post-Biblical Judaism* (New York: Schocken, 1967), 6.

16. Joseph Blenkinsopp argues for the existence of a temple at Mizpah. The

The king's prophets exulted at the inception of the Persian rule. In the collective memory of the Jewish people, and even in the later Zadokite historiography, the return under Cyrus would remain associated forever with the fulfillment of the prophecy of Jeremiah (Jer 25:11-12; 29:10; cf. Ezra 1:1; 1 Esd 1:57–2:1; 2 Chr 36:21; *Ant* 11:1) and with the words of Second Isaiah who celebrated Cyrus as "God's messiah" (Isa 44:24–45:8; cf. *Ant* 11:5-6). The local population of "Judah" and "Benjamin" and "all their neighbors" enthusiastically welcomed the returned king and "aided" the projects of reconstruction "with silver vessels, with gold, with goods, with animals, and with valuable gifts, besides all that was freely offered" (Ezra 1:5-6).

In the context of conflicting opinions developed over the Babylonian exile about the role of the monarchy and the nature of the priesthood, the tradition of Jeremiah could celebrate its victory against those who dared say that "the two families that YHWH chose have been rejected by him" (Jer 33:24). The Davidic monarchy and the Levitical priesthood are the two institutions of Israel whose existence is guaranteed forever by God's covenant. The restoration would vindicate the Levitical priests' rights, as well as the king's. "In those days . . . I will cause a righteous Branch to spring up for David. . . . For thus says YHWH: David shall never lack a successor to sit on the throne of the house of Israel, nor shall the priests of Levi ever lack a man to offer holocausts before me, to burn cereal offerings, and to sacrifice victims. . . . If you can break my covenant with day, and my covenant with night . . . then can my covenant with my servant David also be broken . . . and my covenant with the priests of Levi" (Jer 33:14-26).[17] For some time it seemed that Jeremiah's, not Ezekiel's, program of restoration was about to be fulfilled.

But soon the climate changed, and proved that the Zadokites had large support among the Jewish exiles, influential connections at the Persian court, and the capability to turn into their own advantage the political interests of the empire. Under Cambyses, the construction project initiated by Sheshbazzar languished and was never completed (Hag 1:4, 9; Ezra

---

Deuteronomistic legislation required the existence of only one temple, not necessarily in Jerusalem. See Blenkinsopp, "The Judaean Priesthood during the Neo-Babylonian and Achaemenid Periods: A Hypothetical Reconstruction," *CBQ* 60 (1998): 25-43. See also Jeffrey R. Zorn, "Mizpah: Newly Discovered Stratum Reveals Judah's Other Capital," *BAR* 23/5 (1997): 28-38, 66.

17. On the dating of this passage to the early postexilic period, see Pomykala, 42-45.

5:16). The restoration envisaged by Ezekiel 40–48 was indeed an ideal program but soon proved to be neither a vain hope nor a desperate illusion. Some 18 years later, under Darius I (522-486), a new wave of returning exiles left Babylon, this time under the dual leadership of the Davidic king Zerubbabel, the nephew of Sheshbazzar, and of the Zadokite priest Joshua, the son of Jehozadak (Hag 1:1). The disgrace the Zadokites suffered at the time of Zedekiah was vindicated and the house of David paid its defection with interest: the grandson of Jehoiachin, the king who sat at the table with Evil-merodach, now shared power with the grandson of the "chief priest" Seraiah whom the Babylonians executed as a traitor.

Whereas Cyrus had merely taken over the existing administrative structures of the Babylonian Empire, Darius's policy marked a major change in the region as it reveals the attempt to reconstruct a political authority within the old boundaries of the former kingdom of Judah. Scholars of the Persian Empire would once again say that this "was not an isolated act of favor by the imperial court, but part of a larger strategy in the Levant" of relocating exiled communities and installing loyal representatives of the indigenous populations — a strategy designed to reorganize the satrapies and "integrate more completely the political and the social order of a conquered territory into the imperial system."[18]

The Persian goal was to prevent insurrection and foster loyalty; however, for the social relations within the Israelite people, the shift of imperial favor from the remainees to the returnees meant a revolution. It was now the Zadokite priests who set the agenda: the recognition of the exclusive leadership of the exiles and the construction of a new temple in Jerusalem under a new priesthood. Indeed, it would be a temple as it had never been before in Israel.

The house of David had to bear the humiliation of sharing its power and priestly prerogatives with the house of Zadok, and capitulated to their plans of reconstruction. Yet, the prophet Zechariah underlines the terms of a still acceptable compromise. "The word of YHWH came to me: Collect silver and gold from the exiles. . . . Take the silver and gold and make crowns, and set [them] on the head of [the king Zerubbabel and] the high priest Joshua son of Jehozadak. Say to him [= Zerubbabel]: Thus says the Lord of hosts: Here is a man whose name is Branch, for he shall branch out

18. Hoglund, 25, 27. See also John M. Cook, *The Persian Empire* (New York: Schocken, 1983), 61, 71.

in his place, and he shall build the temple of YHWH. . . he shall bear royal honor, and shall sit and rule on his throne. There shall be a priest [= Joshua] by his throne, with peaceful understanding between the two of them. And crowns shall be in the care of Heldai . . . as a memorial in the temple of YHWH" (Zech 6:9-14).[19]

For the house of David, the presence of the house of Zadok was a bitter pill to swallow, as Zechariah's anxious invitation to a "peaceful understanding between the two" suggests. The prospects for the king's power, however, remained intact and even were strengthened by the alliance with a powerful ally. The monarchy maintained its primacy over the priesthood. In ancient sources the name of Zerubbabel always precedes that of Joshua, and the king sits "on the throne" while the priest stands "by his throne." Most significantly, the Davidic king did not lose his own right to be directly involved in temple affairs. All ancient sources concur to give to Zerubbabel, although in association with the priest, the same role of temple-builder as Sheshbazzar (Ezra 5:2; Hag 1:1-4; 2:1-5). In line with the ancient monarchic ideology, Zechariah boasts the king's central role in the construction of the temple: "the hands of Zerubbabel have laid the foundation of this house; his hands shall also complete it" (Zech 4:9; cf. 6:12-13). As Herbert Niehr has pointed out, the prophetic words "He shall bring out the top stone amid shouts of 'Grace, grace to it!'" (Zech 4:7) are "to be understood as an allusion to a temple building ritual. . . . All over the Ancient Near East kings acted as temple-builders and the building of a temple was a royal initiative . . . It was the royal authority of Zerubbabel which sufficed to fulfil this task, while conversely he needed a temple for the cultic dimensions of his royalty."[20]

The alliance between the house of David and the priests of Levi, which

19. The text as handed down by the later Jewish tradition is corrupted. It requires making two "crowns" (one of gold and one of silver) but then setting "it" on the head of the high priest only. The invitation to "a peaceful understanding between the two of them," that is, between the Branch and the priest, makes sense only if the words of God are addressed to the king (not to the high priest) and the priest "by the king's throne" is Joshua himself. When the reference to Zerubbabel is properly restored, the text regains immediately its consistency. It describes the coronation and enthronement of the king and the contemporaneous coronation of the high priest "by his throne," and defines the terms of their relationship and sharing of power. See Sacchi, *The History of the Second Temple Period,* 67-68.

20. Niehr, 234-35.

the tradition of Jeremiah proclaimed would last forever (Jer 33:14-26), was seriously compromised on the altar of the new balance of power. The Levitical priesthood in Judah and Samaria lost the support of the king, their only source of legitimacy. The new imposed laws of purity disqualified them from serving as priests: "these people . . . are unclean, and so every work of their hands, and what they offer" (Hag 2:10-14). The prophecy in Jeremiah, however, was not fully contradicted: Zerubbabel was "the righteous Branch from David" and the Zadokites were, after all, a line of Levitical priests. The king could hope that the loss of a loyal yet weak priesthood would be compensated by the gain of a recalcitrant yet powerful one.

The "peoples of the land" (the local population, including the Samaritans, who "had been sacrificing to YHWH since the day of King Esarhaddon of Assyria") were no longer welcomed as having responsibilities in the temple leadership: "You shall have no part with us in building a house to our God, but we alone will build to YHWH, the God of Israel" (Ezra 4:1-3). In sharp contrast with what happened at the time of Sheshbazzar (Ezra 1:5-6), the text of Zechariah requires the gold and silver for the royal and priestly crowns now be collected among the exiles exclusively, and not be offered by the local population of Judah and Benjamin and all their neighbors. To the peoples of the land, however, the king and his prophets remained a precious token of continuity. Zechariah 7–8 presents a delegation from "the people of Bethel" that comes to "entreat the favor of YHWH" and seek authoritative instruction from "the priests of the house of YHWH of hosts and the prophets" (Zech 7:2-3). This is "in the fourth year of King Darius" (7:1), that is, two years after the arrival of Zerubbabel and Joshua, and significantly the king's prophets are still associated with the Zadokite priests. The answer the people of Bethel received by Zechariah was a message of peace and welcome: "Many peoples and strong nations shall come to seek YHWH of hosts in Jerusalem, and to entreat the favor of YHWH" (8:22). The exclusion from the new temple leadership did not mean that the peoples of the land (including the Samaritans) now had to cut off their ties with Jerusalem. They continued to be regarded, and to look at themselves, as part of the same religious community.

These elements of continuity made the king's prophets also look at the diarchy of Zerubbabel and Joshua with enthusiasm and hope. When the work of reconstruction began, the prophets were there, directly involved, "helping" the king and the priests (Ezra 5:1-2). Haggai and Zechariah present Zerubbabel and Joshua as instruments of God for a common task — "the two anointed ones who stand by YHWH of the whole earth" (Zech 4:10b-14).

The balance of power between the house of David and the house of Zadok, between the remainees and the returnees, did not last long, however, and not to the priests' regret. When the new temple was dedicated in 515, only the returned priests performed the rituals: Zerubbabel had vanished and with him his fragile coalition of priests and prophets. What happened to the last Davidic king of Judah is largely a mystery; what is certain is the gain for the Zadokites. The ceremony of dedication of the new temple was attended only by the exiled families and by those "who had joined them and separated themselves from the pollutions of the nations of the land" (Ezra 6:15-22; cf. *Ant* 11.79). The king's prophets looked at the events with despair: "Your holy people took possession for a little while; but now our adversaries have trampled down your sanctuary" (Trito-Isaiah 63:18). The political power of the king was absorbed by the governor; both Malachi and the tradition of Nehemiah confirm the presence of "governors" before the appointment of Nehemiah (Mal 1:8; Neh 5:15). Accepting the disputed antiquity and authenticity of the bullae published by Avigad, André Lemaire suggests that after Zerubbabel the office of governor was held by his brother Hananah and then by Elnathan, the husband of Hananah's sister, Shelomit.[21] If Lemaire's reconstruction is correct, the end of the political role of the house of David was an even more gradual process than indicated in Jewish literary sources. After Zerubbabel, however, there is no evidence that Davidic governors were granted the title and the cultic role of "kings." The religious functions associated with the Davidic kingship were absorbed by the priest; the Zadokites were left alone as the supreme and unchallenged religious authority in Jewish society.

The diarchy with the house of David was gone, but its royal symbols, such as the hereditary succession and the anointing, which the house of Zadok had inherited by their brief association with the monarchy, re-

21. André Lemaire, "Histoire et administration de la Palestine à l'époque perse," in *La Palestine à l'époque perse,* ed. Ernest-Marie Laperrousaz and Lemaire (Paris: Editions du Cerf, 1994), 11-54; cf. Naḥman Avigad, *Bullae and Seals from a Post-Exilic Judean Archive* (Jerusalem: Hebrew University, 1976). The antiquity of the bullae is called in question by Francesco Bianchi, "Monete giudaiche di età ellenistica," *RSO* 63 (1989): 213-29.

mained and marked, also visually, the Zadokites' supersession of kingship.[22] "The old monarchical state had been transformed into a much-reduced theocracy with the high priest as the main native spokesman and leader."[23]

The priestly historiography did its best to hide the role that the Davidic monarchy played during the Babylonian exile and the early Persian period. The Priestly writing transfers back to Sinai the royal status of the priesthood: before and during the monarchy, the high priest was appointed not by human choice but by divine right (Exod 28:1), was anointed (Exod 29:7; Lev 8:12), wore an official robe (Exod 28:2-43; 39:1-31) and a crown (Exod 28:36-38; 39:30-31), was the mediator between God and the people (Lev 17), and served for life before passing the office to his eldest son (Num 20:22-29).

The traditions of both Ezra and Chronicles blame the Babylonian conquest for the end of the Davidic monarchy. Zedekiah is singled out as the last Davidic king of Judah (2 Chr 36:11-21; 1 Esd 1:46-58). Jehoiachin is quickly dismissed as merely the predecessor of Zedekiah: "he reigned three months and ten days in Jerusalem" and "did what was evil in the sight of YHWH" (2 Chr 36:9-10; 1 Esd 1:43-46). The narrative is drastically abridged from 2 Kings; nothing is said of the small court of relatives and officials that accompanied the king in exile (2 Kgs 24:8-17) or of his second, and more successful, political career as the vassal king of Judah under the Babylonians in the years following the death of Zedekiah (2 Kgs 25:27-30). Chronicles goes as far as to turn Jehoiachin into a child king who "was eight years old when he began to reign," the prepubertal age of the king making impossible that he fathered an heir during the "three years and ten days" of his kingdom (2 Chr 36:9).[24]

As for Jehoiachin's successors Sheshbazzar and Zerubbabel, in Chronicles they are only inconspicuous names in the genealogy of the sons of David (1 Chr 3), deprived of any political role. In the tradition of Ezra, where they do have a major political role, nothing is said about their royal ances-

22. Joseph Blenkinsopp, *Sage, Priest, Prophet: Religious and Intellectual Leadership in Ancient Israel* (Louisville: Westminster John Knox, 1995), 80.

23. Lester L. Grabbe, *Priests, Prophets, Diviners, Sages: A Socio-Historical Study of Religious Specialists in Ancient Israel* (Valley Forge: Trinity, 1995), 50.

24. That Jehoiachin was "eighteen years old when he began to reign" is confirmed not only by the agreement between 2 Kgs 24:8 and 1 Esd 1:43, but also by the reference to "the king's wives" in 2 Kgs 24:15 and by tablets from Babylonian archives that testify how by 592 Jehoiachin already had five sons.

try; without a critical analysis of ancient sources, one would never guess that the two illustrious "governors" were from the house of David.

Yet, the Zadokites still needed the Davidic monarchy "to legitimate the temple and cultic traditions current in [their] own time."[25] After all, it was David who conquered Jerusalem and his son Solomon who built the first sanctuary, and it was their descendants who for generations watched over the place the Zadokites regarded as the only legitimate place of the only legitimate temple, which they had rebuilt after the Babylonian exile and in which they now served as high priests.

The providential role played by the Davidic monarchy for the establishment of the Zadokite order is at the center of the Chronicles' rewriting of the ancient history of Israel. The text summarizes the period from Adam to the death of Saul in lengthy genealogies (1 Chr 1–9) and focuses on the kingdom of David (1 Chr 10–29). Radically departing from the tradition, Chronicles exalts David, not Solomon, as the true founder of the Jerusalem temple. It was David who planned the construction of the sanctuary in all details, organized the priesthood (1 Chr 23–24), and gave to Solomon the "plan of all the works" (28:19).

The shift of emphasis from Solomon to David and the unprecedented expansion of the king's functions as the patron and organizer of the temple cult are not accidental. In the Chronicles' view, the divine task of the Davidic monarchy was to establish in Jerusalem the only sanctuary that God required to be built in the land of Israel and to organize the priesthood according to the dictates of the Mosaic torah. Accordingly, the rise of the house of David and the establishment of the house of YHWH had to be brought together; the synchrony stresses the Zadokite view that the Davidic king was chosen by God only to be instrumental in the building of the Jerusalem temple.

As William Riley has demonstrated in a monographic study on the relationship between king and cultus in Chronicles, the notion that the Jerusalem kings were called "to exercise the role of temple-builders and to bear the responsibility for the temple's maintenance" guides Chronicles' understanding of the entire monarchic age.[26] David's plans of construction were carried out by Solomon (2 Chr 1–9), but one must wait until the reforms of

25. Pomykala, 110.

26. William Riley, *King and Cultus in Chronicles: Worship and the Reinterpretation of History,* JSOTSup 160 (Sheffield: JSOT, 1993), 155.

Hezekiah (29–32) and Josiah (34–35) in order to see the priestly structure completed in all its details and David's orders about the priesthood finally executed. Chronicles wants its readers to feel a profound sense of accomplishment and fulfillment before watching the fall of the house of David. Nothing that had to be done was left out: "After all this, when Josiah had set the temple in order" (2 Chr 35:20), he died in battle. Josiah's death was the beginning of the end; the last chapter of Chronicles (2 Chr 36) is a dry narrative of the final agony of the monarchy in the hands of the Babylonians.

The fall of the house of David does not seem to disturb the Zadokite confidence in God's promises. Chronicles recognizes that David and his descendants received the divine right to reign: "the Lord God of Israel gave the kingship over Israel forever to David and his sons by a covenant of salt" (2 Chr 13:5). However, the Mosaic covenant makes the divine promise to David conditional on the righteousness of his children, as Solomon reminds himself: "O Lord, God of Israel . . . you promised my father David, saying, 'There shall never fail you a successor before me to sit on the throne of Israel, if only your children keep to their way, to walk in my law as you have walked before me'" (2 Chr 6:16; cf. 7:17-18). As long as the Davidic monarchy had to carry out its providential task to build the temple and establish the priesthood, God passed over the tormented and often unfaithful succession of Davidic kings. But after everything was fulfilled with Josiah, the survival of the monarchy depended exclusively on their righteousness.

The ancient historiography of Kings, which focused on the eternal covenant between God and the house of David according to the prophecy of Nathan (2 Sam 7), ended with the good news of the liberation of King Jehoiachin. Chronicles also mentions the genealogy of the house of David far beyond Zedekiah, including Jehoiachin, Sheshbazzar, and Zerubbabel, up to its own times (1 Chr 3). Yet, it offers a completely different happy ending — the edict of Cyrus. In its view, the house of David lost the kingship not because the royal family was exterminated by external enemies, but because, after they had fulfilled their mission, their sins made them unworthy of ruling. "The Davidic rule, having finished its cultic task, had given way to a new regime with God's approval because of the dynasty's unfaithfulness."[27]

The Babylonian exile affected the personal destiny of the members of the house of David by barring them from the way to kingship. Yet, it did not cancel what the Davidic kings accomplished. The Zadokites held it

27. Riley, 203.

would remain forever, with or without the king — the temple and the priesthood. Offering an astonishing example of theological supersession, Chronicles claims that the end of the Davidic monarchy did not mean the end of God's promise to David as it "sees that promise to have its enduring reality in the temple and cultic community of God's post-exilic people."[28]

This was in the eyes of the Zadokites the major accomplishment and the divine mission of the Davidic monarchy, the very and only reason of their election — to establish the Zadokite order. So, ironically the house of David ended up in the Zadokite tradition being praised for empowering those who replaced their authority and priesthood.

Now that it was merely an institution of the past, the Davidic monarchy lost definitively any residual cultic function in the Zadokite worldview. In its discussion of the duties of priests and of laity, the Priestly writing, unlike Ezekiel, gives no place to the king; he would be simply another lay person. Equally lost is any reference that might suggest a special sacral relationship between God and the king. Chronicles systematically omits the formula "for the sake of my servant David" (1 Kgs 11:13, 32; 2 Kgs 19:34; 20:6), which would challenge the cult's unique foundational role for the stability and welfare of Jewish society.

Chronicles erases any surviving reference to the priestly functions of the king, which would conflict with the exclusiveness of the Zadokite priesthood. The "sons of David," who in 2 Sam 20:25-26 are "priests," are transformed into "chief officials in the service of the king" (1 Chr 18:17).

In order to make it plainly clear what God feels about the relationship between the priest and the king, Chronicles has also an original and quite educational story about King Uzziah. The king "grew proud . . . and entered the temple of YHWH to make offering on the altar of incense" (2 Chr 26:16). Reacting as no preexilic priest would ever dare or dream to do, the priest Azariah warned the king by asserting back over the centuries the eternal validity of the Zadokite principles: "It is not for you, Uzziah, to make offering to YHWH, but for the priests . . . who are consecrated to make offering" (26:18). Uzziah did not listen, and as punishment "a leprous disease broke out on his forehead . . . and he was leprous to the day of his death" (2 Chr 26:20-21). The house of David is a respected institution of blessed memory and their role as temple-builders and patrons was providential, but worship is the priest's business, and woe betides those who forget it.

28. Riley, 204.

3. Sons of Levi, Sons of Aaron, Sons of Phinehas

While the confrontation with the Davidic monarchy resulted in an astonishing triumph that went far beyond their rosiest expectations, the attempt of the Zadokites to conquer the leadership in the Jerusalem temple gave mixed results. The Zadokites reached their primary goal: the rebuilt temple was not simply the restoration of the old sanctuary but a new one with new rules and a new priesthood. The Zadokites also succeeded in excluding most of their Levitical rivals from the priesthood and in establishing the principle of a distinction within the temple personnel between "priests" and "levites," a distinction that, unknown in preexilic Judaism, became normative in postexilic sources. As Blenkinsopp argues, "levites as *clerus minor* are not unambiguously attested before the Neo-Babylonian period. . . . The displacement occurred as a result of conflict within priestly circles in the Neo-Babylonian and early Persian periods, the context no doubt being control of worship in the Babylonian Diaspora and especially of the preparations for resuming worship after return to the homeland."[29]

However, some Levitical families proved to be strong and influential enough to resist the Zadokite claim of being left "alone" as priests. The showdown resulted in accommodation and compromise. The priestly genealogies, cold and pedantic as they may seem, are the product of hot conflicts, and when critically examined and decoded, offer a fascinating glimpse at the evolution of Jewish leadership in the early Second Temple period. Many details may escape our viewing, but the general picture looks clear.

The earliest lists of returnees mention four classes of "priests": Jedaiah, Immer, Pashhur, and, less frequently, Harim (Neh 11:10-14; 1 Esd 5:24-25 = Ezra 2:36-39 = Neh 7:39-42; 1 Esd 9:18-22 = Ezra 10:18-22). Only the first class is associated with the house of Zadok; nothing is said about the origin of the other three classes. Over time, the situation became more and more complex with the addition of new families, as shown by the conflicting names and numbers of Neh 12:1-7, 12-21; 10:3-9[Heb 4-10] and Ezra 8:2. Eventually the priestly classes added up to 24, the partition that Chronicles attributes to David (1 Chr 24:1-19) and that would remain standard in the later Second Temple period ("until this day," says

29. Blenkinsopp, *Sage, Priest, Prophet,* 93-94.

Josephus in *Ant* 7:365-66 — a fact also confirmed by the sectarian literature of Qumran and by *m. Sukkah* 5:6).[30]

While acknowledging that originally "four classes returned from the exile: Jedaiah, Harim, Pashhur, and Immer," rabbinic literature explains the multiplication of priestly classes as a subdivision of them for merely practical purposes: "the prophets among them then arose and made twenty-four lots and cast them in an urn. [Jedaiah, Harim, Pashhur, and Immer] came and drew five lots each, each making six including himself" (*y. Ta'an.* 68a; cf. *t. Ta'an.* 2:1-2; *b. Arak.* 12b). This seems to be also the sense of Josephus's passage in *Contra Apionem* when he speaks of the Jews having "four tribes of priests" (*C. Ap.* 2:108).

A critical analysis of ancient sources shows a much less irenic picture behind the multiplication of priestly classes. The earliest lists can still be understood as made of Zadokite families, or at least of families who accepted to be recognized as such. But when in the final partition of Chronicles we see enrolled families who claimed descent from Ahimelech and Abiathar (1 Chr 24:3, 6), we face a qualitatively different situation. Abiathar and Ahimelech were representatives of a priestly family, that of Eli, which was traditionally rival to that of Zadok. Abiathar was priest with Zadok under David (2 Sam 20:25), but was later banished by Solomon for his part in supporting Adonijah (1 Kgs 1:7), while Zadok (2:35) and his son Azariah after him (4:2) were Solomon's priests.

The ancient tradition presented the exile of Abiathar as "fulfilling the word of YHWH that he had spoken concerning the house of Eli in Shiloh" (1 Kgs 2:27; cf. 1 Sam 2:27-34; 3:11-14). Because of their sins, the house of Eli lost the right to the priesthood that was given to them by God's choice "in Egypt when they were slaves to the house of Pharaoh" (1 Sam 2:27). 1 Sam 2:35-36 compares the humiliation of the house of Eli to the glory of the house of "the faithful priest" Zadok, and without pity forecasts that "every one who is left in your family shall come to implore him for a piece of silver or a loaf of bread."

We do not know when the rehabilitation of the house of Eli occurred or under what circumstances they saw their rights as priests vindicated. We

30. H. G. M. Williamson, "The Origins of the Twenty-Four Priestly Courses: A Study of 1 Chronicles xxiii-xxvii," *VTSup* 30 (1979): 251-68. On the Qumran calendrical documents that incorporate the priestly courses, see James C. VanderKam, *Calendars in the Dead Sea Scrolls: Measuring Time* (London: Routledge, 1998), 77-87.

can only conjecture that their opposition to the house of David made them natural allies of the Zadokites during the exile and helped overcome the ancient grudge and rivalry. However, the listing of the descendants of Abiathar along with the descendants of Zadok shows not only how proudly they refused to be assimilated to the Zadokite genealogy, but also how powerful they must have been, as they succeeded in maintaining a separate identity. The Zadokites would have never compromised and co-opted their former rivals (to whom the tradition prophesied only a destiny of beggars), if they had not been somehow compelled to do so in order to keep, consolidate, or strengthen their power.

Such an explicit compromise with the house of Eli in fact denied the Ezekielian principle that the descendants of Zadok alone had the right to be priests and would have entirely disrupted the foundations of the Zadokite primacy, if some changes were not introduced in the genealogical structure of the priesthood in order to accommodate the newcomers. The answer was to widen the boundaries of the priesthood as to embrace the "priests" as an intermediate class, and make them share common descent from a particular branch of Levites, the "sons of Aaron." As a result, a distinction arose between the sons of Zadok (now referred to as the "high priests"), who were enlisted as the direct descendants of Aaron's grandson Phinehas, and the other descendants of Aaron's sons Eleazar and Ithamar (the "priests"), and between them and the rest of the descendants of Levi (the "levites"). The Ezekielian bipartition between the "sons of Levi" and the "sons of Zadok" developed into a tripartition, within the temple personnel, of "sons of Levi," "sons of Aaron," and "sons of Phinehas."

A. *The Sons of Aaron*

The creation of the Aaronite priesthood was a postexilic phenomenon. In the earlier tradition the role of Moses' brother, "Aaron the Levite" (Exod 4:14), was that of a thaumaturge and leader in the Exodus story who served primarily as an interlocutor in what dialogue the narrative required (Exod 4:14-16; 7:1ff.). Aaron was never referred to as a priest, or father of priests; on the contrary, he opposed Moses in cultic matters (Exod 32; Num 12). Remarkably, while the "sons of Zadok" by the time of the Babylonian exile were acknowledged to be "sons of Levi" also (Ezek 40:46; cf. 43:19; 44:15), nothing is said in Ezekiel 40–48 about their Aaronite descent. Aaron and the "sons of Aaron" are not even mentioned. "Indeed, no tradition of Judaean origins which can plausibly be regarded as ancient, that is, preexilic, so much as mentions Aaron occupying a priestly role or discharging priestly functions."[31]

Still, in the traditions of Nehemiah and Ezra dealing with the early return to Judah we find only scant and ambiguous references to Aaron and Aaronite priesthood. It was the Priestly writing and Chronicles which legitimized and standardized the new threefold structure of priestly power by transferring it back to both the mythical and the historical past of Israel. What better way to consolidate a revolution than to show that there was no revolution and this was the way things had always been! The rabbinic chain of tradition that traces the origins of their movement back to Sinai has illustrious antecedents in the priestly genealogies.

The Priestly writing links the privileges of the "sons of Aaron" as priests to the Mosaic revelation. "YHWH spoke to Moses: . . . You shall bring Aaron and his sons to the entrance of the tent of meeting . . . and anoint them . . . that they may serve me as priests; and their anointment shall admit them to a perpetual priesthood throughout all generations to come" (Exod 40:1-35 [P]). The later tradition would commonly refer to the priests as the "sons of Aaron" or the "house of Aaron" as distinct from the rest of the people of Israel (Ps 115:9-11; 118:2-4; 135:19-20; Sir 45:6-22).

On principle, no one not belonging to the "house of Aaron" by birth could be admitted to it; and no one belonging to it through legitimate birth could be excluded from it. In reality, the tradition is full of stories of priestly families that suddenly were able to prove their ancestry, while others were pitilessly excluded (Ezra 2:61-63 = Neh 7:63-65). Until the situation became more stabilized, which occurred only at the end of the Persian period, being in or out was more a matter of power than of principle.[32]

The new order also implied some changes in the genealogy of the descendants of Aaron in order to accommodate the ancestors of those priestly families who succeeded in being associated with the Zadokites af-

31. Blenkinsopp, *CBQ* 60 (1998): 36. See also Aelred Cody, *A History of the Old Testament Priesthood,* AnBib 35 (Rome: Pontifical Biblical Institute, 1969), 146-56.

32. Even later, priestly genealogy would remain hardly reliable. The "public archives," which Josephus mentions against the "detractors of [his] family," did not restrain him from embellishing his own genealogy (*Vita* 1-6). On the difficulties regarding Josephus's priestly genealogy, see Schürer (rev. Vermes), *The History of the Jewish People,* 1:46n.

ter the Babylonian exile. The most remarkable and pitiless choice was the replacement of the original two sons of Aaron, Nadab and Abihu, with Eleazar and Ithamar. In the earliest narrative, Nadab and Abihu are mentioned as the only sons of Aaron; together with their father and 70 of the elders of Israel, they accompanied Moses on the summit of Mount Sinai where "they beheld God, and they ate and drank" (Exod 24:1, 9-11). The Zadokite tradition (Lev 10 [P]) explains how Nadad and Abihu were later consumed by a heavenly fire for their sin of making an unauthorized offering before YHWH, and how Eleazar and Ithamar and their descendants were summoned in their place, while "Nadab and Abihu died before their father, and had no sons" (1 Chr 24:2). Eleazar and Ithamar became the ancestors of Zadok and Ahimelech, respectively (1 Chr 24:3). In this way it was possible to give equal legitimacy to the descendants of both priestly lines, while each maintained its separate identity.

The link with Eleazar guaranteed to the Zadokites their superiority over the sons of Ithamar. As the elder brother, Eleazar had already under the ministry of Aaron greater cultic responsibilities than Ithamar (Num 4:16, 28, 33 [P]), and when Aaron died, it was Eleazar who succeeded his father as the new high priest (20:25-28 [P]) and served under Moses and Joshua (25:11; 26:1; 31 [P]). Besides, of the 24 priestly classes, 16 are said to be of the "sons of Eleazar," while only eight are of the "sons of Ithamar" (1 Chr 24:4). There remained, however, the problem of preserving the primacy of the sons of Zadok among the descendants of Eleazar.

B. *The Sons of Phinehas*

The uniqueness of the Zadokites was saved by elevating them above the other "sons of Aaron," as they had already elevated themselves above the ordinary "sons of Levi," and by transferring back their ancestry from the time of David to the time of Moses. From "priests" the Zadokites became "high priests," and from "sons of Zadok" they became "sons of Phinehas."

Historically, the office of the "high priest" has its roots in the functions of the preexilic "chief priests" who likely were royal appointees, not necessarily related by blood and with no right to hereditary succession.[33]

33. Grabbe, *Priests, Prophets, Diviners, Sages,* 60-62; John R. Bartlett, "Zadok and His Successors at Jerusalem," *JTS* n.s. 19 (1968): 1-18.

Joshua, the first "high priest" of the Second Temple, was the grandson of Seraiah, the last "chief priest" of the First Temple under Zedekiah (2 Kgs 25:18-21). Chronicles takes for granted that the high priesthood was a preexilic office and that all the preexilic chief priests were sons of Zadok, such as, for instance, the chief priest Azariah at the time of King Hezekiah (2 Chr 31:9-10). That the Zadokite list of preexilic "high priests" omits some of the most influential chief priests of the First Temple, such as Ira the Jairite (2 Sam 20:26), Jehoiada (2 Kgs 11–12), Uriah (2 Kgs 16:10-16; Isa 8:2), Zephaniah ben Maaseiah (Jer 21:1; 29:25-26; 37:3), and others, is plain evidence of its artificial and anachronistic character. The hereditary office and the title of "high priest" are postexilic, the first primary evidence stemming from the Elephantine papyri at the very end of the 5th century.[34] In the context of the Second Temple, the high priesthood must be regarded as a new institution, now that there was no longer a functioning monarchy, and priests and levites were hierarchically subordinated to a higher authority which the Zadokites held as hereditary from father to son.

As the partition between Levites and Aaronites is clearly secondary to that between Zadokites and Levites, so is the division between Aaronites and Zadokites. Originally, the source of Zadokite authority was their link with Zadok, not with Aaron. Preexilic and exilic texts were so uninterested in the problem that they fail to provide any detailed genealogical information on Zadok. The text of 2 Sam 8:17, which makes Zadok "son of Ahitub," is clearly corrupted as Zadok was certainly not of the house of Eli. Many hypotheses have been made about the origin of this priest; the fact is that ancient sources, as in the case of Melchizedek, are totally silent.[35]

The question of Zadok's ancestry was a postexilic theological problem. Now that the Aaronite descent and the Sinaitic investiture were prerequisites for priesthood, the connection that Ezekiel 40–48 had established between Levi and Zadok was no longer sufficient. The Zadokites had to become "sons of Aaron," and the hereditary office of the high priest had to be as ancient as the Sinaitic revelation. Levi provided the model; the patriarch was the ancestor of both the levites and, through his descendant Aaron, the priests. Following the same pattern, Aaron could be the ancestor of both

34. Bezalel Porten and Ada Yardeni, *Textbook of Aramaic Documents from Ancient Egypt*, 1 (Jerusalem: Hebrew University, 1986), A4.7:18; A4.8:17.

35. See Grabbe, *Priests, Prophets, Diviners, Sages*, 61. See also Cody, 88-93.

the priests and, through one of his descendants, the Zadokite high priests. It was only a matter of finding a suitable descendant who would link Aaron to Zadok.

The Priestly writing solved the problem by introducing a new hero: Phinehas, son of Eleazar, son of Aaron the priest.[36] In the Priestly worldview, Aaron was now the first high priest, so much so that he is often referred to simply as "the priest" (Exod 29:30; 31:10; Num 3:6). His ministry was distinguished by special cultic functions, special laws (Lev 21:10-15), and special garments (8:7-9). As the high priesthood was hereditary and Aaron's sons Eleazar and Ithamar were the ancestors of the "priests," it was necessary to skip that generation and clarify who among the grandchildren of Aaron was granted the privilege to carry on the high priesthood, and why. The genealogy of Exod. 6:14-25 (P) already singles out Phinehas and makes the readers foresee the unique role to which he is destined above the other "sons of Aaron." The story of an incident at Shittim, when "the people began to have sexual relations with the women of Moab" and "yoked themselves to the Baal of Peor" (Num 25:1-5), then provided the setting for a spectacular performance (25:6-18 [P]). "As one of the Israelites came and brought a Midianite woman into his family . . . Phinehas took a spear in his hand . . . and pierced the two of them" (Num 25:6-8). Pleased by Phinehas's zeal, God "turned back [his] wrath from the Israelites . . . and granted him [his] covenant of peace," with the promise that "it shall be for him and his descendants after him a covenant of perpetual priesthood, because . . . he made atonement for the Israelites" (Num 25:12-13). Thus Phinehas became the point of departure of the autonomous Aaronite line chosen to perform the highest priestly function — atonement. Now, it was enough to connect Zadok backwards to Phinehas. The result was the creation of an unbroken genealogical chain of high priests that through Aaron, Eleazar, Phinehas, and Zadok reaches out to

36. Commentators agree that the reference to Phinehas in Judg 20:27b-28a is a late editorial insertion. Aside from the chronological absurdity that makes Phinehas still active at the end of the era of the Judges, a literary examination shows that verses 27b-28a are interpolations that break the continuity of the recital. See Abram Spiro, "The Ascension of Phinehas," *PAAJR* 22 (1953): 91-114. Phinehas the high priest son of Eleazar was unknown to the ancient Jewish historiography before the character was created by the Priestly writing. See Blenkinsopp, *CBQ* 60 (1998): 35. According to Cody, the character may well be inspired by the "Phinehas, son of Eli" of 1 Samuel (1:3; 4:4, 17). See Cody, 171.

Jehozadak, whose son Joshua was the first to officiate in the Second Temple (1 Chr 6:1-15[Heb. 5:27-41]; Ezra 7:1-5).

The Zadokites reached their goal. It did not matter that the ancestors of Zadok, like his descendants, did not include some of the best-known figures of ancient "priests" recorded in the previous Jewish historiography, such as Eli and his sons (1 Sam 1:1–3:18; 1 Kgs 2:27). Despite any exclusion, Zadok had now a noble pedigree, instead of an obscure genealogy, and from now on he would be remembered not only among the "sons of Eleazar" (1 Chr 24:3) but also as a distinguished member of the "family of Phinehas" (cf. *Ant* 8.11). More importantly, while it was agreed that all the sons of Aaron, through Eleazar and Ithamar, had the right to the priesthood, the high priesthood was limited to the descendants of Eleazar's son Phinehas, that is, the sons of Zadok.

C. *The Sons of Levi*

The Priestly writing also argues that the distinction between "the priests, the sons of Aaron" and ordinary "levites" had its foundation in the divine order at Sinai, when "YHWH spoke to Moses, saying: Bring the tribe of Levi near, and set them before Aaron the priest, so that they may assist him. . . . You shall give the levites to Aaron and his descendants; they are unreservedly given to him from among the Israelites" (Num 3:5-10 [P]). Accordingly, Moses enrolled the Levites "by ancestral houses and by clans. . . as YHWH commanded [him]" (Num 3:14–4:49 [P]), and in Chronicles David appointed "the divisions of the priests and of the levites" to serve in the First Temple (1 Chr 23–26), and the "good" kings Hezekiah and Josiah re-established them and saw they were provided for (2 Chr 31:2-19; 35:7-15).

Whoever dare change this order is severely punished by God. The Priestly writing makes plainly clear that those who would challenge the Aaronite power deserve nothing but death. "You shall make a register of Aaron and his descendants; it is they who shall attend to the priesthood, and any outsider who comes near shall be put to death" (Num 3:10 [P]). The story of the rebellion of Korah, as it results from the Priestly redaction (Num 16), is a warning against those, levites and laypeople, who will challenge the Aaronite order and seek full priestly status for all the sons of Levi. Moses was outraged by their demand: "Hear now, you levites! Is it too little for you that the God of Israel has separated you from the congregation of Israel, to allow you to approach him in order to perform the duties of YHWH's tabernacle, and to stand before the congregation and serve them? He has allowed you to approach him, and all your brother levites with you; yet you seek the priesthood as well!" (Num 16:8b-10 [P]). God was not less displeased; the ordeal set up by Moses ended in a terrifying punishment. "The earth opened its mouth," and Korah and his associates "went down alive into Sheol. . . . And fire came out from YHWH and consumed the two hundred fifty" levites who dared "offer the incense" (Num 16:32-35 [P]). Then God commanded "Eleazar son of Aaron . . . to take the bronze censers that had been presented by those who were burned, and to hammer them out as a covering for the altar — a reminder to the Israelites that no outsider, who is not of the descendants of Aaron, shall approach to offer incense before YHWH, so as not to become like Korah and his company" (Num 16:37-40[Heb. 17:4-5] [P]). The message is clear, direct, the supernatural elements of the story advisedly aimed to impress and frighten the readers. The division between sons of Levi and sons of Aaron is from God and by God protected.

Considering the pitiless anti-Levitical stance of the Priestly writing, it is not surprising that the tradition records how difficult it was for the priests to recruit their servants, the "levites." While the competition for being recognized among the sons of Aaron was wildly open with plenty of ambitious candidates, being a "levite" was a much less sought goal. "Since levites who chose to return would have to resign themselves to a subordinate role in temple affairs, it is understandable that few chose to do so."[37]

The shortage of levites remained a major concern for a long time. When Ezra first gathered "by the river that runs to Ahava" those who would come with him from Babylon, he was disappointed to "find there none of the descendants of Levi" and had to set a special mission, and even so he was able to recruit only "38" of them (Ezra 8:15-20). The list of Ezra 2 = Neh 7 encompasses a mere handful of 74 levites as against 4289 priests. The proportion is even more remarkable when considering the larger availability of non-Levitical temple personnel (148 musicians and 138 gatekeepers).

The priestly aristocracy responded to this situation with a series of measures, such as the (occasional?) lowering of the age of admission to the

37. Blenkinsopp, *Sage, Priest, Prophet,* 94.

levitical rank, which some sources fixed at 25 (Num 8:24-26) or 20 years (1 Chr 23:24, 27; 2 Chr 31:17; Ezra 3:8) against the 30 years of Numbers 4 and 1 Chr 23:3. Eventually, the best way to deal with the shortage crisis was to broaden the definition of levites as to include temple personnel, such as "gatekeepers" and "liturgical musicians," who originally were not classed as levites (Ezra 2:40-42 = Neh 7:43-45; Ezra 7:7; Neh 13:10). Our sources allow us even to reconstruct an intermediate stage that first welcomed into the levitical rank (Neh 11–12) the "liturgical musicians" only; later, the gatekeepers also were accorded the honor (1 Chr 23:4-5; 25:1–26:19). This shows, once again, how flexible and fluid the genealogical theories of the Second Temple were behind their apparent rigidity. The adaptability of the system was one of the reasons for the Zadokite success.

But the major reform was to secure financial support for the assistant "levites" independently of the emoluments due to the priests for the sacrifices. The Deuteronomistic legislation provided emoluments for the priests, that is, for "all the sons of Levi" (Deut 18:1-8); the rest of the temple personnel, then composed of non-Levites, were excluded. Ezekiel 40–48 made higher claims regarding the priests, that is, the sons of Zadok (44:28-30), and ignored the needs of the levites. Obviously, in their being assimilated to the servants of the priests, the levites had to bear also a financial punishment. Thus, while Deuteronomy and Ezekiel disagree on who the priests are, they share the principle that only the priests who perform sacrifices have the right to receive emoluments.

There is strong evidence that this situation did not change up to the time of Nehemiah. On the eve of Nehemiah's mission, Malachi is concerned only about the precarious moral and financial situation of the sons of Levi who were "priests" (Mal 2:1; 3:6-12); again, not a word is said about the sons of Levi who were not priests. Nehemiah was apparently the first to realize that the autonomy of the temple could not be fully guaranteed without providing emoluments to the levites too. He made an assembly of returnees approve a decree in which they obligated themselves "to bring to the levites the tithes from our soil," and the Levites in turn agreed to pay to the priests "a tithe of the tithes" (Neh 10:37-38[Heb. 38-39]). He also made the treasury of the temple the storage room of the contributions to both the priests and the levites, and appointed both priests and Levites as supervisors (Neh 13:13; cf. 12:44-47). It was an innovative and very controversial step. Many people were discontent that they had to maintain not only the priests but also the servants, even more so now that gatekeepers and musicians were also included. Nehemiah had to fight hard to impose his will (Neh 13:10-14).[38]

As usual, the Priestly writing transfers back Nehemiah's legislation to the Sinaitic revelation. It was Moses who commanded the Israelites to give tithes to the levites (Num 18:21-24) and the levites in turn to pay "a tithe of the tithe" to the Aaronite priests (18:25-32). Chronicles would then attribute to King Hezekiah the institution of store-chambers in the temple under the supervision of priests and levites, where the tithes for the priest and the levites were stored before being distributed (2 Chr 31:11-21).

Thanks also to these arrangements, as time passed and the new order became widely accepted, the tone of the anti-Levitical polemics that often characterized the earliest Zadokite literature softened. The Chronicles repeatedly praise the faithfulness of the levites and their loyalty to the Jerusalem temple. In particular, when the schism of the northern tribes occurred, the levites are said to have "left their common lands and their holdings [to] come to Judah and Jerusalem" (2 Chr 11:13-14). In this climate of harmony and fair play, Chronicles is not afraid of stressing the autonomy and dignity of the sons of Levi, or even exalting their superior zeal over the priests (2 Chr 29:34).

The more positive view of the levites in Chronicles does not signal the emergence of a pro-Levitical anti-Aaronite party, but the cessation of hostilities. During the early Second Temple period, the levites remained a class of lower priesthood under the control of the "sons of Aaron" and the "sons of Phinehas." We have no evidence yet of conflicts between levites and priests, such as those that would arise in Roman times and lead, for example, "the singers of hymns" to claim the right "to wear linen robes on equal terms with the priests" — a request that, eventually accorded by King Agrippa II, was labeled by the priest Josephus as "contrary to the ancestral laws" and "liable of punishment" (*Ant* 20:216-18).

It is unquestionable, however, that already under the Zadokites the higher degree of integration among the different classes of Jewish priesthood brought about a corresponding increase in the power and influence of the levites. As the range and dignity of their past functions expanded in the historical narratives of Chronicles, so did the range and dignity of their present functions. Of prime importance for the future was Chronicles' recognition of their public role as "administrators and judges" (1 Chr

38. For a discussion of the episode in its historical context, see the following chapter.

26:29) and, in particular, as "scribes" (2 Chr 34:13) and "teachers of the book of the law of YHWH . . . through all the cities of Judah" (2 Chr 17:7-9; cf. Neh 8).

Not improperly, Flavius Josephus would define the structure of power following the Babylonian exile as "a form of government that was aristocratical, but mixed with oligarchy, for the high priests were at the head of their affairs, until the posterity of the Hasmoneans set up kingly government" (*Ant* 11:111). Since the beginning the Zadokite oligarchic power had indeed an "aristocratical character" as it so largely depended on the support of their fellow priests, the Aaronites (and to a lesser extent of the levites). What began with Ezekiel as a Zadokite revolution resulted in an Aaronite hegemony. Ellis Rivkin perceived it long ago: "A coalition of Levitical families . . . join[ed] together as a privileged class, the sons of Aaron, against other priestly families. At the same time, by . . . allocating to the high priest the special privilege of being the Grand Expiator . . . the powerful Zadokite family was allowed to enjoy priestly supremacy, although not the monopoly accorded to them by the last chapters of Ezekiel. Such a coalition could beat down the claims of the other Levitical families for altar rights."[39] This aristocratic aspect would prove to be providential for the survival of the priestly hierarchy when the Zadokite leadership "imploded," mostly as a result of its own internal strife, in the first half of the 2nd century. Then, the Aaronite aristocracy would prove to be self-sufficient and strong enough to support a change in the leadership.

All of this, however, belongs to the future of Judaism after the Maccabean Revolt. Since members of the house of Zadok kept the hereditary high priesthood in the early Second Temple period, we may call "Zadokite Judaism" the form of Judaism that was predominant up to the Maccabean Revolt. Wherever and whenever a proto-rabbinic tradition began, its roots must be traced back neither in the legendary institutions of Rabbinic Judaism nor in the vacuum of elusive oral traditions but in the actual dynamics of the priestly society the Zadokites created after the Babylonian exile.

39. Ellis Rivkin, "The Revolution of the Aaronites," *The Shaping of Jewish History: A Radical New Interpretation* (New York: Scribner, 1971), 21-41 (quotation, 36-37).

CHAPTER TWO

Zadokite Judaism and Its Opponents

1. The Zadokite Worldview

Zadokite Judaism was a society that unceasingly and persistently defined the boundaries of cosmic and social structure; rules and regulations were enforced to restrict or control interaction and avoid trespassing.

The Priestly writing tells how the Creator turned the primeval disorder into the divine order (Gen 1:1–2:4a [P]). At the beginning was chaos ("a formless void," 1:2), but through a seven-day process of creation boundaries of division were set to organize the cosmos. God separated light from darkness on the first day, the waters above from the waters below on the second, water from dry land on the third, and day from night on the fourth. As time unfolded, the spaces that progressively came into existence (heavens, water, air) were filled with the living beings that belong to them (stars, fish, birds, respectively), so that all creatures might fit their proper environment. Then God placed on earth the creature it was destined for — the "human being . . . male and female" (1:27). The refrain that scans the creation story, "God saw that it was good" (1:10, 12, 18, 21, 25), repeats that everything was made advisedly according to God's will, until the climactic conclusion of the sixth day when "God saw everything that he had made, and indeed, it was very good" (1:31). At this point, God finally "rested from all the work that he had done . . . and blessed the seventh day and sanctified it" (2:2-3).

By creation, therefore, the Priestly writing means the process through which God organized the cosmos by defining the boundaries of time, space, and society. A coherent mechanism of "graded holiness" preserves the harmony of the system and makes the created world an orderly and closely related hierarchy of living beings, spaces, and times. In the cosmic ecology, each element is assigned a unique role within the graded scale of purity.[1]

(a) *Society.* At the top of the social hierarchy are the Zadokite high priests, followed by the Aaronite priests, the levites, male Jews, female Jews, Gentiles, clean and unclean animals. Such a division makes each class of living beings subject to different purity laws and defines their mutual relations as well as their cultic responsibilities toward God. Indeed, as commentators have not failed to notice, there is a correspondence, even linguistic, between the structure of the world as set up in Genesis and the social hierarchy of living beings in Leviticus based on diminishing levels of purity. "I am YHWH your God; I have separated you from the peoples; so you must separate between clean and unclean animals. . . . You shall be holy to me, for I YHWH am holy. I separated you from the peoples that you may be mine" (Lev 20:24-26). In the Zadokite worldview, social distinctions, within and outside the temple personnel, are not the result of historical processes, but of divine command.

(b) *Space.* The Zadokite order defines not only a hierarchy of living beings, but also a sacred geography. The holiness of the earth is concentrated in the highest degree in the Jerusalem temple. This produces areas of decreasing sanctity as one moves away from that center — a concept that Zadokite literature visualizes either in the form of boxed squares (Ezekiel 40–48) or of concentric circles (Num 2:1-34; 10:13-28 [P]) around the sanctuary. Accordingly, a higher degree of purity separates the temple from the city of Jerusalem, the city of Jerusalem from the land of Judah, and the land of Judah from the rest of the inhabited world.

(c) *Time.* Time, as well as society and space, is structured and graded, resulting in a division between sacred and ordinary days. Many of the Jewish festivals, as in the neighboring nations, were originally linked to the natural rhythms of the agricultural year, and in fact the Priestly

1. See Philip Peter Jenson, *Graded Holiness: A Key to the Priestly Conception of the World,* JSOTSup 106 (Sheffield: Sheffield Academic, 1992).

writing recognizes for both the sun and the moon the calendrical function to "be for signs and for seasons and for days and years" (Gen 1:14). The Zadokite creation story, however, takes as the central structure of time a cycle independent of any natural cycle, solar or lunar, that is, the regular seven-day cycle of the week, culminating in the holiest time of sabbath (Gen 2:2). The number seven is in fact the unifying element of the priestly calendar, the key element in regulating the orderly succession of sacred and ordinary days conforming to the set times of the cosmos.[2] Both textual evidence and logic point to the conclusion that the Zadokite cultic calendar was some sort of perpetual sabbatical calendar in which each feast fell on the same day of the week, year after year, with no conflict with the sabbatical cycle and, most importantly, no overlapping of sacred and ordinary times.[3]

As the Priestly narrative of the Flood knows only months of 30 days each (Gen 7:11, 24; 8:3-4), it is apparent that equinoxes and solstices were not counted as "days" but as intercalary times between seasons so that the sabbatical cycle knew no interruption in a perpetual 360+4–day calendar.[4] The medieval historian al-Biruni was quite correct when he claimed that the Jews introduced the lunar calendar and began to compute the dates of the new moons "nearly 200 years after Alexander the Great" in the aftermath of the Maccabean crisis and

2. The seventh day (the sabbath) was a special day of rest marked by additional sacrifices (Num 28:9-10). The seventh month was the one with the greatest number of festivals, as well as the most important ones. The seventh year (the sabbath of years) had a special festival character, as "a sabbath of complete rest for the land" (Lev 25:2-7). The seventh sabbath of years, the 49th year, was a special year marked "on the day of atonement" by the celebration of "the fiftieth year . . . a jubilee" (Lev 25:8-12). See Jenson, 192-95.

3. On the sabbatical nature of the Zadokite calendar, see Annie Jaubert, "Le calendrier des Jubilés et de la secte de Qumrân: Ses origines bibliques," *VT* 3 (1953): 250-64; "Le calendrier des Jubilés et les jours liturgiques de la semaine," *VT* 7 (1957): 35-61; James C. VanderKam, "The Origin, Character, and Early History of the 364-Day Calendar: A Reassessment of Jaubert's Hypotheses," *CBQ* 41 (1979): 390-411; "2 Maccabees 6,7a and Calendrical Change in Jerusalem," *JSJ* 12 (1981): 52-74.

4. Gabriele Boccaccini, "The Solar Calendars of Daniel and Enoch," in *The Book of Daniel: Composition and Reception,* ed. John J. Collins and Peter W. Flint (Leiden: Brill, 2001) 2:311-28.

that "before that time" their calendrical calculations were based "on the *tekufoth,* i.e. the year-quarters."[5]

The process of creation did not eliminate the disruptive forces of chaos, but confined them within precise boundaries. Even as a physical place, the abyss still exists in contrast to the orderly creation, and so does the wilderness populated by demons (Lev 16:8, 10; 17:7) in contrast to the inhabited world and Sheol, the neverland where the dead live, in contrast to the land of the living. There is therefore a strict connection between the cosmic and the moral order. To cross God's boundaries without proper rituals or without being in the proper state, or for any element of the cosmos to lose the integrity of its proper place, is to jeopardize the stability of the entire system and to invite disaster.

The ancient narratives of primeval history, which the Priestly writing inherited by the previous Jewish tradition, told of a fragile balance, of a universe always dangerously on the verge of collapse. There was a time in which the "sons of God" trespassed the boundary between heaven and earth, humans did what was evil, and for a while with the Flood the chaos seemed to retake the world (Gen 6). But the Priestly writing claims that this is not going to repeat. The covenant of Noah (Gen 9:8-11) between God and the earth (9:13) assures that God's order is forever. This does not mean that God will remain indifferent. On the contrary, God will take any necessary step to protect the order of creation — ordinary steps in ordinary circumstances and extraordinary steps in extraordinary circumstances, including allowing the king of Babylon to destroy the sanctuary (2 Chr 36:11-21). Even the most dramatic punishment, however, leads only to peace and restoration; the narrative of Chronicles ends with the good news of the rebuilt temple (2 Chr 36:22-23). God is perfectly capable of controlling and suppressing any rebellion without destroying the work of creation. There is no room in the Zadokite worldview for extreme measures that would lead to the end of times and a new creation. Despite any odds, this world is and remains the good and orderly universe created by God, and there is no reason God should destroy God's most perfect accomplishment.

God's commitment and care for the created world urge people's active

5. Al-Biruni, *The Chronology of Ancient Nations,* ed. C. Edward Sachau (London: W. H. Allen, 1879), 68.

cooperation. It is in the very interest of human beings to avoid God's punishment and enjoy the benefits of stability and order. The Zadokite civil and cultic laws share "a common concern for boundaries, sanctions, maintenance and correction" so that the world would remain "a stable and enduring sphere of ordered relations."[6]

The covenantal relationship between God and Israel, as understood by the Zadokites, is a pact for the stability and welfare of the universe. Compliance with the purity and moral laws of the covenant brings about stability and survival for the Jewish society as well as stability and survival for the entire world. The covenant is also the foundation of an orderly and balanced relationship between God and his people, once again by providing precise and not arbitrary boundaries. The Jewish people agreed to submit themselves to God's law, including the hardships of punishment in case of transgression. In return, God also agreed to put the divine punitive power under the restraints of the covenant and to guarantee protection and well-being to those who are faithful to God's laws.

Zadokite Judaism strongly believed in the power of human freedom. People have the duty and the capability of maintaining the distinction between right and wrong, holy and profane, pure and impure, and therefore each generation is accountable for its own actions. The earliest traditions of Israel allowed God a great deal of discretion in distributing reward and punishment within the span of some generations (Exod 20:5; Deut 5:9-10; 1 Kgs 21:28-29). Accordingly, it was not considered unfair to punish the entire family or group with the guilty, as for instance in the case of "Achan, son of Zerah" whom Joshua executed "with his sons and daughters" (Josh 7:24-26).

The Deuteronomistic legislation, however, prohibited humans to use this same criterion of God's justice in their relationships: the death penalty shall not apply to the family of the guilty (Deut 24:16; 2 Kgs 14:6). This created a contradiction between divine and human behavior.

The tension is apparent in Jeremiah at the time of the Babylonian exile. The prophet knows that the actual covenant grants God broad discretion: "You show steadfast love to the thousandth generation, but repay the guilt of parents into the laps of their children . . . rewarding all according to their ways and according to the fruit of their doings" (Jer 32:18-19). But Jeremiah cannot help seeing the unfairness of God's justice and longs for

6. Jenson, 217-18.

the time when God would establish a new covenant whereby the same principle of individual accountability, which regulates covenantal relations within the Jewish people, would also be applied in the relations between God and humans. "In those days they shall no longer say, 'The parents have eaten sour grapes, and the children's teeth are set on edge.' But all shall die for their own sins" (Jer 31:29-30).

Ezekiel turned Jeremiah's wishful thought into the general rule, claiming that God does hold each generation accountable only for their own actions: "What do you mean by repeating this proverb concerning the land of Israel, 'The parents have eaten sour grapes, and the children's teeth are set on edge'? As I live, says the Lord God, this proverb shall no more be used by you in Israel. . . . It is only the person who sins that shall die" (Ezek 18:2-4).

The only way for the individual to defer punishment is to repent and make atonement. This is not in itself a new principle: when provoked to anger, God is just but not cruel; repentance can make God change his mind. What is new in Ezekiel is that the righteous children have now nothing to fear. In 1 Kings, that Ahab humbled himself only meant that the punishment pending on his house was simply deferred from "his days" to "his son's days." Ezekiel stresses that when the sinner is either forgiven or punished, that is the end of God's wrath: "The righteousness of the righteous shall be his own, and the wickedness of the wicked shall be his own" (Ezek 18:20).

In their rewriting of Jewish history, the Priestly writing and Chronicles scrupulously applied the principles of Ezekiel as the foundation not only of human fair behavior (2 Chr 25:4 = 2 Kgs 14:6) but also of God's behavior toward God's people. The way in which Chronicles copes with the experience of the Babylonian exile offers a clear example of Zadokite revisionism. Kings had offered two reasons for the fall of Jerusalem, blaming either the evil kings of the past or Zedekiah. Neither reason was compatible with the principle of individual retribution.

The accumulation of the sins of the kings in general (2 Kgs 23:37b), and Manasseh in particular, was a key argument in Kings' effort to provide a theological explanation to the catastrophe. "Surely this came upon Judah at the command of YHWH, to remove them out of his sight, for the sins of Manasseh, for all that he had committed, and also for the innocent blood that he had shed; for he filled Jerusalem with innocent blood, and YHWH was not willing to pardon" (2 Kgs 24:3-4). But Manasseh had a long life and a successful kingdom that lasted "fifty-five years" (2 Kgs 21:1). He "did what was evil in the sight of YHWH" (2 Kgs 21:2), yet he did not experience God's wrath; it was the future generations who paid for his sins. How can this unequal treatment be fair and acceptable?

Chronicles straightens things out. Based on the principle that the sins of past generations have an effect only on rebellious children, Chronicles is committed to review the lives of the kings case by case. Manasseh was, yes, evil, but later he "humbled himself greatly before the God of his ancestors. He prayed to him, and God received his entreaty [and] heard his plea" (2 Chr 33:12-13). Manasseh's repentance explains the length of his kingdom in accordance with the words of Ezekiel: "if the wicked turn away from all their sins that they have committed and keep all my statutes and do what is lawful and right, they shall surely live; they shall not die" (Ezek 18:21).

Kings also established a more direct link between the sins of Zedekiah and God's anger against "Jerusalem and Judah" (2 Kgs 24:18-20). The king was made personally accountable for the destruction of Jerusalem, and this was surely more acceptable from the Zadokite point of view, but his sin meant the ruin of the entire nation; the leader's guilt fell upon the people. Once again, is it fair that the innocent paid for sins they had not committed?

The Zadokite historiography obviously agreed that Zedekiah was guilty "in the sight of YHWH his God" (2 Chr 36:12) and deservedly lost his power. To the religious sins against God Chronicles adds also the political act of rebellion "against King Nebuchadnezzar, who had made him swear by God" (2 Chr 36:13; cf. Ezek 17:16). Of course, the Zadokites had no sympathy whatsoever for the memory of the Babylonian king who executed Seraiah and exiled Jehozadak, but they did not want to miss the opportunity to stress their gratefulness and loyalty to the new "foreign kings" by whom they had been so generously treated and under whom they happily prospered.

What the Zadokites could not accept, however, was Kings' stance that innocent people paid for the sins of their king. In contrast, Chronicles points out that "all the chief priests (LXX: all the leaders of Judah and the priests) and the people also were exceedingly unfaithful, following all the abominations of the nations; and they polluted the house of YHWH that he had consecrated in Jerusalem" (2 Chr 36:14). From the perspective of hindsight, the Ezekielian principle that "it is only the person who sins that shall die" (Ezek 18:4) was confirmed. Collective catastrophe can be provoked only by collective guilt.

In the Zadokite reinterpretation of the Mosaic covenant, people's accountability is enhanced and God's discretion limited. Generation after generation, people can only blame themselves for their physical and moral failures, and God can no longer miss or delay the chance of punishing the wicked and rewarding the righteous. The Zadokite sense of order was fully satisfied: misfortune always follows transgression and well-being is always a sign of obedience.

At the core of the Sinaitic covenant is now the Jerusalem temple. In Kings the foundation of the sanctuary was a corollary of God's promise of eternal kingship to David and his successors. In the Zadokite worldview the house of YHWH has taken the place of the house of David, the priesthood has replaced the monarchy, and Aaron has superseded Moses. Priestly sources stress the absolute continuity between the tent in the wilderness and the First and the Second Temple, as well as the continuity and legitimacy of their institutions and rituals. God's one and exclusive temple, led by God's one and legitimate priesthood, is ideally at the center of the world. Its architecture and internal structure, its hierarchically disposed personnel, and the regularity of its liturgical calendar were intended to replicate the sacred geography of creation, the social hierarchy of humankind, and the eternal times of the cosmos. As the temple so closely mirrors the divine order of heaven, "to enter the Temple and take part in the Temple cult is therefore to participate in some degree in the unceasing worship going on in heaven."[7]

A replica of the divine and the human realms, the temple is also the place of interaction between the two. The regularity of its rituals is ultimately the main guarantee that creation would not collapse, the cult having the dual function of maintaining and restoring the creative order, by reminding God of God's commitments and removing sin and impurity from the worshipers.

The Priestly writing views the objects and acts of worship as a "memorial for the children of Israel before YHWH" (Exod 12:14; 28:12, 29; 30:16; 39:7; Lev 23:24; Num 10:10; 16:40[Heb. 17:5]; 31:54), so that, as Num 10:9 explains about the ritual sounding of the trumpets, Israel will be remembered before God and God will intervene in their favor. Sacrifices are "the

7. Joseph Blenkinsopp, *Sage, Priest, Prophet,* 113.

food of their God" (Lev 21:6; passim); they do not feed the deity, however, but appeal to God's sense of smell through the pleasant and reminding fragrance of burning offerings (Gen 8:21; Lev 2:2). In essence, while the previous Deuteronomistic tradition stressed the value of worship as a reminder for future generations (Deut 16:3; cf. 16:9-12; Exod 13:3-10; Josh 4:1-9), for the Zadokite tradition worship regards not human memory but God's memory, so that God will continue to remember and sustain the divine order of creation.[8]

Since some sort of evil and impurity, deliberately or undeliberately, individually or corporately, could not be avoided, the cult played an essential role also in providing rituals of atonement and purification, so averting God's wrath and punishment. The sacrifices "are the means by which the divine order, disturbed by impurity or sin, is restored to an original harmony."[9] People are offered a way back to their proper status provided that in their freedom they are eager to fulfill the required conditions for purification.

The Day of Atonement was indeed the climax of the temple cult and the highlight of Zadokite theology. On that occasion, in the holiest time of the year, the holiest space on earth was entered by the holiest living being on earth to provide atonement and purification of the sins and impurities of Israel. The sacredness and power of the day were exactly in its realigning in a perfect and unique coalescence, year after year, the social, spatial, and temporal axes on which the order of the universe is based.[10]

This was what the temple, the Mosaic Torah, and the Jewish priesthood were ultimately for. From their role as the keepers of the holiest place on earth, the interpreters of the sacred laws, and the ministers of the sacred times the Zadokites derived both their power at the top of Jewish society and the responsibility of adhering to the strictest rules of purity and the highest level of morality. Where modern historians see a mixture of social conservatism, national pride, and even obsession to cultic minutiae, the Jerusalem priests looked at themselves as the chosen to a hard service on be-

8. See Gabriele Boccaccini, "Il tema della memoria nell'ebraismo e nel giudaismo antico," *Hen* 7 (1985): 1-26 (esp. 11-13); Brevard S. Childs, *Memory and Tradition in Israel,* SBT 37 (Naperville: Allenson, 1962); and Willy Schottroff, *Gedenken im Alten Orient und in Alten Testament,* WMANT 15 (Neukirchen-Vluyn: Neukirchener, 1964).

9. Jenson, 164.

10. Jenson, 197-208.

half of the entire cosmos. "The high priest . . . and his priestly kinsmen served as the human community that established and maintained connection between the various orders of being. Their labor in the temple preserved all other orders of beings from collapse. Upon them, the people of Israel, the land of Israel, and, ultimately, the entire cosmos and its population all depended."[11]

2. Early Opponents: Samaritans, Tobiads, Prophets

The progressive establishment of the Zadokite order was accompanied by obscure conflicts with large sections of Israelites who had remained in the homeland — the "peoples of the land," often alluded to in Ezra-Nehemiah (Ezra 4:4-5; 6:21).

The conflict was not only political but also religious. The land of Israel that welcomed the returned exiles was not an estranged land, and most of its inhabitants were not pagans but people of Israelite descent and worshipers of YHWH. The Babylonian exile affected only the upper strata of the Jewish society — the political, military, religious, and economic elites. The rural and poor constituencies remained in Judah; their way of life and their religious practices were not significantly altered. With the establishment of the Second Temple and the Zadokite rise to power, the returnees came to dominate the province of Judah by transforming the strategies of survival they had developed in Babylon in a context of exile and minority into an effective means of social control over against their neighbors and former compatriots.[12]

The remainees were required to conform to the new order. Those who were unwilling to join the process of "restoration" and to accept its logic were banned from participating in the "reconstruction" of the temple and from intermarrying with the returnees, and finally outcast as "foreigners" from the cultic community of Jerusalem. Fringe phenomena of survival of the ancient religion of Israel, like the presence of a Jewish

11. Martin S. Jaffee, "Ritual Space and Performance in Early Judaism," *Early Judaism*, 164-212 (quotation, 171).

12. Joseph Blenkinsopp, "Temple and Society in Achaemenid Judah," in *Second Temple Studies*, ed. Philip R. Davies, 1: *The Persian Period*, JSOTSup 117 (Sheffield: JSOT, 1991), 22-53.

temple in Egypt at Elephantine, were tolerated for some time, provided that they recognized the authority of the Jerusalem priesthood, and then gradually reabsorbed.[13]

The victory of the Zadokite party defined the new Jewish identity as the "sons of the exile" (Ezra 4:1; 6:19-21; 8:35; 10:7, 16) and led to the myth in Chronicles that the Babylonian conquest left behind an empty land, all the inhabitants of Judah being either killed or exiled (2 Chr 36:17-21; cf. Lev 26:27-39).[14] "By their own self-definition, the returnees were the only surviving community with the right to call themselves the sons of Israel."[15]

Such an extreme retroactive glance at the historical events of the return from the exile shows the depth of the struggle. Many indeed tried to resist. Nehemiah lists his enemies: "Tobiah and Sanballat . . . and also the prophetess Noadiah and the rest of the prophets who wanted to make me afraid" (Neh 6:1-14; cf. 2:10, 19-20; 4:1-4[Heb. 3:33-36]).

A. *The Samaritans*

The roots of the conflict between Judah and Samaria go back to the monarchic period. At stake was the hegemony in the region — a situation that repeated after the Babylonian exile. In spite of their common religious roots, the Samaritans found themselves in the front line against any attempt at restoring an autonomous political or religious power in Judah, which would have diminished the hegemony they had gained in the region. Eventually, they could not stop the exiles' plan of reconstruction of the Jerusalem temple, nor effectively challenge the Zadokite refusal to share control of the rebuilt sanctuary with any local priesthood. The support the returnees received from the Persian administration under Darius I was a decisive factor in the setback. The political and economic power in the region, however, remained largely in the hands of the Samaritans.

13. Bezalel Porten, *Archives from Elephantine: The Life of an Ancient Jewish Military Colony* (Berkeley: University of California Press, 1968).

14. Robert P. Carroll, "The Myth of the Empty Land," in *Ideological Criticism of Biblical Texts,* ed. Tina Pippin, Semeia 59 (Atlanta: Scholars, 1992), 79-93.

15. John H. Hayes and Sara R. Mandell, *The Jewish People in Classical Antiquity: From Alexander to Bar Kochba* (Louisville: Westminster John Knox, 1998), 1.

The change in religious policy by Darius's son, Xerxes, revealed how precarious the situation of the returned exiles was. With a poor economy and without the military protection of walls, Jerusalem was defenseless and the temple heavily depended on the support of outsiders. As governors of Samaria, the Sanballats regained some control in Jerusalem with a covert and judicious policy of patronage. Had their influence not been strong in Jerusalem, they would never have succeeded in infiltrating even the Zadokite family structure of power through intermarriage. The lamentations of Malachi reflect the growing concerns of the Zadokite party over the objective weakness of the temple administration (Mal 1:6–2:9) and the priesthood's tendency to compromise and establish economic and familiar links with "foreign people" (2:10-12). Without a decisive change in the balance of power in the region, the outcome would probably have been some political and religious accommodation between the Sanballats and the Zadokites.

The Babylonian diaspora ran to the rescue, and thanks to personal connections with the Persian court and the new king, Artaxerxes, Nehemiah was able to reverse the situation. It is fairly obvious that Sanballat was upset at seeing Jerusalem gaining political, economic, and military autonomy, and frustrated at his failure to sabotage Nehemiah's plan. The walls of Jerusalem were a barrier against any hope of compromise with the Jerusalem priesthood. Now, it was just a matter of time before the political struggle turned into a religious schism.

At the end of the second mission of Nehemiah, the Zadokite party was strong enough to sever any residual tie with the Sanballats. A critical incident involved a distinguished member of the Zadokite family. "One of the sons of Jehoiada, son of the high priest Eliahib, was the son-in-law of Sanballat the Horonite; I chased him away" (Neh 13:28; cf. Josephus *Ant* 11:302-12).

Josephus adds to the story many interesting details, including the names of Manasseh and Nicaso as the banned couple. However, the chronological and genealogical framework he provides differs significantly, the episode being dated almost one century later. This does not imply an improbable repetition of events.[16] Josephus also knew from his source that the incident occurred "under Darius" (*Ant* 11:311) and involved a Sanballat. He ignored, however, that the Sanballats were an ancient dy-

16. See Paolo Sacchi, *The History of the Second Temple Period,* 152-59.

nasty, with several individuals bearing the same name, and not a single individual.[17] The only Sanballat Josephus knew was the "one who was sent by Darius, the last king (of Persia), into Samaria" (*Ant* 11:302). It was therefore obvious for Josephus to believe that the Darius mentioned in his source was Darius III, not the successor of Artaxerxes I, Darius II. He adjusted the historical and genealogical framework of the episode accordingly.

As the marriage between members of influential families was a public and calculated political act, so was the request for divorce. The Zadokite leadership signaled to the world their freedom from the patronage of the Sanballats.

As a good politician, Sanballat made the best of his defeat. According to Josephus, he promised his son-in-law "not only to preserve to him the honor of the priesthood but to procure for him the power and dignity of a high priest . . . and that he would build him a temple like that at Jerusalem upon Mount Gerizim" (*Ant* 11:310). Since the Deuteronomist legislation required only one sanctuary but did not specify its location, a member of the dominant priestly family was just what was needed to give equal legitimacy to a religious schism and to a rival temple, and to create embarrassment to their adversaries by means of the similarities between the two traditions. Significantly, the source of Josephus speaks only of Sanballat's "promise" of a temple and provides no description of its actual construction; archaeological evidence shows it probably happened only "about the end of the fourth century BCE."[18]

Although the boundaries of separation between the two communities remained somewhat uncertain for a long time, the wound in the Israelite body would never be healed. The destruction of the Samaritan temple on Mount Gerizim by John Hyrcanus in 128 B.C.E. only ratified the impossibility of reconciliation. Today, the Samaritans still survive as a separate branch of Israelite religion.[19]

17. Frank M. Cross, Jr., "Aspects of Samaritan and Jewish History in Late Persian and Hellenistic Times," *HTR* 59 (1966): 201-11.

18. Henk Jagersma, *A History of Israel from Alexander the Great to Bar Kochba* (Philadelphia: Fortress, 1985).

19. On the Samaritans, see Reinhard Pummer, *The Samaritans* (Leiden: Brill, 1987); Nathan Schur, *History of the Samaritans*, BEATAJ 18 (Frankfurt: Lang, 1989); John MacDonald, *The Theology of the Samaritans* (Philadelphia: Westminster, 1964).

B. *The Tobiads*

Among those who tried to "intimidate" Nehemiah and sabotage the reconstruction of the walls of Jerusalem, Tobiah emerges as an even more insidious enemy than Sanballat (Neh 2:10, 19-20; 4:1-5[Heb. 3:33-37]; 6:1-19). Nehemiah derogatorily labels him as "the Ammonite official" (Neh 2:10, 19), but the Tobiads were an Israelite family with a respectable Yahwist name; they only lived in the old Ammonite region, in Transjordan, where they had a rich estate. Because of their wealth, they could boast an impressive credit of connections in Jerusalem, consolidated by matrimonial ties with prominent Jewish nobles (Neh 6:18), including the Zadokite family (13:4).

The Tobiads were part of that class of landowners who had risen to power in Judah during the exilic period. The control the "nobles of Judah" exerted on the Judean economy as moneylenders was the major obstacle to the Zadokite power. The loyalty of priests and levites had to be anchored to a mechanism of economic autonomy in which the temple, not the landowners, was the center of Jewish economy through the collection of tithes. Nehemiah was determined to avoid any compromise and impair the economic interests of the "nobles of Judah" by forcing them to remit all previous debts and forbidding them from the taking of interest (Neh 5:1-13). It is no surprise that "the nobles of Judah sent many letters to Tobiah, and Tobiah's letters came to them. For many in Judah were bound by oath to him. . . . And Tobiah sent letters to intimidate me" — as Nehemiah complains (Neh 6:17-19). "Tobiah was a leading representative of the native Jews who had remained in the land and thus of particular danger to Nehemiah's plans."[20]

Nehemiah prevailed and imposed a system of tithes that for the first time included also the subordinate levites (Neh 9:38–10:39[Heb. 10:1-40]). In so doing he reached a double goal: to reward those levites who accepted the new order, and to free them from the economic dependence on the landowners.

It was enough for Nehemiah to leave Jerusalem for a few years, however, and at his return, with great disappointment, he found Tobiah being allotted in the temple by the high priest Eliashib "a large room where they had previously put . . . the tithes . . . [for] the levites . . . and the contribu-

20. Lester L. Grabbe, *Ezra-Nehemiah,* 176.

tions for the priests" (Neh 13:4-9). Tobiah's countermove had been to take control of the temple's treasure, so nullifying the effects of Nehemiah's economic reforms. Controlling the treasure, Tobiah could disrupt the social bloc that Nehemiah had built around the Zadokite power. That the point was the economic status of the subordinate "levites" is proved by the fact that they were the ones to suffer the most from the change. While the priests could survive thanks to the emoluments associated with the sacrifices, the levites and singers, deprived of their source of income, "had gone back to their fields" (Neh 13:10), where they were once again at the mercy of the landowners. Nehemiah reacted with timeliness and energy. He cast the Tobiads out of the temple and restored the tithes to the temple staff (Neh 13:8-9, 11-14). He won the day, but the struggle was yet far from over. Unlike the Sanballats, the powerful Tobiads remained a cumbersome presence in Judah, too strong and powerful to be destroyed. The tradition of Ezra does not accord them full membership in the new religious community, yet still cannot get rid of them completely. "The descendants of Tobiah" are listed among those returned exiles who "could not prove their ancestral houses or their descent, whether they belonged to Israel" (Neh 7:61-62). The limbo in which the Tobiads were confined did not prevent them from playing an important political role in Jewish society, which — as we will see — was only to increase in Hellenistic times.

C. *The Prophets*

As for the third opposition group, that of the prophets, Nehemiah maliciously insinuates that "Tobiah and Sanballat had hired them" (Neh 6:12). But the prophets had their own reasons to complain.

The Zakokite order drastically reduced the cultic and religious importance of the prophet. The preexilic prophets had a recognized role in the monarchic society and a close association with the temple. The ancient Jewish tradition portrayed the prophet and Levite Moses as a priest performing with his associates elaborate rituals and sacrifices at the foot of the mountain of God and inside the tent of meeting (Exod 24:4-8; 33:7-11; cf. Ps 99:6). The book of Judges even testifies to the existence of a priestly line descended from Moses: "Jonathan son of Gershom, son of Moses, and his sons were priests to the tribe of the Danites until the time the land went into captivity" (Judg 18:30).[21] In the monarchic age, prophets of non-Levitical descent, like the Ephraimite Samuel (1 Sam 1:1), were priests, and members of priestly families, like Jeremiah (Jer 1:1), were prophets. The boundary between priesthood and prophecy was not clearly drawn, and leaders of the prophetic movement were very much interested and often deeply involved in temple affairs as performers of cultic functions.

In the early Second Temple period, Third Isaiah and Ruth still testify to the vitality of the prophetic movement faithful to the heritage of the Davidic monarchy, and to their opposition against Zadokite exclusiveness. This explains not only Nehemiah's ruthless lack of respect for the prophet, but also the stubbornness of the Priestly writing in denying any priestly status to Moses. The Zadokite attitude toward Moses and the prophets was indeed ambivalent. They needed the prophetic mediation of Moses in order to set a divine foundation for the priesthood and the sanctuary and, accordingly, exalted the role of the prophet at Sinai. But once the revelation was completed, the tent of meeting was sealed off and turned by Moses himself into Aaron's tabernacle (Exod 40:1-35 [P]). It was time for the prophet to step back. The Aaronite line cut off the descendants of Moses from any priestly function; the genealogy of the descendants of Levi in Exod 6:16-25 (P) ignores the line of Moses completely, as if he had no sons. The role of forerunners of the priesthood deprived the prophet of any ambition of power and autonomy; Moses was the greatest prophet, as he established the priesthood of Aaron.

A credible anti-Zadokite opposition, however, did not build up around the prophets. With the end of the monarchy and the centralization of the cult, the prophets had already lost the most important war, that of survival. The social and political environment that for centuries had sustained their fortunes and authority in the Jewish society had vanished. The motives of the prophets did not fail; it was the prophets who failed as an autonomous social class and a dependable means of expression of those motives. Even before they could stand up, the prophets were doomed; others would carry on the cause of opposition.

As the voice of the prophets as an autonomous group weakened, gradually their opposition was reabsorbed and accommodated within the

21. The reading "Manasseh" *(mnsh),* instead of "Moses" *(msh),* is an ingenious yet obvious scribal correction aimed to eradicate an embarrassing tradition. See Lester L. Grabbe, *Priests, Prophets, Diviners, Sages,* 43.

Zadokite structure of power. The aura of celebration that surrounded the glorious accomplishments of the ancient prophets covered their current subordination to the priesthood. Like the king, the prophet became a highly regarded institution of the past whose main credit was to have contributed so much to the success of the priesthood.

Chronicles pursues the Zadokite program of *damnatio memoriae* by erasing any historical reference to the cultic functions of the prophets, but also shows a less polemical and more inclusive attitude. The confrontation was over. Chronicles recruits the former cult prophets (1 Chr 25:1) and even the forgotten "sons of Moses" (23:14) into the Levitical ranks. Accordingly, "the prophets" who went up with King Josiah to the temple (2 Kgs 23:2) are transformed by 2 Chr 34:30 into "levites." Now that the priests had won the war, they could even allow themselves the luxury of being gracious. They celebrated the prophet Moses who gave the Torah to Aaron, with the same sense of gratitude they had reserved for King David who built the Jerusalem temple.

3. The Priestly Opposition: Enochic Judaism

In spite of its accomplishment and undeniable authority, the Zadokite hegemony was not without its critics. Specialists in ancient Jewish apocalypticism and mysticism concur in identifying the presence of a priestly opposition active in Jerusalem since the early Second Temple period.[22] The strength of the movement is proved by the impressively high level of sophistication of its literature, which is now preserved mostly in the modern collection of the Old Testament Pseudepigrapha and has the Book of the Watchers, Aramaic Levi, and the Astronomical Book as its earliest pieces of evidence. The recognition of the existence of such a "movement of dissent" is becoming a key element for any general reconstruction

22. John J. Collins, *The Apocalyptic Imagination;* Paolo Sacchi, *Jewish Apocalyptic and Its History,* JSPSup 20 (Sheffield: Sheffield Academic, 1990); Paul D. Hanson, *The Dawn of Apocalyptic,* rev. ed. (Philadelphia: Fortress, 1979); Ithamar Gruenwald, *From Apocalypticism to Gnosticism,* BEATAJ 14 (Frankfurt: P. Lang, 1988); *Apocalyptic and Merkavah Mysticism,* AGJU 14 (Leiden: Brill, 1980); Martha Himmelfarb, *Ascent to Heaven in Jewish and Christian Apocalypses* (New York: Oxford University Press, 1993); *Tours of Hell: An Apocalyptic Form in Jewish and Christian Literature* (Philadelphia: Fortress, 1985).

of the development of Jewish thought in the Second Temple period, and for the understanding of Qumran and Christian origins in particular.[23]

We do not know what this party was called, or what it called itself in antiquity. However, since the priestly opposition to the Zadokites first coalesced around ancient myths with Enoch as their hero, the term "Enochic Judaism" seems quite appropriate and satisfactory as a modern label. What must be certainly avoided are denominations like "early Jewish apocalypticism" or "early Jewish mysticism," which are descriptive of much broader phenomena. Enochic Judaism was indeed (yet not exclusively) an apocalyptic and mystical party, but the history of early Jewish apocalypticism and mysticism is the comprehensive history of two literary genres and their respective worldviews, whose influence went far beyond the boundaries of Enochic Judaism. There are, for example, clear apocalyptic and mystical motifs in Zadokite Judaism.[24] Since the beginning, mysticism and apocalypticism in Judaism have never been tied to one single ideology or group.[25]

The catalyst of Enochic Judaism was a unique concept of the origin of evil that made the "fallen angels" (the "sons of God" also recorded in Gen 6:1-4) as ultimately responsible for the spread of evil and impurity on earth.[26] According to the Book of the Watchers, despite God's reaction and

23. Mark Adam Elliott, *The Survivors of Israel;* Sacchi, *The History of the Second Temple Period;* Boccaccini, *Beyond the Essene Hypothesis;* Shemaryahu Talmon, "The Community of the Renewed Covenant: Between Judaism and Christianity," in *The Community of the Renewed Covenant: The Notre Dame Symposium on the Dead Sea Scrolls,* ed. Eugene C. Ulrich and James C. VanderKam (Notre Dame: University of Notre Dame Press, 1994), 3-24; Florentino García Martínez, *Qumran and Apocalyptic: Studies on the Aramaic Texts from Qumran,* STDJ 9 (Leiden: Brill, 1992).

24. See in particular Stephen L. Cook, *Prophecy and Apocalypticism: The Postexilic Social Setting* (Minneapolis: Fortress, 1995).

25. This has been recognized in particular by specialists of Jewish apocalypticism. "We conclude that the apocalyptic writers were to be found not in any one party within Judaism but throughout many parties, known and unknown, and among men who owed allegiance to no party at all"; D. S. Russell, *The Method and Message of Jewish Apocalyptic,* OTL (Philadelphia: Westminster, 1964), 27. "The apocalyptic framework is not itself tied to a particular ideology"; Collins, *The Apocalyptic Imagination,* 255.

26. For a description of the early Enochic literature, see Collins, *The Apocalyptic Imagination;* Sacchi, *Jewish Apocalyptic and Its History;* and James C. Vanderkam, *Enoch, A Man for All Generations* (Columbia: University of South Carolina Press, 1995); *Enoch and the Growth of an Apocalyptic Tradition,* CBQMS 16 (Washington:

the subsequent Flood, the divine order of creation was not restored. The cosmos did not return to what it was. The good angels, led by Michael, defeated the evil angels led by Semyaz and Azaz'el; however, the victory resulted not in the death or submission of the rebels but in their confinement "in the wilderness which was in Dudael," where the fallen angels were imprisoned "in a hole . . . underneath the rocks of the ground" (1 En 10:4-6, 11-12). The mortal bodies of the giants, the offspring of the evil union of immortal angels and mortal women, were killed (1 En 10:9-10); however, their immortal souls survived as evil spirits and continue to roam about the world (1 En 15:8-10). Humankind was decimated with the Flood but not annihilated, as Noah's family survived (1 En 10:1-3). Creation was cleansed but not totally purified, as God used water and not the "fire" that is reserved only for "the great day of judgment" (1 En 10:6). As disturbing as this idea can be, God's reaction limited but did not eradicate evil. A time of "seventy generations" was set "until the eternal judgment is concluded" (1 En 10:12).

The anti-Zadokite implications of the Enochic myth are obvious. First, against the Zadokite idea of stability and order, the Enochians argued that God's order was no more, having been replaced by the current disorder. In their view, the rebellion of the "sons of God" was not simply one of the primeval sins that characterized the ancient history of humankind; it is the mother of all sins, the original sin which corrupted and contaminated God's creation and from which evil relentlessly continues to spring forth and spread. By crossing the boundaries between heaven and earth, the angels broke apart the divisions set by God at the time of creation. The consequent unleashing of chaotic forces condemns humans to be victims of an evil they have not caused and cannot resist.

Second, against the Zadokite idea of stability and order, Enochic Judaism introduced the concept of the "end of days" as the time of final judgment and vindication beyond death and history. What in the prophetic tradition was the announcement of some indeterminate future event of God's intervention became the expectation of a final cataclysmic event that will mark the end of God's first creation and the beginning of a second creation — a new world qualitatively different from, and discontinu-

---

Catholic Biblical Association of America, 1984); Matthias Delcor, "Le mythe de la chute des anges et de l'origine des géants comme explication du mal dans le monde dans l'apocalyptique juive: Histoire des traditions," *RHR* 190 (1976): 3-53.

ous with, what was before.[27] Such an idea has become so closely associated to Judaism (and Christianity) that it is difficult for us even to imagine a time when it was not. But that God's creation has not only a "beginning" but also an "end" contradicts the infallibility of God and God's unchallenged control over creation. No one needs to build a new house if the old one is perfect. Why should God feel compelled to remake what God said was "very good"? Which mistake has God made to make creation deteriorate so rapidly that God cannot fix it anymore? And if the infallible God did not make any mistake, how can the almighty God have allowed the creature to spoil God's work? The concept of new creation implies that something went wrong in the first creation — a disturbing and quite embarrassing idea that the Zadokites could not accept without denying the very foundations of their theology and power.

Third, against the Zadokite idea of stability and order, the Enochians openly challenged the legitimacy of the ruling priesthood. In a seminal article in 1976, Michael A. Knibb was the first to notice, almost with surprise, that according to the Enochic literature the Babylonian exile has not ended yet: Israel is still in exile.[28] The attribution to Enoch of priestly characteristics as the intercessor in heaven between God and the fallen angels as well as the warnings of Aramaic Levi about his apostate descendants assume the existence of a purer pre-Aaronite priesthood and disrupt the Sinaitic foundations of the Zadokite structure of power as a later degeneration. When transferred within the Enochian worldview, the Zadokite claim of being the faithful keepers of the cosmic order sounds like the grotesque and guilty pretentiousness of evil usurpers.

Finally, against the Zadokite idea of stability and order, the Enochians questioned the correspondence of the cultic calendar with the cosmic structure, as attested by the existence, at least by the 3rd century B.C.E., of calendrical discussions. The Astronomical Book claims that "people err" in not reckoning equinoxes and solstices as "days" of the months and the year as the angel Uriel reveals to Enoch. In place of the 360 days plus four intercalary times between seasons of the Zadokite calendar, Enochic Judaism promoted a year of 364 "days" with a seasonal cycle of two 30-day and

27. Jean Carmignac, "La notione d'eschatologie dans la bible et à Qumrân," *RevQ* 7 (1969): 17-31.

28. Michael A. Knibb, "The Exile in the Literature of the Intertestamental Period," *HeyJ* 17 (1976): 253-72.

one 31-day months.[29] The discussion was more theoretical than practical; as it did not alter the sabbatical cycle, it affected only marginally the succession of sacred days and the regularity of the cult. However, even the dimension of time is compounded to the Enochians' list of complaints against the Zadokite priesthood — a factor that would have dramatic developments after the Maccabean Revolt, when the lunar calendar was enforced in the temple.

While the anti-Zadokite character of Enochic Judaism seems to be unquestionable, the origins of such an opposition party remain largely obscure. Before the discovery of the Dead Sea Scrolls, the pre-Maccabean origin of Enochic literature was the authoritative yet still minority stance of some distinguished specialists in ancient Judaism. In particular, the multiple stages of composition of the Book of the Watchers led Robert H. Charles to believe that the document might have had a long and complex prehistory before its final redaction in the 2nd century B.C.E.[30]

The publication of the Aramaic fragments of 1 Enoch by Josef T. Milik in 1976 provided the breakthrough.[31] It was no longer possible to claim that Enochic Judaism generated in the wake of the Maccabean Revolt as a reaction to the process of Hellenization. The oldest manuscript of the Book of Astronomy went back "to the end of the third or the beginning of the second century BCE," and the Book of the Watchers was already attested in its final shape by "the first half of the second century BCE."[32] Milik was also convinced that the relationship between Genesis and the Book of the Watchers (or at least its oldest stratum, chs. 6–19) had to be reversed. Far from being an expansion of the biblical text, the Enochic version of the myth of the fallen angels was the original source and predated the composition of the "Yahwist." Making the Genesis passage (Gen 6:1-4) a shortened form of the Enochic text implied a very ancient, preexilic origin for the Enochic movement.

Accordingly, Margaret Barker presented Enochic Judaism as a survival

29. See Boccaccini, "The Solar Calendars of Daniel and Enoch"; cf. Paolo Sacchi, "The Two Calendars of the *Book of Astronomy*," *Jewish Apocalyptic and Its History*, 128-39; "Testi palestinesi anteriori al 200 a.C. con particolare riguardo al problema dei due calendari solari del Libro dell'Astronomia," *RivB* 34 (1986): 183-204.

30. R. H. Charles, "Book of Enoch," *APOT* 2 (1913): 163-281.

31. Josef T. Milik, *The Books of Enoch: Aramaic Fragments of Qumran Cave 4* (Oxford: Clarendon, 1976).

32. Milik, 22.

form of the religion of the First Temple, which the Zadokites replaced and tried in vain to eradicate. "What we have in Enoch is the writing of a very conservative group whose roots go right back to the time of the first temple."[33]

Barker is certainly right when she warns against having "a double standard when it comes to the dating of non-biblical texts." It cannot be assumed that "biblical texts" are necessarily old unless the opposite is proven, while "non-biblical texts" are necessarily late unless the opposite is proven. The problem of dating the different parts of 1 Enoch needs to be addressed "with open minds" by asking the proper questions: "when [the documents] might have been written, where the ideas originated, and who cherished them sufficiently to preserve and transmit them."[34] The actual composition of these documents could be earlier, even much earlier, than the end of the 3rd century B.C.E., when the texts were copied in the scrolls found at Qumran.

Barker is also correct when she argues that "the Genesis account of the fallen angels. . . has also been heavily edited."[35] On the one hand, the Genesis texts are abridged versions of stories of which the authors knew more than they chose to include: the logic is confused, the language does not run smoothly, and one cannot help smelling embarrassment and censorship. On the other hand, the Enoch texts can hardly be characterized simply as additions or expansions of Genesis; the author is interested neither in clarifying the obscurity of the biblical texts nor in using Genesis as a source of legitimacy. His theological agenda seems to rest on completely autonomous sources. "1 Enoch preserves ancient ideas that have dropped from the Old Testament."[36]

Scholars have long recognized the antiquity of the traditions about the fallen angels. These traditions go back to the Babylonian milieu of the exilic age and to the preexilic mythological and polytheistic heritage that the ancient Israelite religion shared with the other peoples of the Near East.[37]

33. Margaret Barker, *The Lost Prophet: The Book of Enoch and Its Influence on Christianity* (Nashville: Abingdon, 1988), 19.

34. Barker, 105.

35. Barker, 19.

36. Barker, 108.

37. A. Kirk Grayson, *Babylonian Historical-Literary Texts* (Toronto: University of Toronto Press, 1975).

The myth of fallen "sons of gods" was also well known by the early Greek mythology, where the cosmic battle between Olympians and Titans led to Zeus' rise to power and to the defeat and ensconscement of the Titans in Tartaros far below earth.[38] When later the titan Prometheus gave humankind the fire he stole from Zeus and the titan Epimetheus married Pandora, the result was the Great Flood and the spreading of every sort of evil on earth.[39] The giants also were familiar, transcultural characters; even Josephus knew this: "the deeds that tradition ascribes to [the *nephilim*] resemble the audacious exploits told by the Greeks of the giants" (*Ant* 1.73).[40]

The antiquity of these traditions, however, cannot be used to support an ancient, preexilic origin for Enochic Judaism. Dating traditions is not the same as dating documents, social groups, and systems of thought, exactly as the age of a building cannot be dated by the age of its bricks. Using such a criterion acritically, one should conclude that most romanesque churches go back to pre-Christian times as they are often built out of the ruins of ancient pagan temples, and that Christianity already existed before Jesus as so many traditions in the New Testament clearly predate the 1st century C.E. The evidence that Enochic literature is rooted in very ancient oral and literary traditions does not give an exact clue to the time of the emergence of Enochic Judaism as an established movement.

Moreover, there are some compelling reasons that prevent us from seeing Enochic Judaism as a conservative pre-Zadokite movement, and that indicate a more likely post-Zadokite setting.

First, the theological problem that the Book of the Watchers wants to address, that of the origin of evil, makes sense only within the monotheistic context of Second Temple Judaism as an attempt to absolve the one, all-good and all-powerful God from being the source of evil. We simply do not know what the meaning of the story of the fallen angels was within the ancient polytheistic religion of Israel in which it originated. The function the myth now exercises within the Book of the Watchers belongs to a later stage of reinterpretation which parallels that testified to in Genesis.

38. See Timothy Ganz, *Early Greek Myth: A Guide to Literary and Artistic Sources* (Baltimore: Johns Hopkins University Press, 1993), 44-56.

39. Ganz, 152-66.

40. Ganz, 445-54.

In the biblical text the story of the fallen angels was first taken as an example of the ancient sins that characterized the primeval history of humankind — a regrettable incident but without lasting consequences. The Zadokite historiography, which inherited the story, shows the concern of further downplaying the already demythologized narrative. There was in fact a dangerous potential of disruption in the idea that both angels in their sin and God in God's punishment trespassed the boundaries of creation that separate heaven from earth and the waters of below from the waters of above, respectively. The story of the covenant with Noah was advisedly added to reassure people that never again would God either tolerate or cause any trespassing (Gen 8:21-22).

What makes Enochic Judaism differ from Zadokite Judaism is not the reference to the fallen angels but the different meaning given to the same ancient story. The narrative was developed according to an opposite trajectory, to the extent of making it the central paradigm for the origin of sin and evil. In itself the myth of the fallen angels is neither Enochic nor Zadokite, but belongs to the common polytheistic heritage of both movements.

Second, the beginning of Enochic Judaism is the link that the Book of the Watchers established between Enoch and the story of the fallen angels. It was the presence of the heavenly seer that made it possible to use the polytheistic myth in order to solve a monotheistic problem, by giving a new theological meaning to the ancient narrative and fully exploiting its subversive potential.

Living in heaven, Enoch had a firsthand knowledge of the secrets of heaven and a continuous ability to communicate with his son Methuselah, the grandfather of Noah. The heavenly dwelling and the familial ties made Enoch the perfect forerunner of a tradition that claimed to have survived the Flood and reached the present of Israel. The antiquity of Enoch also made him the perfect vehicle for a revelation that claimed to be over and above that of Moses. But if the presence of Enoch is so crucial for the birth of Enochic Judaism, when did the association between the fallen angels and the heavenly seer occur?

There are strong indications that "Enoch was developed as a Jewish counterpart of such heroes as Enmeduranki . . . the Mesopotamian seventh king . . . [who] was the founder of a guild of diviners and a recipient of revelations."[41] The character of Enoch therefore is as pre-Zadokite as

41. Collins, *The Apocalyptic Imagination*, 44-47.

the fallen angels; his origins lie in the ancient Mesopotamic tradition.[42] However, there is no evidence that Enochic Judaism inherited the connection between Enoch and the fallen angels as something that already belonged to an earlier stage of the tradition. Both the parallel versions of the myth of the fallen angels in the Book of the Watchers (1 En 6-11) and Genesis (6:1-4) do not contain any reference to Enoch and make perfect sense without him. Before Enochic Judaism, Enoch and the fallen angels were autonomous mythological characters, belonging to autonomous cycles of narrative.

This view is confirmed by the fact that Enoch and the fallen angels entered the Torah at different stages. While the story of the fallen angels belongs to an earlier layer of the Genesis narrative, the character of Enoch was only a postexilic addition by the Priestly writing. According to Gen 5:18-24 {P}, Enoch was the seventh in the genealogy of Adam. His father, Jared, "lived after the birth of Enoch eight hundred years. . . . When Enoch had lived sixty-five years, he became the father of Methuselah. Enoch walked with the *elohim* [= angels] after the birth of Methuselah three hundred years. . . . Thus all the days of Enoch were three hundred sixty-five years. Enoch walked with the *elohim* [= angels]; then he was no more, because Elohim [= God] took him."

In no way does the character of Enoch affect the previous and subsequent narrative. Enoch is an erratic meteor once met in a close encounter and then lost in the depths of outer space. According to the Priestly writing, however, Enoch lived immediately before the Flood, which happened to make him contemporaneous to the episode of the fallen angels. The Priestly writing did not make the connection; yet it created the chronological framework that made it possible.

The chronology of the Book of the Watchers depends on the Zadokite narrative. After presenting its version of the ancient myth of the fallen angels without any reference to Enoch (1 En 6–11), the text continues: "Before these things (happened) Enoch was hidden, and no one of the children of the people knew by what he was hidden and where he was. And his dwelling place as well as his activities were with the Watchers and the holy ones; and (so were) his days" (1 En 12:1-2). The Enoch who witnessed the

42. Helge S. Kvanvig, *Roots of Apocalyptic: The Mesopotamian Background of the Enoch Figure and of the Son of Man*, WMANT 61 (Neukirchen-Vluyn: Neukirchener, 1988).

sin of the fallen angels is clearly the same Enoch introduced by the Priestly author, the one who spent his days with the *elohim*. The synchrony is strengthened by the specification that the fallen angels descended "in the days of Jared," the father of Enoch (1 En 6:6 [4Q201 (4QEnoch a) and Greek; the Ethiopic is corrupted]).

Paolo Sacchi disagrees on this point. He argues that the original context of the Book of the Watchers implies that Jared is the son of Enoch, not his father, because "Enoch was hidden *before* these things happened" (1 En 12:1). In his view, 1 Enoch followed the chronology of the Yahwist (Gen 4:18), not that of the Priestly writing.[43] But this is not the case. According to the chronology of the Priestly writing, Jared was still alive when "Enoch was taken by God," which invalidates the argument that the fall of the angels may not have happened after Enoch's ascent to heaven and still "at the time of Jared." Besides, according to the Zadokite interpretation, Enoch "walked with the angels" even before he was taken away by God.[44]

This seems to be the most likely perspective of the Enoch texts, for which Enoch acted for some time as a mediator between heaven and earth. He received the revelation from the angels, while he was still in contact with his earthly family. According to the Book of Astronomy (1 En 81:6), after Enoch received divine revelation, a period of one year was granted to him to dwell with his son Methuselah ". . . and teach [his] children . . . and in the second year, [he] shall be taken away from (among) all of them." The time when Enoch "was hidden . . . and his dwelling place was among the Watchers" (1 En 12:1-2) may well refer to the time when he walked with the *elohim*, not to the time when he was taken away by God. The chronology of chs. 106-7, which is held to be a very ancient fragment of the Book of Noah, also depends on the priestly chronology, according to which Noah was born 69 years after Enoch was taken away by God.[45] Consistently, this time it was not Enoch who visited his family but rather Methuselah who had to go and visit his father's "dwelling place . . . among the angels . . . at the ends of the earth" (1 En 106:7-8). The only chronolog-

43. See Sacchi, *Jewish Apocalyptic and Its History*, 157.

44. See VanderKam, *Enoch and the Growth of an Apocalyptic Tradition*, 31; and Devorah Dimant, "The Biography of Enoch and the Books of Enoch," *VT* 33 (1983): 14-29.

45. García Martínez, *Qumran and Apocalyptic*, 27-28.

ical framework that the Enoch literature knows and uses, even in its most ancient texts, is that provided by the Priestly writing.

Thanks to Enoch, myths that in the Zadokite Torah resurfaced only in the form of obscure and theologically inert allusions were given new life and were turned into the cornerstone of an autonomous and alternative system of thought. However, it was only thanks to the Zadokite Torah that Enoch was connected to the story of the fallen angels and to the primeval history of Israel. Also from the literary point of view, Enochic Judaism was a side-effect of the Zadokite editing of the ancient biblical narrative.

Third and finally, not only are Enochic and Zadokite Judaism rooted in a common mythological legacy, not only does the Enochic narrative depend on the Zadokite chronology, but both traditions share the same priestly background. Scholars have not failed to emphasize the many parallels between Ezekiel and the Book of the Watchers (esp. chs. 21–36), so much so that both Enochic and Zadokite Judaism can legitimately claim a father-child relationship with the exiled prophet-priest.[46]

There is now a widespread scholarly consensus that in the Enochic literature the myth of the fallen angels is a mirror of intrapriestly conflicts. The story reflects an experience of exclusion and disorder that interrupts a brief period of order, exactly as a "plot" of evil forces came shortly after the creative act of God.[47] As Benjamin G. Wright III has effectively said, Enochic Judaism voices "groups of priests and scribes who feel marginalized and even disenfranchised vis-à-vis the ruling priests in Jerusalem."[48]

The strong antipriestly attitudes of the Enoch books do not signal that this literature came from nonpriestly circles, as Paul D. Hanson believed.[49] Enochic Judaism was not the reaction of outsiders against the Zadokite order, but rather was the cry of insiders who (after a brief period of order) had seen denied (lost) (what they claimed were) their rights within the divine order. In the priestly worldview, the exclusion of legitimate priests from the earthly sanctuary could only mean that a "rebellion in heaven" had occurred; humans had now to cope with "the collapse of the order of

46. Gruenwald, *Apocalyptic and Merkavah Mysticism.*

47. David W. Suter, "Fallen Angel, Fallen Priest: The Problem of Family Purity in 1 Enoch 6–16," *HUCA* 50 (1979): 115-35.

48. Benjamin G. Wright, "Fear the Lord and Honor the Priest: Ben Sira as Defender of the Jerusalem Priesthood," in *The Book of Ben Sira in Modern Research,* ed. Pancratius C. Beentjes, BZAW 255 (Berlin: de Gruyter, 1997), 189-222 (quotation, 218).

49. Hanson, *The Dawn of Apocalyptic.*

creation, with pugnacious forces unleashed in a vicious process of degeneration and decay."[50]

Enochic Judaism was a post- and anti-Zadokite phenomenon, a reaction to their claims, made by people who viewed themselves as priests and shared the same worldview and traditions as the Zadokites, while denouncing a present of degeneration and disorder due to the rebellion of evil usurpers which caused the collapse of the divine order. Hence, the birth of Enochic Judaism must be located somewhere between the Priestly writing and the 3rd century B.C.E., after the return from the exile and the establishment of Zadokite order, before the writing of the earliest extant copies of 1 Enoch found among the Dead Sea Scrolls. Can we be even more specific?

Scholars generally point to the Hellenistic period. "The fallen angels induced culture shock in the prediluvian generation. Similar culture shock in Israel in the Hellenistic period gave rise to the apocalyptic visions ascribed to Enoch."[51] More specifically, George W. E. Nickelsburg has suggested that we should detect in the myth of the fallen angels a reflection of the wars of the Diadochi.[52]

The 4th-century origin of Enochic Judaism is strongly articulated and advocated by Paolo Sacchi and the Italian school of apocalypticism.[53] To the arguments already proposed by Charles and Milik about the complex textual prehistory of the document and its multiple stages of composition, Sacchi adds ideological considerations, pointing to the similarities between the Book of the Watchers and Chronicles. He sees Qoheleth as the terminus ad quem: "[The Book of the Watchers] must be earlier even than Qoheleth, who would not have spoken ironically of those who believe in the immortality of the soul if certain ideas had not circulated, and with a certain frequency, in the Jerusalem of his time."[54]

50. Paul D. Hanson, "Rebellion in Heaven, Azazel, and Euhemeristic Heroes in 1 Enoch 6–11," *JBL* 96 (1977): 195-233 (quotation, 199-200).

51. Collins, *The Apocalyptic Imagination,* 51.

52. George W. E. Nickelsburg, *Jewish Literature between the Bible and the Mishnah* (Philadelphia: Fortress, 1981).

53. Sacchi, *Jewish Apocalyptic and Its History,* 13-108; *The History of the Second Temple Period,* 174-82; cf. Gabriele Boccaccini, "Jewish Apocalyptic Tradition: The Contribution of Italian Scholarship," in *Mysteries and Revelations: Apocalyptic Studies since the Uppsala Colloquium,* ed. John J. Collins and James H. Charlesworth, JSPSup 9 (Sheffield: JSOT, 1991), 33-50.

54. Sacchi, *Jewish Apocalyptic and Its History,* 61.

In light of my reconstruction of Zadokite origins, the 4th century appears to be a more likely setting for the emergence of a movement like Enochic Judaism than the early Hellenistic period. We have no evidence that the Hellenistic conquest provoked any "culture shock" in the Jerusalem priesthood in the 3rd century. At the beginning, Hellenism produced more attraction than rejection within the priestly circles; the rise of Jewish nationalism and of a militant anti-Hellenistic party belongs only to the Seleucid period.[55]

Against the turmoil(s) that in the 5th and 4th century accompanied the Zadokite rise to power, the 3rd century appears as a period of stability and order. There was struggle and fighting about the political role of the priesthood, but no significant change occurred in the structure of the priestly hierarchy, as described by Chronicles. No one questioned the legitimacy of the hereditary Zadokite high priesthood or the threefold distinction of sons of Levi, sons of Aaron, and sons of Phinehas. There may have been some minor changes in the order of priestly and Levitical classes, but no class was added or expelled. On the contrary, the 4th century was indeed a critical period of controversy and division within the priesthood — a time of flexibility and uncertainty, when the boundaries between being in or out were not yet clearly defined, and the hope of being included was no less than the fear of being excluded.

As we have seen in the previous chapter, the Zadokite struggle for power in the Persian period was marked by the production of genealogical lists that aimed to justify their authority while enlarging the basis of consensus. But the process worked also through exclusions and purges. The same genealogical lists through which the Zadokites co-opted (or were forced to co-opt) some of their most powerful adversaries as allies functioned as lists of proscription against their weakest adversaries. Translated into the bureaucratic language of census and accountability, it was certified that some families "proved" their genealogical right to the priesthood, while others never did or suddenly could no longer prove it.

One of the several lists that have survived (1 Esd 5:38-40 = Ezra 2:61-63 = Neh 7:63-65) keeps memory of some "of the priests," namely "the descendants of Habaiah, Hakkoz, and Jaddus (Barzillai)," who "had assumed the priesthood" (1 Esd 5:38); but when the Jerusalem temple authorities

55. Doron Mendels, *The Rise and Fall of Jewish Nationalism* (1992, repr. Grand Rapids: Wm. B. Eerdmans, 1997).

"looked for their entries in the genealogical records, they were not found there, and so they were excluded from the priesthood as unclean. . . . [Hence], the governor told them not to share in the holy things until a [high] priest [Ezra] with Urim and Thummim should come."

This ancient priestly document is certainly not the faithful list of the returned exiles under Zerubbabel and Joshua that it pretends to be. Yet, its archaic distinction of the priesthood in four classes and only two additional classes of levites, as well as its archaic reference to Urim and Thummim, makes the text belong to an early stage in the development of Zadokite Judaism. Since the division of priesthood into four classes is consistent with the tradition of Ezra (cf. Ezra 10:18-22 = 1 Esd 9:18-22), the passage most likely reflects the situation at the beginning of the 4th century, before Chronicles and its 24 classes of priests.

The condition of those priests who were excluded was far more miserable than that of most Levitical families. These are not people who tried to make a claim to the priesthood and failed. These are people who did serve as priests for some time in the Second Temple, only to be excluded later. They were reckoned among the priests and, according to an enlightening detail that resurfaces only in 1 Esdras, "had assumed the priesthood" (1 Esd 5:38), that is, had ministered in the Second Temple for a while, yet for reasons that remain unknown to us they were doomed with the worst possible punishment. While they saw some other Levitical families gain the priesthood, they experienced a traumatic devolution in their status.

We are not claiming, of course, that the Enochians were indeed "the descendants of Habaiah, Hakkoz, and Jaddus," but the passage offers a very likely 4th-century context for the origins of the conflict that opposed the Zadokites (and their Aaronite allies) to members of dissident priestly families.

Unlike the situation with the Samaritans, we have no evidence that the Enochians formed a schismatic community, in Palestine or elsewhere. John J. Collins agrees: "It does not appear . . . that the bearers of the Enoch tradition before the Maccabean revolt were separated from the rest of Judaism in the manner of the later Qumran community."[56] The Enochians were an opposition party within the Jerusalem aristocracy, not a group of separatists. The words of Robert A. Kugler about Aramaic Levi apply to the entire Enochic literature in pre-Maccabean times: it testifies to "a period

56. Collins, *The Apocalyptic Imagination*, 79.

of time when there was a dispute regarding the proper character of the priestly office, but when the discussion was still quite tame, and there was yet room for differences of opinion."[57] It was only the Maccabean Revolt that caused Enochic Judaism to grow and expand into something different and larger — a movement of dissent that would be ultimately known as Essenism.[58] What at the beginning was probably only the experience of exclusion of a few priestly families generated a sophisticated theological alternative that would attract a large portion of the Jewish population and become a powerful and potentially schismatic component of ancient Jewish thought, ultimately fostering the most radical schism of all, that of Christianity.

4. The Lay Opposition: Sapiential Judaism

The Enochians were not the only opposition party in early Second Temple Judaism. "Instruction must not perish from the priest, nor counsel from the wise, nor the word from the prophets" — said Jeremiah (Jer 18:18; cf. Ezek 7:26), seeking a future and balanced coexistence for the religious authorities of preexilic Judaism. In its disproportionate growth, postexilic priesthood silenced the prophet but did not suffocate nor domesticate the wise. Indeed, the early Second Temple period was the golden age for Jewish wisdom traditions. Unlike Enochic Judaism, Sapiential Judaism was a form of Judaism that originated in the monarchic period prior to, and independently of, Zadokite Judaism, and was able to flourish and maintain its autonomy in the Zadokite society. The books of Ahiqar, Proverbs, Job, and Jonah testify to the continuity of scribal schools from preexilic times throughout the Persian period. The dual structure of postexilic Jewish society, with the Zadokite priests in charge of the temple and an autonomous Persian administration led by a governor in charge of political affairs, gave the proper setting for the development of Sapiential Judaism as an autonomous movement.

The most striking feature of Sapiential Judaism is the absence of any

57. Robert A. Kugler, *From Patriarch to Priest: The Levi-Priestly Tradition from Aramaic Levi to Testament of Levi,* Early Judaism and Its Literature 9 (Atlanta: Scholars, 1996), 135.

58. See Boccaccini, *Beyond the Essene Hypothesis.*

reference to the Mosaic covenant and, more generally, to the priesthood. The authority on which Sapiential Judaism relies is that of the accumulated knowledge of teachers and parents (both father and mother), attentive observation of everyday experience, moral consensus, and, above all, deference to tradition.[59] We see the typical sapiential attitude in the saying the book of Job attributes to Bildad the Shuhite: "Inquire now of bygone generations, and consider what their ancestors have found; for we are but of yesterday, and we know nothing, for our days on earth are but a shadow" (Job 8:8-10). The assumption of Sapiential Judaism is that human survival and well-being (health, wealth, fame, honor, longevity, progeny) depend on the ability to live in harmony with the cosmos and all living beings, to understand the complexity of human relationships, and to cope with reality in any circumstance of daily experience. The form of knowledge Sapiential Judaism promoted demands human inquiry and initiative, rather than obedience to sacred laws or conformity to cultic acts.[60] The result was a rich legacy of parental and traditional teaching passed on from one generation to the next, from parents to children and from teachers to disciples, in families and in schools, outside the control of the priesthood.

Equally striking is the cosmopolitan attitude of the wise, their assumption being that "truth applies universally and thus [is] not confined to private experience or limited to any geographical area."[61] The search for wisdom unites the wise of Israel to the wise of the neighboring nations. Ahiqar is an Assyrian, Job (and his friends) are from the land of Uz, and Proverbs proudly hosts the sayings of Solomon's foreign peers, "Agur, son of Jakeh the Massaite," and "King Lemuel" (Prov 30:1-33; 31:1-9). The debt of wisdom literature to foreign cultures and secular education is massive, and is marked by an impressive series of literary and conceptual borrowings from foreign wisdom (Egyptian, Mesopotamian, and later, Greek). Sapiential Judaism passes over any particularity of Jewish history and tradition and views human beings simply as creatures of one God regardless of their ethnic origin, cultural identity, or cultic affiliation.[62]

59. John J. Collins, *Jewish Wisdom in the Hellenistic Age,* OTL (Louisville: Westminster John Knox, 1997), 2.

60. James L. Crenshaw, *Education in Ancient Israel: Across the Deadening Silence* (New York: Doubleday, 1998), 121.

61. Crenshaw, *Education in Ancient Israel,* 64.

62. John G. Gammie and Leo G. Perdue, eds., *The Sage in Israel and the Ancient Near East* (Winona Lake: Eisenbrauns, 1990).

Not unexpectedly, the hero of Sapiential Judaism is neither a priest nor a prophet or a seer but a lay person, and the most cosmopolitan among the Jewish heroes: the wise King Solomon. The reason for this choice is manifest: the ancient Jewish tradition claimed that "Solomon's wisdom surpassed the wisdom of all the people of the East, and all the wisdom of Egypt," and magnified his worldwide reputation in the epic of the Queen of Sheba (1 Kgs 10:1ff.). "For [Solomon] was wiser than all others: than Ethan the Ezrahite, and Heman, Calcol and Darda, the sons of Mahol; his fame spread throughout all the surrounding nations. . . . People came from all peoples to hear the wisdom of Solomon; they came from all the kings of the earth who had heard of his wisdom" (1 Kgs 4:29-34[Heb. 5:9-14]).[63]

The book of Ahiqar unveils the cosmopolitan nature and the polytheistic roots of the Jewish concept of Wisdom. The preexilic document is one of the most widespread and popular narratives of the ancient Near East. Its influence is well attested also in ancient Judaism. An Aramaic version of it, possibly from the 7th-6th centuries B.C.E., was found in the ruins of the Jewish colony of Elephantine. Proverbs has many parallel sayings, and Tobit quotes it explicitly. References to the character of Ahiqar would find their way down to the rabbinic and Islamic literature.[64]

In Ahiqar, Wisdom is introduced as a goddess who is inaccessible to human beings, yet beneficial to them through the mediation of Baal Shamayn, the Canaanite Lord of Heaven. "From Shamayn the peoples are favored; Wisdom is of the gods. Indeed, she is precious to the gods; her kingdom is et[er]nal. She has been established by Shamayn; yea, the Holy Lord has exalted her" (Ahiqar 6:13). Because of her special relationship with the Lord of Heaven, Wisdom rules forever, and her enthronement as queen of an eternal kingdom is a sign of Shamayn's benevolence toward the peoples.

In postexilic Jewish texts, such as Job 28 and Proverbs 1–9, the language is still largely that of polytheism, although now in a context of a henotheistic exaltation of the God of Israel, which identifies YHWH with

63. James L. Crenshaw, "Solomon as Sage par excellence," *Old Testament Wisdom: An Introduction* (Atlanta: John Knox, 1981), 42-54.

64. On Ahiqar, see James M. Lindenberger, "Ahiqar," *OTP* 2 (1985): 479-507; Avinoam Yellin, *The Book of Ahiqar the Wise,* 2nd ed. (Jerusalem, 1937), 13 [Hebrew]; Anis Furayhah, *Ahiqar: Wise Man of the Ancient Near East* (Beirut: American University of Beirut, 1962) [Arabic].

the father of the gods in the Canaanite pantheon, El(ohim).[65] As in Ahiqar, the starting point is given by the theme of the inaccessibility of Wisdom. Humans search the entire universe for precious metals; they explore paths that no animal has ever seen or trodden, and succeed in "bringing hidden things to light" (Job 28:1-11). Yet Wisdom remains hidden. "But where shall wisdom be found? Where is the place of understanding? Mortals do not know the way to [it], and it is not found in the land of the living" (28:12-13).[66] Inaccessible to mortals, wisdom is also unapproachable to gods. Four places of the earth (and former gods of the Canaanite pantheon) are called as witnesses. Tehom (Deep) and Yam (Sea) both say that "she is not with me" (28:14). Abaddon (Destruction) and Muet (Death) admit that they only "have heard a rumor of her with [their] ears" (28:22). What humans and (other) gods cannot do, Elohim did: "Elohim understands the way to it and he knows its place. For he . . . sees everything under the heavens. When he gave to the wind its weight, and apportioned out the waters by measure . . . then he saw her and declared her; he established her, and searched her out. And he said to humankind, 'Truly, the fear of YHWH, that is wisdom; and to depart from evil is understanding'" (28:23-28).

Proverbs 1–9 also praises Wisdom for her collaborative role in creation. "YHWH by wisdom founded the earth; by understanding he established the heavens" (Prov 3:19). God "acquired" (Heb. *qanah*) her before anything else (8:22) and through her gave order to the primordial chaos: "When [God] established the heavens, I was there, when he drew a circle on the face of the deep . . . when he marked out the foundations of the earth, then I was beside him" (8:27-31). The search of Wisdom therefore is the search of "the divine logic by which the universe took shape, the structuring of things into a coherent order."[67] And since humans have life, prosperity, and divine favor by conforming to the order of creation, seeking wisdom is the essence and the goal of religious life. That "the fear of YHWH is the beginning of wisdom" (Prov 9:10; cf. 1:7) is the central theme of Proverbs 1–9. Through creation, God made the inaccessible Wisdom close to humans, desirable to their eyes, necessary to their well-being.

65. Diana Vikander Edelman, ed., *The Triumph of Elohim;* Margaret Barker, *The Great Angel: A Study of Israel's Second God* (Louisville: Westminster John Knox, 1992).

66. The text is corrected according to the Greek (Heb. "its price").

67. Crenshaw, *Education in Ancient Israel,* 70.

Although largely practical and secular in character, sapiential knowledge therefore is not autonomous from the divine. "The world is never experienced as purely secular, as apart from YHWH who controls it and who is revealed in it."[68] Not only is God wiser than any human being, but God is the ultimate source of wisdom, for "God gives wisdom" (Prov 2:6). The humanistic attitude of Sapiential Judaism, its optimism regarding human potential, springs from this conviction that it was God who first took the initiative and created the world orderly, concealing valuable truth within nature itself. Experience is a means of knowledge because God made the universe in itself pregnant with signs,[69] and the Wisdom of the world longs to be known and to gratify her searchers with the abundance of her gifts. "I love those who love me, and those who seek me diligently find me. Riches and honor are with me, enduring wealth and prosperity" (Prov 8:17-18).

If since its earliest stages Sapiential Judaism tends to dismiss claims of heavenly revelation, it is not out of skepticism for the divine. On the contrary, it is the revelatory exclusiveness of divine creation that gives no more room for additional revelations beyond the secrets of the universe which were implanted there at the moment of creation. The quest of the wise is an empirical yet religious inquiry; the search for wisdom is the attitude of those who "fear God."

Unlike Enochic Judaism which directly challenged the legitimacy of the Zadokite priesthood, the lay movement of the wise was "indifferent rather than hostile to the priestly and cultic establishment."[70] With Zadokite Judaism, the wise shared the idea that the universe was divinely ordained and basically good, and posited a system of retribution on the assumption that "the world has been programmed to reward virtue and punish vice."[71] "What the wicked dread will come upon them, but the desire of the righteous will be granted. . . . Whoever is steadfast in righteousness will live, but whoever pursues evil will die" (Prov 10:24; 11:19; cf. 10:27, 30; 11:8, 20; passim). As in the Zadokite tradition (1 Chr 21:1), the "satan" of Sapiential Judaism is an agent of God, a member of God's heav-

68. Roland E. Murphy, *The Tree of Life: An Exploration of Biblical Wisdom Literature,* 2nd ed. (Grand Rapids: Wm. B. Eerdmans, 1996), 114.

69. Crenshaw, *Education in Ancient Israel,* 120.

70. Blenkinsopp, *Sage, Priest, Prophet,* 99.

71. Crenshaw, *Old Testament Wisdom,* 55.

enly court (Job 1–2), not a rebellious Prometheus, the "devil" of Enochic Judaism, whose sin brought about evil and impurity on earth.[72] The Enochic notion of corruption and disorder was rejected, as well as any solution that would have implied the existence of another world or of an afterlife (Job 14:10-14).

The criticism of Sapiential Judaism did not confront directly the authority and stability of Zadokite power but, more subtly, the foundations of their covenantal theology. Indeed, in the Persian and even more so, as we will see, in the early Hellenistic period, more and more decidedly Sapiential Judaism assumed the form of a nonconformist, increasingly skeptical tradition. Irony became one of the distinguished elements of sapiential narratives, of which Job and Jonah offer two outstanding examples.

The problem of Sapiential Judaism is that it does not see any correspondence between the order of the universe as revealed by God through creation and the order of the universe as supposedly revealed on Sinai and interpreted by the priests. Since the effects of the covenant are not confirmed by experience, the wise cannot help denying that retribution is regulated through obedience to the Zadokite Torah. This is not the way things are. The rules of partnership between God and humans as established by the Mosaic covenant simply do not work.

The personal experience of Job, the suffering righteous man who protests before God his right to happiness and well-being, is already emblematic in itself. According to the criteria of the covenant, Job was "blameless and upright, one who feared God and turned away from evil" (Job 1:1), yet God allows his righteousness to be tested to the extreme.

The revolt of Job, even in its most original and polemical aspects, does not part from the principles of traditional wisdom; it is in the name of experience and rational analysis. "I have intelligence as well as you . . . my eye has seen all this; my ear has heard and understood it. What you know, I also know" (Job 12:3; 13:1-2), reminds Job to his wise friends. What now adds a nontraditional skeptical dimension to the sapiential analysis is the presence of an actual target — the Zadokite concept of individual retribution.

The logic of the Zadokite covenant would require Job to acknowledge

72. See Paolo Sacchi, "The Devil in Jewish Traditions of the Second Temple Period (c. 500 BCE–100 CE)," *Jewish Apocalyptic and Its History,* 211-32; cf. Peggy L. Day, *An Adversary in Heaven:* śāṭān *in the Hebrew Bible,* HSM 43 (Atlanta: Scholars, 1988).

his sinfulness, as his friends repeatedly invite him to do for his own sake and for the sake of the entire theological system. Job steadfastly refuses; he will never ask forgiveness for a sin he did not commit (Job 27:1-6).

Job's innocence is the unbearable contradiction that unveils the inherent weakness of the Zadokite concept of covenant. What justice can humans expect when the other party is at the same time partner and judge?[73] "[God] is not a mortal, as I am, that I might answer him, 'Let's go to trial together,' for there is no umpire between us who might lay his hand on us both" (Job 9:32-33). However, Job equally refuses to attribute to God any wrongdoing or falsehood. His skepticism is not against God or God's authority. Job will not curse God to whom he concedes the right to send the good as well as the bad, as God wishes (2:9-10).

Now, if both Job and God are innocent, then there must be something wrong in a theology that would make either guilty. Job struggles to find an answer. In vain he seeks for an explanation, only to recognize at the end that God's freedom and omnipotence allow no explanation. God's silence is not a sign of impotence and embarrassment; on the contrary, it is the ultimate proof of God's unlimited power and human frailty. Job's desire for a confrontation with God (Job 23:3-7) would therefore remain unanswered. If God is almighty — and God is almighty — then God cannot be limited by a covenant. If God is good — and God is good — then God does not need to be limited by a covenant. God need not give reasons to anybody, and no one can force God to answer. Job has finally discovered why his innocence does not make God guilty, nor does God's innocence make Job guilty. Contrary to what Zadokite Judaism claims, the almighty and good God is not bound by the covenant.

The happy ending of the book of Job still concedes an appeal to the Zadokite covenantal theology. Although in a tortuous and painful way, the righteous Job eventually got what the covenant promised him — "twice as much as he had before" (Job 42:10). After all, the reward was only delayed and its abundance may make one forget the hardships of an unmerited ordeal.

As commentators have not failed to notice, Jonah functions as the logical counterpart to Job. While Job shows that God's punishment may not follow strictly the rules of the covenant, Jonah explores the other (and no

73. Paolo Sacchi, "Giobbe e il Patto (Giobbe 9, 32-33)," *Hen* 4 (1982): 175-84; "Job," *The History of the Second Temple Period,* 186-91.

less disturbing) side of the coin: "are God's compassionate actions just?"[74] Written probably at the dawn of the Hellenistic age, the book of Jonah ridicules the ancient figure of the prophet, confirming that during the Persian period the prophetic movement lost any role as a reliable catalyst of anti-Zadokite opposition.

The prophet preaches God's justice but is afraid of subjecting its validity to the test of experience. He tries to "flee away from the presence of YHWH" (Jonah 1:3), only to discover that the "fear of God" is abundant also outside the Western boundaries of Israel and the pagan sailors are wiser than the Jewish prophet. When finally the reluctant prophet decides to move eastwards, he sees the arch-enemies of God, the oppressors of Israel, the people of the city that more than any other city deserves God's punishment, welcoming his appeal to conversion and making atonement. Even more disappointingly, he sees that "God changed his mind about the calamity that he had said he would bring upon them" (3:10). The prophet discovers that the "divine attributes" of "freedom, power and sovereignty over all creation . . . are beyond the bounds of any human notions of justice, mercy or logic."[75] To Jonah, like Job, this means that life itself is meaningless in a world where there is no justice: "I knew that you are a gracious God and merciful . . . please take my life from me, for it is better for me to die than to live" (Jonah 4:2-3). The recognition that God is not bound by any pronouncement, even pronouncements God has made, is simply unbearable to him.

As in the case of Job, the Zadokite covenantal theology is not entirely denied; at the end the sailors are spared because they "offered a sacrifice to YHWH and made vows" (Jonah 1:16) and the Ninevites are saved because they "believed God . . . and everyone, great and small, put on sackcloth" (3:5). The emphasis of Sapiential Judaism, however, is not on the covenant but on God's freedom to use unexpectedly the covenant as God likes. Job's conclusion is that humans have no right to question the justice of God's punishment. Jonah now shows that God has broad discretion in rewarding, too: "Should I not be concerned . . . ?" (Jonah 4:11).

74. Terence E. Fretheim, *The Message of Jonah: A Theological Commentary* (Minneapolis: Augsburg, 1977), 23; see also Bruce Vawter, *Job and Jonah: Questioning the Hidden God* (New York: Paulist, 1983).

75. Thomas M. Bolin, *Freedom Beyond Forgiveness: The Book of Jonah Re-Examined,* JSOTSup 236 (Sheffield: JSOT, 1997), 183.

Job's and Jonah's unique experiences can still be read as the classical exceptions that prove the general rule. There remains the disturbing recognition, however, that even the most wicked can be graciously offered the opportunity to repent, while the most righteous may suffer for reasons that are hidden to them. At any moment God has the power, the right, and the freedom to deviate from the established terms of God's relationship with humans.

CHAPTER THREE

The Rapprochement between Zadokite and Sapiential Judaism

1. The Beginnings of Hellenistic Rule under the Ptolemies

The impact of the Greek conquest in the Middle East was monumental. "The Greek conquerors were the bearers of an exceptional vitality that few historical periods have witnessed."[1] Greek culture, political forms, and language spread widely throughout the eastern Mediterranean region, especially among prominent elements in the cities, creating a new cosmopolitan culture, of which the Jews also would soon become an important component.[2]

At the very beginning, however, nothing changed in Jerusalem with the coming of Alexander the Great. The transition from Persian to Greek rule went smoothly; Alexander took over the Persian system of adminis-

1. Paolo Sacchi, "Hellenism," *The History of the Second Temple Period,* 203-12 (quotation, 208); cf. Moses Hadas, *Hellenistic Culture: Fusion and Diffusion* (New York: Norton, 1972).

2. See John J. Collins, *Between Athens and Jerusalem: Jewish Identity in the Hellenistic Diaspora,* 2nd ed. (Grand Rapids: Wm. B. Eerdmans, 2000); Erich S. Gruen, *Heritage and Hellenism: The Reinvention of Jewish Tradition* (Berkeley: University of California, 1998); J. M. G. Barclay, *Jews in the Mediterranean Diaspora from Alexander to Trajan (323 B.C.E.–117 C.E.)* (Edinburgh: T. & T. Clark, 1996); Arnaldo Momigliano, *Alien Wisdom: The Limits of Hellenization* (Cambridge: Cambridge University Press, 1975); Martin Hengel, *Judaism and Hellenism.* 2 vols. (Philadelphia: Fortress, 1974); Victor Tcherikover, *Hellenistic Civilization and the Jews* (1959, repr. Peabody: Hendrickson, 1999).

tration and followed the same policy of religious tolerance. Unlike Samaria, which rebelled and experienced the sting of Alexander's revenge, Judah surrendered peacefully.[3]

Josephus narrates how the high priest Jaddua welcomed Alexander and went to meet him outside Jerusalem, and how Alexander in return visited Jerusalem and offered sacrifice in the temple. The substance of Josephus's narrative, full of legendary traits and further embellished in the later rabbinic literature, is that the new power recognized the Jews' right to live according to their ancestral laws, just as the kings of Persia had allowed before (*Ant* 11:326-339; cf. *b. Yoma* 69a).[4] The only change was that political loyalty and taxes were now due to a new ruler.

The situation, however, became complicated after the death of Alexander, with Ptolemy I and Seleucus I competing for possession of the Syrian satrapy. Ancient Jewish sources speak of a divided society. Ptolemy took Jerusalem by "deceit and treachery . . . for he came into the city on a Sabbath day . . . and when he had gained the city, he reigned over it in a cruel manner" (*Ant* 12:4). The harsh treatment he inflicted on the Jews, with mass deportations of prisoners to Egypt (*Ant* 12:4-7; Aristeas 10-12), suggests that there was among the people and especially among the leaders in Jerusalem an active anti-Ptolemaic opposition. It is no surprise that many in Judah sided with Seleucus, because of their traditional links with the Eastern diaspora. However, Josephus also speaks of "not a few other Jews who, on their own accord, went into Egypt, as invited by the goodness of the soul and by the liberality of Ptolemy" (*Ant* 12:9) and "were willing to assist him in his affairs" (*C. Ap.* 1:186). If Josephus is to be believed in this report from Hecateus of Abdera, the split crossed priestly families, possibly the same Zadokite family: among those who went to Egypt was also a certain "Hezekiah, a chief priest of the Jews, a man of about sixty-six years of age, and in great dignity among his own people, intellectual, and moreover an able speaker and very skillful in the management of affairs" (*C. Ap.* 1:187).

The struggle for the possession of the Syrian satrapy did not last long.

3. On the rebellion of Samaria, see Henk Jagersma, *A History of Israel from Alexander the Great to Bar Kochba*, 13-14.

4. On the visit of Alexander to Jerusalem, see Arnaldo Momigliano, "Flavius Josephus and Alexander's Visit to Jerusalem," *Athenaeum* 57 (1979): 442-448; S. J. D. Cohen, "Alexander the Great and Jaddua the High Priest According to Josephus," *AJSR* 7-8 (1982-83): 41-68.

In the aftermath of the battle of Ipsus in 301 B.C.E., the satrapy was de facto divided; the Ptolemies held the southern part (including Judah), but the Seleucids never surrounded their claims to the entire region. The legal dispute over ownership was never settled and would soon lead to a new period of confrontation at the end of the 3rd century.[5]

The war of the Diadochi and the Ptolemaic rule threw Judah from "the periphery of world empires . . . into the vortex of political and military activity."[6] In the Persian period, the political influence of the Zadokite priesthood outside the boundaries of the temple appears to have been very limited. Judah was politically and economically so insignificant, its international relevance so negligible, that the historical and geographical description of the Near East provided by Herodotus in the 5th century skips over Jerusalem and its sanctuary. This can hardly be accidental from the perspective of a professional historian who was eager to record even the rarest ethnographical curiosities, and cunning enough to know that the powerful were not to be overlooked.

Now Judah was no longer insulated from the outside world; it was at the juncture of two powerful and competing empires, in an age of global market and booming economy. Many welcomed this change. Lee I. A. Levine points out that archaeological findings, including the coins minted in Jerusalem during the Ptolemaic period with their vivid Hellenistic style, prove the powerful attraction of the new economy, as well as the eagerness and enthusiasm of the Jerusalem authorities and large segments of the Jewish population to embrace the opportunities for integration and economic development.[7]

Culturally and religiously, Hellenism was no less pervasive and appealing. Convenience and persuasion, rather than force and persecution, were the foundations of the success of the cultural revolution Alexander the Great consciously initiated with his conquest of the Persian Empire. The new culture spread mainly through the founding of new cities or the voluntary transformation of an already existing city into a polis by adopt-

5. See Dov Gera, "Between Ptolemies and Seleucids," *Judaea and Mediterranean Politics, 219 to 161 B.C.E.* (Leiden: Brill, 1998), 3-35.

6. Lee I. A. Levine, "The Age of Hellenism: Alexander the Great and the Rise and Fall of the Hasmonean Kingdom," in Hershel Shanks, *Ancient Israel,* 231-64 (quotation, 232).

7. Levine, 233-34.

ing a Greek constitution and introducing Hellenistic educational and entertainment institutions. The market, or agora, was not only the motivating force of the new economy but also, with the theater, the center for discussion and promotion of Hellenistic ideals and values. The gymnasium and the ephebium were the core of a sophisticated system of education. Speaking Greek was much more than a necessity for trade and business; it was the mark of emancipation from "barbarianism" — the passport to the new cosmopolitan society of educated people. "The concept of 'barbarian' . . . shift[ed] from being the opposite of 'Greek' to being the opposite of *pepaideumenos,* that is those who know the language and practise the customs of the Greeks."[8] By teaching Greek and the Greek way of life, the network of schools and other institutions for youth provided a powerful means of cultural integration and social advancement, which, at least ideally, was accessible to individuals regardless of their ethnic or religious background. Finally, religious and cultural syncretism offered the many religions and cultures the possibility not only to survive in peace but also to prosper and coexist in a climate of freedom and mutual tolerance.[9] The many gods, the result of ancient and autonomous traditions, could be conveniently seen as different names for the same deity. The synchronic comparison of cultures could reveal that the mythical founders and spiritual leaders of different nations were the same figures, or were related by means of genealogy or discipleship.

For some time it appeared that Judaism also could blend into the melting pot in which Hellenistic culture tried to harmonize the diversity of its cultural, ethnic, and religious components. The first step had to be the translation of the Torah into Greek, which according to Jewish tradition (Letter of Aristeas) took place under the auspices of Ptolemy II Philadelphus (285-246). However, the emancipation of a local culture from its "barbaric" origins was not only a matter of language. In order to become susceptible of syncretistic absorption, Jewish culture and history had also to be translated into the established categories of Hellenistic culture and interpreted according to the established criteria of Hellenistic scholarship. By the time of Ptolemy IV Philopator (222-205), Jewish authors like Demetrius the chronographer fulfilled the task, providing that

8. Sacchi, *The History of the Second Temple Period,* 205.

9. See Louis H. Martin, *Hellenistic Religions: An Introduction* (Oxford: Oxford University Press, 1987).

synchrony between Jewish history and the histories of other peoples that was the necessary premise to any comparison or fusion.[10]

Chronology made it possible, for example, to "discover that the Spartans and the Jews . . . are brothers and are both of the seed of Abraham," as King Arius of Sparta supposedly wrote to the high priest Onias (1 Macc 12:7-8, 19-23; *Ant* 12:226-27; 13:167). According to Josephus, the Pergamenes also "found set down in [their] public records," and wrote down in a formal decree of alliance, that their "ancestors had friendly relations with the Jews, even in the days of Abraham" (*Ant.* 14:247-55). Beyond their actual historicity, the documents are important evidence of diplomatic syncretism; they testify to the high degree of integration reached by the Jewish people during the early Hellenistic period.

The process of acculturation of Jewish traditions into Hellenistic society had the potential of even more profound developments from the religious point of view. At the end of the 3rd century, the portrait Artapanus offers of Moses shows how advantageously the criteria of Hellenistic syncretism could be used in order to promote Judaism as a form of inclusive monotheism. "As a grown man [Moses] was called Mousaeus by the Greeks. This Mousaeus was the teacher of Orpheus. . . . [Moses] bestowed many useful benefits on mankind, for he invented boats and devices for stone construction and the Egyptian arms and the implements for drawing water and for warfare, and philosophy. Further he divided the [Egyptian] state into 36 nomes and appointed for each of the nomes the god to be worshiped, and for the priests the sacred letters, and that they should be cats and dogs and ibises. . . . He did all these things for the sake of maintaining the monarchy firm. . . . On account of these things then Moses was loved by the masses, and was deemed worthy of godlike honor by the priests and called Hermes, on account of the interpretation of the sacred letters" (Artapanus, fr. 3).[11]

While combining Jewish and foreign mythologies with great freedom and without prejudice, Artapanus was not polytheistic and had no intention to sell off cheaply the uniqueness of Jewish religion. On the contrary, his work offers a very sophisticated example of "competitive historiogra-

10. On Demetrius, see Collins, *Between Athens and Jerusalem*, 27-30; J. Hanson, "Demetrius the Chronographer," *OTP* 2 (1985): 843-54.

11. On Artapanus, see John J. Collins, "Artapanus," *OTP* 2 (1985): 889-903; *Between Athens and Jerusalem*, 37-46.

phy." The goal was to exploit other mythologies in order to put his own mythology on the highest level of authority and antiquity.

The first element is the most obvious. Moses, the lawgiver of the Jews, was the superhero of humankind, the true initiator of "modern" civilization. He was the founder of Egyptian culture and religion. He was called Mousaeus by the Greeks, and this Mousaeus was the teacher of Orpheus (not his disciple as in the Greek tradition). Consequently, as it was commonly held that Orpheus brought wisdom from Egypt to Greece, Moses-Mousaeus was the founder of Greek wisdom too.

The reference to Moses as the champion of the monarchy and the organizer of the kingdom, as well as the patron of local cults, also contributes to the exaltation of the wisdom of the Jews while stressing their loyalty to the king and their respect of pagan institutions as inventions that were "useful benefits on mankind" (fr. 3).

Finally, the identification of Moses with Hermes (the latter being identified with the Egyptian god Thoth) does not deify Moses into the Hellenistic pantheon, but euhemeristically demythologizes the character of Hermes. The humanization of Hellenistic gods opens the door to the participation of Jews in Hellenistic rituals and festivals, which now can be seen not as acts of idolatry but as celebrations in honor of ancient heroes.

During the 3rd century, the possibility that Judaism might develop in the Hellenistic world as a form of inclusive monotheism was a feasible and fascinating option, a possibility that — as the events that preceded the Maccabean Revolt would prove — was to find many enthusiastic supporters in Jerusalem, even among the members of the ruling priesthood.

The beginnings of Ptolemaic rule, however, were not so easy for the Jerusalem priesthood; they led initially to a decreasing influence for the Zadokites. The Ptolemies were much less interested in religious affairs than were their Persian predecessors, who often employed priestly aristocracies in pursuit of their political goals. On the contrary, "the Macedonian monarchs did not seem to pay attention to the religious practices of those under their dominion save when those practices were baneful to the state or to the monarch."[12] For a priestly class who had greatly benefited from the support of Persian kings, the end of monarchic interference in religious affairs was not necessarily a blessing.

12. John H. Hayes, and Sara R. Mandell, *The Jewish People in Classical Antiquity,* 19.

Even most importantly, the office of governor disappeared and was replaced by a system of tax farming. It was now the highest bidders who could purchase the right to collect taxes in royal auctions (*Ant* 12:169). This was a very expensive job, not only to get but also to keep. Presents and bribes had to be offered frequently to the king and his officials to strengthen personal relations and exclude rivals. But at the end it was also a very lucrative job. There were no actual limitations to the extent tax farmers could exploit the local population on behalf of the king and for their own profit.

The system enhanced the power of the wealthiest families in the various districts of the Ptolemaic kingdom. They had the money and the skill to serve as local instruments of the king's exploitative policy, at the expense of the small farmers. The gap between the few and the many, between the city and the countryside deepened. Judah was no exception.[13]

In the long run the Jerusalem high priesthood would greatly benefit from the system. However, in the short term the power vacuum was filled by those who had the actual economic power to collect taxes in the region, and in the first half of the 3rd century these did not happen to be the Zadokite high priests. It is certainly striking to see how, when between 260 and 258 a Ptolemaic officer, Zenon, visited Judah in an official mission, he ignored the Jerusalem priesthood and dispatched all his business outside Jerusalem with a certain Tobiah, who was manifestly the one in charge of the political, economic, and military affairs of the region on behalf of the Ptolemies. Tobiah headed a military colony in Transjordan with a garrison of Macedonian and Judean troops. The friendly tone of his correspondence and the liberality of gifts he exchanges with both the king and his finance minister are the clearest indications of Tobiah's power and wealth.[14]

Tobiah was a descendant of that "Tobiah the Ammonite" whose influence in Jewish society Nehemiah and Ezra struggled to minimize (Neh 7:61-62; 13:4-9). From the turmoil of the early Hellenistic period, the Tobiads re-emerged as the wealthiest family and therefore de facto as the civil rulers of the region.

The spread of Hellenistic ideals and the greater autonomy of the civil

13. Jagersma, 25; Hayes and Mandell, 35.

14. C. C. Edgar, *Zenon Papyri I-IV* (Cairo: Institut français d'archéologie orientale, 1925-1940, repr. 1971); William Linn Westermann et al., *Zenon Papyri* (New York: Columbia University Press, 1934-1940, repr. 1987).

power from religious affairs gave to Sapiential Judaism new strength and an unprecedented freedom from the Jerusalem priesthood. It was in this climate that the book of Qoheleth or Ecclesiates was composed, in Ptolemaic Jerusalem, in the first half of the 3rd century.

Qoheleth belongs to the same tradition of skeptical wisdom as Job and Jonah. "All three emphasize the pain of an existence under the rule of an omnipotent but inscrutable deity. All three emphasize the futility of the foundational religious and theological issues of prayer, sacrifice, repentance and right living."[15] Faithful to the sapiential method, Qoheleth also puts the Zadokite theology under the scrutiny of experience. "I applied my mind to seek and to search out by wisdom all that is done under heaven" (Eccl 1:13). As in Job and Jonah, the revolt is in the name of practical experience.

Yet Qoheleth's skepticism is much more radical; it shows no restraint. In comparison, the earlier books of Sapiential Judaism were quite moderate and indirect in their criticism and gave to the doubts of the protagonists a happy ending that did not openly contradict the principles of Zadokite Judaism. With Qoheleth, any semblance of compromise and accommodation disappears. Irony turns into bitterness and sarcasm. The crisis is complete and the conceptual impossibility of a covenantal theology affirmed.

Qoheleth's analysis is lucid, almost merciless. The righteous suffer while the unrighteous triumph too frequently for us to believe in any rule that guarantees vindication for those who obey the Mosaic covenant. "There are righteous people who perish in their righteousness, and there are wicked people who prolong their life in their evil-doing" (Eccl 7:15). Too often the lives of the righteous and the wicked are undistinguishable for us to believe that this is not the general rule. "There are righteous people who are treated according to the conduct of the wicked, and there are wicked people who are treated according to the conduct of the righteous" (8:14). Too often a righteous life is not even accompanied by the comfort of an everlasting memory. "There is no enduring remembrance of the wise or of fools" (Eccl 2:16). Meanwhile, the inherent difficulties in people's efforts to be righteous appear more and more insuperable. "There is no one on earth so righteous as to do good without ever sinning" (Eccl 7:20).

While "lift[ing] penetrating and continuous criticism" against the foundations of Zadokite covenantal theology, Qoheleth does not concede

15. Thomas M. Bolin, *Freedom Beyond Forgiveness,* 185.

anything to Enochic thought. "He was . . . familiar with the early Apocalyptic circles for whom he felt even less sympathy. He does not argue with the Apocalyptics, he only makes fun of them."[16]

To the Enochian search for heavenly knowledge through dreams and visions, Qoheleth opposes the sapiential experience of what exists "under heaven" (Eccl 1:13) or "under the sun" (1:14). He does not invoke the authority of any celestial revelation, which he regards with the utmost skepticism: "When dreams increase, empty words grow many" (5:7). Enoch describes the heavenly voyage that led him to see the throne of God (1 En 14:18-20); Qoheleth reminds its readers that "God is in heaven and you are upon earth" (Eccl 5:2).

To the Enochian pretentiousness to a comprehensive knowledge, Qoheleth opposes the limits of human understanding. Enoch expresses his curiosity and "desire to know everything" (1 En 25:2) and proudly declares that "the boundaries of all" were shown to him (19:3). Qoheleth replies that humans, even the wise, can indeed only partially grasp God's will; "[God] has put a sense of past and future into [human] minds, yet they cannot find out what God has done from the beginning to the end" (Eccl 3:11; cf. 1:8). The work of God is sheer mystery for humans, "for you do not know the work of God, who makes everything" (11:5). In spite of any effort and search, "no one can find out what is happening under the sun" (8:17).

To the Enochic hope of afterlife judgment (1 En 22:9-10), Qoheleth opposes the traditional notion that the experience of death is common to all living creatures. "The fate of humans and the fate of animals is the same; as one dies, so dies the other. . . . All go to one place; all are from the dust, and all turn to dust again" (Eccl 3:19-20). He ridicules the belief that "the life-breath of the children of men goes upward, [while] the life-breath of animals goes downward to the earth" (3:21) and urges people not to delude themselves with vain hopes that the problems of existence may find a solution beyond death, "for there is no work or thought or knowledge or wisdom in Sheol, to which you are going" (9:10).

Above all, against the Enochic idea of corruption and disorder, Qoheleth holds to the notion of the universe as a divine order. He compares God's creation to his own experience of the well-organized Hellenis-

16. Paolo Sacchi, "Qohelet," *The History of the Second Temple Period,* 191-203 (quotation, 192). See also Liliana Rosso-Ubigli, "Qohelet e l'Apocalittica," *Hen* 5 (1983): 209-34.

tic kingdom of the Ptolemies. "If you see in a province the oppression of the poor and the violation of justice and right, do not be amazed at the matter; for the high official is watched by a higher, and there are yet higher ones over them. But all things considered, this is an advantage for a land: a king for a plowed field" (Eccl 5:8-9). The difficulty for the individual to experience justice does not mean that there is no ruler. It only proves the difficulty for ordinary people to understand the superior rationale to which they are subjected — the king's justice may have indeed the taste of injustice for his subjects.

Some would rather "curse the king" and "the rich" (Eccl 10:20), but not Qoheleth. No one can question the king's will, "for he does whatever he pleases" (8:3). The duty of the individual is to "keep the king's command. . . . Whoever obeys a command will meet no harm, and the wise mind will know the time and way. For every matter has its time and way" (8:2-6).

A very convenient political ideology in support of the absolute power of the Hellenistic king and his wealthy allies is turned by Qoheleth into a revelation of God's power. As a kingdom, so is the universe. Not even for a moment does Qoheleth doubt that the universe has an order and that everything happens in conformity with the will of God. The divine power is supreme and unchallenged: "I know that whatever God does endures forever; nothing can be added to it, nor anything taken from it" (Eccl 3:14).

Qoheleth argues that the life of the universe is regulated by the unfolding of a rational yet mysteriously ordained series of times. "For everything there is a season, and a time for every matter under heaven: a time to be born, and a time to die; a time to plant, and a time to pluck up what is planted; a time to kill, and a time to heal [etc.]" (Eccl 3:1-9). As each human experience is followed and compensated by its opposite, the law of the times assumes and annuls the scandal of injustice in the inscrutable unity of divine will.

What Qoheleth denies is the capability of humans to have any influence over the times decided by God. The Zadokite covenant promises a correspondence between human actions and divine reactions; but such a correspondence does not exist. "What do people gain from all the toil at which they toil under the sun? . . . What has been is what will be, and what has been done is what will be done; there is nothing new under the sun" (Eccl 1:3, 9).

Insisting on the validity of the covenant only leads to skepticism and frustration. If the Zadokite Torah is the rule against which the righteous and the wicked are measured, then the only conclusion left is that the same destiny occurs to those who keep the moral, purity, and cultic laws of the covenant and to those who do not. "The same fate comes to all, to the righteous and the wicked, to the good and the evil, to the clean and the unclean, to those who sacrifice and those who do not sacrifice. As are the good, so are the sinners" (Eccl 9:2; cf. 2:14).

Human happiness, the "joy" Qoheleth invites people to seek (Eccl 2:24-26; 3:22; 9:7-9), is not to be found in active partnership but in total submission. "All should stand in awe before him" (3:14); no one "can make straight what [God] has made crooked" (7:13). Qoheleth calls this attitude the "fear of God" (8:12). People's duty is merely to conform to the rhythms of God, of which they have no knowledge or over which they have no control whatsoever. "In the day of prosperity be joyful, and in the day of adversity consider; God has made the one as well as the other" (7:14). The Zadokite covenantal theology, based on the duty to fulfill the cultic and moral acts prescribed by the Mosaic Torah, is pure illusion, "vanity of vanities" *(vanitas vanitatum)*, as it promises what is not possible to maintain. It makes people believe that through their works of obedience they have some power over God, the capability to predict God's action and influence God's reaction — an absurd and blasphemous limitation to the omnipotence of the supreme king of the universe.

Qoheleth is a staunch supporter of the Ptolemaic political and social order. His recommendation not to "curse the king, even in your thoughts, or curse the rich, even in your bedroom; for a bird of the air may carry your voice, or some winged creature tell the matter" (Eccl 10:20) speaks plainly about who now had the power in Jerusalem. The deference to the king and his unquestionable power is complete; any form of criticism is rejected out of hand. The power of the king resembles that of God. "Keep the king's command because of your sacred oath . . . he does whatever he pleases. For the word of the king is powerful, and who can say to him, 'What are you doing?'" (8:2-4). In Qoheleth's worldview there is neither room nor respect but for the king and his wealthy allies.

Josephus confirms that throughout the 3rd century the Tobiads not only continued to prosper but their influence increased. Although his narrative (*Ant* 12:154-236) is based largely on tales and romance, it appears clear that the Tobiads consolidated their power as the tax farmers and civil rulers for the region.

The most significant development was that the Zadokites themselves fell into the sphere of the Tobiads' influence. The Tobiads were now strong enough to renew their political and family ties with the Zadokites. According to Josephus, Tobiah married a sister of the high priest Onias II (*Ant* 12:160); their son Joseph would play a very important role in the second half of the 3rd century as tax collector in Judah.

While Tobiah had maintained the traditional hub in Transjordan, Joseph made Jerusalem the center of his political and economic activity. Thanks to their wealth and their political and economic relations with the Ptolemaic court, the Tobiads made Jerusalem share the booming Hellenistic economy and turned it into an international city, whose importance was now for the first time acknowledged by classical authors.[17]

The merging of Tobiads and Zadokites met with so little opposition that by the end of the century the fluctuating fortunes of the two families appear to be inextricably joined. It was an astonishing comeback for the heirs of that Tobiah who was dismissed by Nehemiah, but also the opening of a new chapter in the history of the Zadokite priesthood. The Zadokites resurfaced as part of the Hellenistic establishment, no longer as the target of the Tobiads' polemical arrows. The Tobiads patronized the Zadokites but also launched them into business and political affairs. Unlike their predecessors, the last generations of Zadokite high priests would be directly involved in the political arena.[18]

2. An Unexpected Supporter of Zadokite Judaism: Tobit

The religious implications of the merging of Zadokites and Tobiads were no less remarkable. It is no accident that the wisdom tradition, which with

17. See Hengel, 1:53.

18. Dov Gera, "The Tobiads: Fiction and History," *Judaea and Mediterranean Politics,* 36-58; Lawrence M. Wills, The Jewish Novel in the Ancient World (Ithaca: Cornell University, 1995), 187-93; Benjamin Mazar, "The House of Tobias," *Canaan and Israel,* 2nd ed. (Jerusalem: Byalik, 1980), 270-90 [Hebrew]; "The Tobiads," *IEJ* 7 (1957): 137-45, 229-38; Jonathan A. Goldstein, "The Tales of the Tobiads," in *Christianity, Judaism, and Other Greco-Roman Cults: Studies for Morton Smith at Sixty,* ed. Jacob Neusner, SJLA 12 (Leiden: Brill, 1975), 3:85-123; C. C. McCown, "The 'Araq el-Emir and the Tobiads," *BA* 20 (1957): 63-76; Adolf Buechler, *Die Tobiaden und die Oniaden* (1899, repr. Hildesheim: Olms, 1975).

Qoheleth in the first half of the 3rd century B.C.E. had never been so distant from, and disrespectful of, the Zadokite tradition, in the second half of the century suddenly became more and more eager to compromise. The Zadokites were now among those rich people against whom one could not even whisper. The process of rapprochement between Zadokite and Sapiential Judaism, fully recognized by scholars with regard to the book of Sirach,[19] is first evidenced a few decades before the end of the 3rd century, during the late Ptolemaic period, with the book of Tobit.

It is difficult not to relate the book of Tobit to the powerful family recorded by Zenon and Josephus. As J. T. Milik fully acknowledged, the document "was designed to enhance the prestige of the family,"[20] and functioned as a legitimization of their association to the high priesthood of Jerusalem. The book of Tobit overturned the verdict of the tradition of Ezra and marked the recognition of the genealogy "of the descendants of Tobiah" as an exiled family from the tribe of Naphtali. The claims of the Tobiads were finally vindicated; "the ancestral descent," which they "could not prove," was now acknowledged, although by means of a special status.

As the boundaries between political and cultic authority weakened in Jewish society, so did the boundaries between wisdom and priestly traditions. The rapprochement between Zadokite and Sapiential Judaism was the religious fallout of the political alliance between the Zadokites and the Tobiads.

The fictional protagonist of the book of Tobit is an Israelite from the northern kingdom of Israel, a member "of the tribe of Napthali, who in the days of King Shalmaneser of the Assyrians was taken captive from Thisbe, which is south of Kedesh Naphtali in Upper Galilee, above Asher toward the west, and north of Phogor" (Tob 1:1-2). Unlike his kindred who "deserted the house of David and Jerusalem . . . [and] sacrificed to the calf that King Jeroboam of Israel had erected in Dan and on all the mountains of Galilee" (1:4-5), Tobit "alone went often to Jerusalem for the festivals, as it is prescribed for all Israel by an everlasting decree . . . and would give [what is commanded] to the priests, the sons of Aaron, at the altar . . . and to the sons of Levi who ministered at Jerusalem" (1:6).

The document shares the Zadokite (and anti-Samaritan) perspective that "Jerusalem . . . had been chosen from among all the tribes of Israel,

19. See Collins, *Jewish Wisdom in the Hellenistic Age.*

20. J. T. Milik, "La Patrie de Tobie," *RB* 73 (1966): 522-30.

where all the tribes of Israel should offer sacrifice and where the temple, the dwelling of God, had been consecrated and established for all generations forever" (Tob 1:4). As in Chronicles, the destruction of the First Temple and the Babylonian exile are described as an experience of total annihilation for the land of Israel. "All of our kindred, inhabitants of the land of Israel, will be scattered and taken as captives from the good land; and the whole land of Israel will be desolate . . . . And the temple of God in it will be burned to the ground, and it will be desolate for a while" (14:4). Tobit agrees that the future of Judaism would belong to the returned exiles, and with enthusiasm foretells the restoration of the Second Temple in Jerusalem (13:9-17; 14:5-7).

In the meantime, the exile did not change Tobit's way of life. While loyal to the Gentile king, he followed scrupulously the purity laws and so the boundaries established by God. Now that he lived among the Gentiles, "I kept myself from eating the food of the Gentiles" (Tob 1:10-17). And when time came, Tobit recommended his son Tobias to "marry a woman from among the descendants of your ancestors" (4:12), as he himself in the land of Israel "married a woman, a member of our own family" (1:9).

In its pro-Zadokite stance, the book of Tobit even bears traces of anti-Enochic polemics. The document knows of the existence and danger of evil spirits, and for many aspects its demonology resembles that of Enochic Judaism. The "wicked demon Asmodeus," who killed Sarah's seven husbands (Tob 3:8) and instantaneously fled from Ectabana in Mesopotamia "to the remotest parts of Egypt" (moving, as the Codex Sinaiticus reads, "through the air," 8:3), has the same features of the evil spirits described in the Book of the Watchers. By connecting the popular belief in demons to the story of the fallen angels, Enochic Judaism understood the evil spirits as the surviving souls of the monstrous children of the fallen angels and women, i.e. the giants, whose bodies perished in the Flood.[21] "The giants who are born from the (union of) the spirits and the flesh shall be called evil spirits upon the earth, because their dwelling shall be upon the earth and inside the earth. Evil spirits have come out of their bodies" (1 En 15:8-9). The demonology of Enochic Judaism provides a good setting for the super powers of Asmodeus, and even for his jealous

21. Interestingly, medieval Jewish folklore (Zoh III 76b) will preserve the idea that Asmodeus is the son of a fallen angel, Shamadon, who had him by a wicked woman, Naamah. See "Asmodeus," *EJ* 3:754-55.

"love" toward Sarah (cf. Tob 6:18). "The spirits of the giants . . . eat no food, nor become thirsty, nor find obstacles. . . . [They] shall rise up against the children of the people and against the women, because they have proceeded forth (from them)" (1 En 15:11-12).

As in the Book of the Watchers, the angels who mediate prayers before the throne of God (1 En 9:1-4; Tob 12:12) are the ones who listen to the cry of the suffering (1 En 8:4; Tob 3:1-6, 11-15) and are sent to fight against the demons (1 En 10:4-15; Tob 12:14-15). The choice of Raphael as the healing hero perfectly fits the framework of Enochic theology as well. Raphael, whose name means "God heals," is the angel who was commanded to "bind Azazel hand and foot (and) throw him into the darkness . . . in the desert" (1 En 10:4-5; cf. 9:1; 22:3, 6). "So Raphael was sent to heal both of them: Tobit, by removing the white films from his eyes, so that he might see God's light with his eyes; and Sarah . . . by setting her free from the wicked demon Asmodeus" (Tob 3:17). Raphael the healer and the exorcist skillfully exploited the medicinal properties of the fish to cure Tobit and its repellent odor to scare Asmodeus. Then, as only a well-experienced bounty hunter could do, he chased Asmodeus "and at once bound him" (Tob 8:3).

Despite the sharing of common traditions, however, the book of Tobit lacks the atmosphere of catastrophe, corruption, and despair of Enochic Judaism. Everything, everywhere, is under God's control and people are not so defenseless. In Nineveh as well in Ectabana, the righteous pray and God listens, "on the same day" (3:7), "at that very moment" (3:16-17). As early as 3:16-17, the reader is reassured of the deliverance of both the characters in distress, Tobit and Sarah; and how this would happen is made explicit even before the story is half told (6:7-9). What has been often criticized as a loss of suspense or surprise in the narrative is equal to a strong theological statement. Against the pessimism of Enochic literature, in Tobit the righteous can trustfully count on the assistance of God who looks after them, listens to their prayers, and sends the good angels to provide them "a medicine" (3:16-17; 6:7-9).

With Zadokite Judaism, Tobit agrees that this world is God's good and eternal creation; reward and punishment are given in one's lifetime. There is no need for an afterlife or the world to come. Blindness is compared to death; Tobit, "who cannot see the light of heaven, . . . lie[s] in darkness like the dead who no longer see the light " (Tob 5:10). As in Job (10:21-22; 38:17), the grave is only a place of eternal darkness.

The book of Tobit, with its emphasis on temple and worship, on tithes and purity laws, and on God's unchallenged control over the world, strenuously supports the Zadokite order. The document repeatedly appeals to the authority of the Jerusalem priesthood, which is referred to in its basic distinction between the sons of Aaron and the sons of Levi (Tob 1:7), and to the authority of the Zadokite Torah, which as in the priestly lexicon is referred to as "the law of Moses" (1:8; 6:13 [some Greek mss]; 7:13; cf. 2 Chr 23:18; 30:16) or "the book of Moses" (Tob 6:13 [other Greek mss]; 7:11, 12; cf. 2 Chr 35:12; Ezra 6:18). Yet there is an important and striking development. The righteousness of Tobit is based on both "the ordinance decreed concerning it in the law of Moses and according to the instructions of Deborah, the mother of my father Tobiel" (Tob 1:8).[22]

This is the first time that the two sets of traditions, the priestly and the familial, are put on the same level as the foundation of Jewish piety. In fact, Tobit fits the parameters of Sapiential Judaism as much as those of Zadokite Judaism. A living family tradition is the life-blood by which Tobit has been nurtured, and he will not fail to pass on the legacy to his son Tobias (14:3-11; cf. 4:3-19). The familial instructions of Tobit are those of Sapiential Judaism, aimed to the practical and moral aspects of being and doing good, and based on personal experience and on the tradition of the wise. "Seek advice from every wise person and do not despise any useful counsel" (4:18). Tobit's teaching to Tobias and Raphael's instructions to father and son (12:6-10) have many close parallels with the earlier documents of Sapiential Judaism as well as with the wisdom literature of the ancient Near East. Tobit even makes explicit and detailed reference to the story of Ahikar (1:21-22; 2:10; 14:10). After all, Tobit is neither a priest nor a levite; he is a layperson and a wise person who "fears the Lord" (14:2). Better, he is a new kind of wise person, a wise person who now actively supports the priest.

As for any compromise, there was a gain and a price to pay for each side. On the one hand, Zadokite Judaism enlarged the basis of consensus by neutralizing a potentially insidious form of opposition and saw the main principles of its covenantal theology accepted and strengthened; yet it had to recognize the value of a teaching generated and passed on outside

22. The reading "my father Tobiel" is according to the Latin version. The Greek has "my father Hananiel." The father of Tobit is Tobiel (Tob 1:1); Hananiel is the grandfather.

the control of the priesthood and independently of the Mosaic revelation. The emphasis shifted from the temple to the family, from worship to charity. Feeding the hungry, clothing the naked, providing the dead a decent burial, preserving dutiful and loving relationships between parents and children, husbands and wives, relatives and neighbors — these are the primary concerns that Sapiential Judaism fostered and that Tobit repeats as the foundations of Jewish morality.[23] "I performed many acts of charity to my kindred, those of my tribe. I would give my food to the hungry and my clothing to the naked; and if I saw the dead body of any of my people thrown out behind the wall of Nineveh, I would bury it" (Tob 1:16-17). In his final instructions, the angel Raphael puts prayer and charity on an equal level and gives to almsgiving the same expiatory power as worship. "Prayer with fasting [and] almsgivings with righteousness" are "better than wealth with wrongdoing. . . . For almsgiving saves from death and purges away every sin" (Tob 12:8-9; cf. 14:10-11).

On the other hand, Sapiential Judaism found legitimacy for its traditions along with the Zadokite Torah, but had to renounce its more cosmopolitan and nonconformist aspects. The Assyrian Ahiqar is now an Israelite, whom Tobit introduces to his son as "the son of my brother Hanael" (Tob 1:21), "my nephew and so a close relative" (1:22). In line with Zadokite thought, universalism belongs to the distant future when "the nations in the whole world will all be converted and worship God in truth" (14:6). Tobit is looking forward to that moment (13:11); in the meantime, however, he confines his own almsgiving to his compatriots (1:3, 8, 16-18; 2:2-3), opposes mixed marriages (4:12), refrains from eating Gentile food (1:11), and seeks the punishment of the nations for their evildoings.

The rapprochement between Zadokite and Sapiential Judaism meant in particular the end of skeptical wisdom. Tobit, Sarah, and Tobias are examples of exactly that kind of people and that kind of situation whose recognition had raised the doubts of Job and Jonah and the protests of Qoheleth.

Tobias is a wiser, unrepentant (and far more confident) Jonah. He would not allow the "big fish" to "swallow" him but would catch and kill it (Tob 6:1-5; cf. Jonah 1:17–2:10[Heb. 2:1-11]).[24] And at the end he would

23. Carey A. Moore, *Tobit,* AB 40A (New York: Doubleday, 1996), 27.

24. See Amy-Jill Levine, "Tobit: Teaching Jews How to Live in the Diaspora," *BRev* 8/4 (1992): 42-51, 64.

not be disappointed by God but would rejoice at the divine revenge finally fallen upon Nineveh (Tob 14:15).

Tobit and Sarah are blameless and innocent people, as was Job (Tob 2:1-7; 3:14). Nevertheless, they must endure much suffering. Sarah saw seven bridegrooms die in the wedding chamber, without having the chance to become a wife and a mother (3:8). Since his birth, Tobit suffered a long series of disgraces: while still a child he was left an orphan (1:9) and later was exiled to Nineveh (1:3); in exile, although his life was spared, he first lost everything except his wife and son (1:18-20), and then became blind and unable to support himself or his family (2:10).

Tobit and Sarah also experienced reproach (Tobit, 2:14b; Sarah, 3:7, 8b-9) as if they were directly responsible for their own misfortune. However, they do not question God's justice, and rather wish they could die (3:6; 3:13; cf. Job 7:15).

Indeed, they would have good reasons to complain against God, Tobit in particular. Sarah is a victim of the evil schemes of a demon, who killed her first seven husbands. As in the case of Job, who lost his "seven sons" (Job 1:2, 13-15) at the instigation of the satan, God may still be viewed as innocent. But in the case of Tobit, the righteous man ironically suffers as a consequence of his good deeds, first at the hand of the king (Tob 1:16-22) and, later, through blindness (2:3-10). There is no satan here who suggested the test of impoverishment and sickness; it was entirely God's decision to allow it to happen.

If Tobias is the anti-Jonah, Tobit is the anti-Job. He never lets his experience clash with his faith in God's covenantal justice. "You are righteous, O Lord; and all your deeds are just; all your ways are mercy and truth; you judge the world" (Tob 3:2). A blind and impoverished man, he restores the unshakeable faith that morality guarantees prosperity, "for those who act in accordance with truth will prosper in all their activities" (4:6; cf. Prov 10:27-30). There is no shadow of irony or regret in his words, even when he teaches his son to give his neighbors a prompt reward, as God does. "Do not keep over until the next day the wages of those who work for you, but pay them at once. If you serve God you will receive payment" (Tob 4:14).

Tobit knows that the God who "shows mercy" is the one who "afflicts" (Tob 13). And because "[God's] judgments are true," Tobit cannot escape the fact that his suffering must be connected with "my unwitting offenses and those that my ancestors committed before you . . . for we have not kept your commandments and have not walked in accordance with truth before you" (Tob 3:3, 5).

There is always a correspondence between human deeds and God's deeds in this world. Israel is punished (3:3-4; 14:4) because it brought punishment upon itself (3:3-5; 13:3-6, 9). The same is true on the individual level, even though the combination of collective and individual sins may produce a disturbing displacement between collective and individual retribution. Righteous people such as Tobit are brought to exile and only "the children of the righteous" will see the restoration (13:9, 13). Tobias, not Tobit, will see the punishment of Nineveh (14:4, 15).

Indeed, all things will be fulfilled "at their appointed times" (Tob 14:4). Although the prayers and the good deeds of the righteous are instantaneously accepted before God (12:12-14), God's providential plans may need some time and take an unexpected (and even sinister) turn before being accomplished. The time of suffering and distress is a time of testing, which only prepares a time of greater joy for all the pious characters of the book, while the villains, Sennacherib (1:18), Asmodeus (3:8), and Nadab (14:10), are defeated and punished (1:21; 8:3; 14:11). The righteous are not guaranteed a life free of suffering, but a happy ending to their misfortunes and an active balance in the vicissitudes of their lives are promised to those who follow the Zadokite Torah and the traditions of the wise.

The relationship between Zadokite and Sapiential Judaism in the book of Tobit was a marriage of convenience, not yet a merging. At this stage, priestly and wisdom traditions remain distinct, and no relationship is established between the two. The pious Israelite was asked to obey both the Zadokite Torah and the wise's instructions as autonomous and nonconflicting sources of God's will. The path was open, however, for more sophisticated exploration and a higher level of compromise.

3. From the Ptolemies to the Seleucids: The Golden Age of Zadokite Priesthood

At the end of the 3rd century, King Antiochus III the Great aggressively renewed the Seleucids' claims over Syria and Phoenicia. As long as Ptolemy IV Philopator was alive, however, the power of the Ptolemies showed no signs of decline. The Jews as well as the other peoples of the region looked almost with indifference at the first military campaign of Antiochus III that ended in 217 with a disastrous defeat at Raphia.

Antiochus III did not lose heart. A series of successful campaigns in the East restored the unity of the Seleucid kingdom and the confidence of the army, while in the meantime the Ptolemaic kingdom entered a period of turmoil and growing uncertainty. When Ptolemy IV died in 204, Antiochus III was ready to reopen hostilities. Now that the balance of power had shifted toward the Seleucids, Antiochus found many friends eager to welcome him.[25]

In Judah also, a strong pro-Seleucid party immediately re-emerged. Jerome explicitly speaks of a split within the Jewish people "into opposite factions — the one favoring Antiochus, and the other favoring Ptolemy" (*Expl. Dan.* 11:4). Josephus's chronological reconstruction is very confused and often unreliable, but agrees in depicting a divided society. This time, however, the civil strife was complicated by the fact that the split was not, like a century before, between the Tobiads and the Zadokites but within the Tobiad-Zadokite family, with some members siding with the Ptolemies and others with the Seleucids. "The elder brothers made war on Hyrcanus . . . and the population was divided into two camps. And the majority fought on the side of the elder brother, as did the high priest Simon [II]" (*Ant* 12:228).

Ancient sources confirm that a majority of Jews actively assisted the Seleucids since the early stages of the revolt, so much so that when the Ptolemies in a counterattack regained temporary control of Jerusalem they had to conquer the city by force. The pro-Seleucid party eventually prevailed and the position of the high priest Simon II, who had chosen the winning side, greatly benefited from the transition of power.

Antiochus III did not fail to show his gratitude to the Jerusalem priestly class (*Ant* 12:145-46). According to Josephus, the king not only "let all of that nation live according to the laws of their own country," but granted a series of provisions and tax exemptions to "the senate and the priests, and the scribes of the temple and the sacred singers" (12:142). Most importantly, Antiochus issued a decree "in honor of the temple." In line with the principles of Zadokite Judaism, he formally recognized the temple and the city as sacred spaces subjected to different degrees of purity. Access to the

25. On the conflicts between Ptolemies and Seleucids, see Gera, *Judaea and Mediterranean Politics*, 3-35.

temple is barred "to all Gentiles and . . . to the Jews also, except to those who, according to their own customs, have purified themselves" (12:145). The city in turn is off limits for "any animal which is forbidden for the Jews to eat"; the law extends also to their "flesh" and "skin" (12:146). By enforcing by royal law the purity boundaries around the temple and the city of Jerusalem, the decree sanctioned the authority of the Zadokites within Jewish society. The decree also acknowledged and strengthened the wealthy of the temple and its administrative role by making "the priests" the payees of the penalty of "three hundred drachmae of silver" against "whoever would transgress any of these orders" (12:146). Antiochus III treated the high priest Simon II not so much as a religious leader, but as a sort of secular prince, having the authority to collect not only the tithes for the temple but also the tributes and taxes owed to the king and to retain part of them.

These financial concessions and economic restrictions were a blow for the Tobiads, as they gave to the high priesthood actual control over the economy of the region. During the Ptolemaic period, the Tobiads had forced the Zadokites to merge by marriage. Now it was the Zadokites who turned the merging to their own advantage. Even in the darkest period of their submission, the Zadokites had retained as their most precious possession — and the Tobiads could neither have nor take away from them — religious authority and control of the temple. In order to subdue the Zadokites, the Tobiads had to share what they had and the Zadokites lacked — economic and political power and wealth. Josephus recognizes that credit goes to the Tobiads, and in particular to "Hyrcanus's father, Joseph," for "bringing the Jews out of the state of poverty and meanness, to one that was more splendid" (*Ant* 12:224). Thanks to their relation with the Tobiads, by the time the Seleucids took over from the Ptolemies, the Jerusalem priesthood had become a political and economic power that could no longer be ignored by the king.

As the Seleucid king restored the political supremacy of the high priesthood, the accumulation of economic and religious power gave unprecedented strength to the Zadokites. The beginning of the Seleucid period was truly the golden age of the Zadokite priesthood, the peak of their power and influence. "The high priest at the time was both the head of the cult and the ruler of the hierarchic state . . . he was the equivalent of a monarch unto himself."[26]

26. Hayes and Mandell, 42.

4. Ben Sira's Synthesis of Zadokite and Sapiential Judaism

At the beginning of the 2nd century B.C.E., before the Maccabean crisis, Ben Sira is an enthusiastic witness of the golden age of the Zadokite priesthood. He salutes the late Simon II as the ideal high priest, who gloriously ministered in the temple, and the ideal leader of a time of peace and prosperity, who "considered how to save his people from ruin, and fortified the city against siege" (Sir 50:1-24).

It was neither nostalgic memory of years gone by, nor the personal and occasional tribute to a charismatic leader. Ben Sira was a faithful and zealous supporter of the priestly establishment of Jerusalem.[27]

In his view, Jerusalem is the "holy city" that God "loves" (Sir 24:11; 36:18; 49:6) and "the place of [God's] dwelling" (36:18-19). There is an unbroken continuity from "the holy tent" of the desert (24:10), to "the lasting sanctuary" established by Solomon (47:13), to the Second Temple rebuilt by "Jeshua son of Jozadak" (49:12) and renovated by "Simon son of Onias" (50:1). The Jerusalem sanctuary is, and always will be, "a temple holy to the Lord, destined for everlasting glory" (49:12). Ben Sira shows his deepest contempt for the Samaritans, who did not recognize the holiness of Jerusalem and worshiped the Lord in the rival temple on Mount Gerizim; "the foolish people that live in Shechem" are "not even a people" (50:25-26).[28]

The Jerusalem temple is the legitimate sanctuary, ruled by the legitimate priesthood. In his review of the Mosaic revelation, Ben Sira repeats and shares the interpretation of the Priestly writing. The first step was the gift of the divine revelation, which needed a prophet, Moses, as the mediator. "[God] gave him the commandments face to face, the law of life and knowledge, that he might teach Jacob the covenant, and Israel his decrees" (Sir 45:5). Moses in turn was instrumental to the establishment of the priestly order by virtue of his relationship with his brother Aaron (45:6-22). The divine covenant made the "sons of Aaron" the legitimate priests forever. "Moses ordained him, and anointed him with holy oil; it was a

27. See, in particular, Benjamin G. Wright III, "Fear the Lord and Honor the Priest"; Saul M. Olyan, "Ben Sira's Relationship to the Priesthood," *HTR* 80 (1987): 261-86; Ellis Rivkin, "Ben Sira and Aaronite Hegemony," *A Hidden Revolution*, 191-207.

28. Cf. James D. Purvis, "Ben Sira' and the Foolish People of Shechem," *JNES* 24 (1965): 88-94.

lasting covenant for him and for his descendants as long as the heavens endure, to minister to the Lord and serve as priest and bless his people in his name" (45:15). Thus the Mosaic Torah became the priestly Torah. "[Moses] gave him authority and statutes and judgments, to teach Jacob the testimonies, and to enlighten Israel with his law" (45:17). The final step was the establishment of the high priesthood, which God granted to one branch of the sons of Aaron, that is, Phinehas and his descendants. "Therefore a covenant of friendship was established with him, that he should be leader of the sanctuary and of his people, that he and his descendants should have the dignity of the [high] priesthood forever" (44:24).

The lack of any reference to the "sons of Zadok" has led some scholars to see in Sirach evidence of a "pan-Aaronite," anti-Zadokite attitude.[29] If this were the case, Ben Sira would have avoided any reference to Phinehas and stressed in his stead the role of Eleazar and Ithamar, the common ancestors of all the Aaronite priestly classes. On the contrary, he advisedly skips the two sons of Aaron to focus on the grandson of Aaron from whom the Zadokites claimed exclusive descent.[30] The original Hebrew ending of the eulogy of Simon II demonstrates that Ben Sira viewed the Zadokites to be the only legitimate "sons of Phinehas" and the only legitimate recipients of the everlasting covenant granted to him and his descendants. "May [God's] kindness toward Simon be lasting; may he fulfill for him the covenant with Phinehas, so that it may be not abrogated for him or for his descendants, while the heavens last" (50:24 [Heb]).

That the covenant with Phinehas was the foundation of the Zadokite high priesthood is confirmed by the later Maccabean propaganda. In their struggle to demonstrate that their line was no less legitimate than that of the Zadokites, the Maccabees compared Mattathias's zeal to Phinehas's (1 Macc 2:26), and by calling the latter "our ancestor" applied typologically to themselves "the covenant of everlasting priesthood" (1 Macc 2:54). It was a new and controversial move by an Aaronite family that was descended from Eleazar only. The embarrassment for the end of the Zadokite line is still apparent at the end of the 2nd century B.C.E. in the Greek version of the book of Sirach. The translator turned the prayer for Simon II and his descendants into a generic wish of prosperity on behalf of the entire people of Israel ("May [God's] kindness remain constantly with us and

29. Olyan, 275.

30. On the "sons of Zadok" as "sons of Phinehas," see above, Chapter 1.

may he save us in our days") rather than repeating a promise that failed, or applying the covenant of Phinehas to the new Hasmonean priesthood.

The idea that the zeal of Mattathias pre-empted the covenant with Phinehas for him and his descendants was an original creation of the Maccabean propaganda not only against the Zadokites but also against the claims of any other Aaronite family. With the end of the Hasmonean rule, the Jewish tradition would rather drop any connection (either direct or indirect) between the covenant of Phinehas and the high priesthood, thus making any Aaronite family eligible for the office. In Roman times, Josephus would say that "it is a custom of our country, that no one should take the high priesthood of God, but he who is of the blood of Aaron" (*Ant* 20:226). The memory of the covenant with Phinehas would fade and be lost, surprisingly even in modern scholarship.

Ben Sira belongs to a generation which is not yet troubled by conflicts within the Aaronite priesthood, or between Aaronites and Zadokites. His admiration for the Jerusalem priesthood is unreserved. He does not hesitate to compare the honor due to the priests to the honor due to God. "With all your soul fear the Lord, and revere his priests. With all your might, love your Maker, and do not neglect his ministers. Fear the Lord and honor the priest, and give him his portion, as you have been commanded: the first fruits, the guilt offering, the gift of the shoulders, the sacrifice of sanctification, and the first fruits of the holy things" (Sir 7:29-31). No Jewish document had ever gone so far.

As Ellis Rivkin has effectively summarized, "Ben Sira spreads before us a hierocratic society. A priesthood consisting exclusively of 'the sons of Aaron' formed its ruling class, and a High Priest, a direct descendant of Aaron, Eleazar, Phinehas, and Zadok, exercised ultimate authority. . . . Undergirding this system was the Pentateuch, which (so it was believed) had been revealed by God to Moses . . . [who] bestowed upon Aaron and his descendants not only an everlasting priesthood but also the *ongoing authority over the Law*."[31]

Ben Sira is more than a witness of the Zadokite power; he is an apologist against their opponents. Their enemies are his enemies. Under the calm and asystematic style of the document smolders a bitter, often acrimonious controversy that divided Jewish society behind the apparent quiet of the early Seleucid period. Ben Sira was aware that there were some

31. Rivkin, *A Hidden Revolution,* 191, 195.

Jews who did not recognize the legitimacy of the Second Temple and of the Jerusalem priesthood, and he did not spare them his most polemical arrows.

That the Enochians are his target is apparent from the strength with which he not only defends the present and future rights of the sons of Aaron but also dismisses the existence of a pre-Aaronite priesthood: "before [Aaron] [the sacred vestments] did not exist. No outsider ever put them on, but only his sons and his descendants in perpetuity" (Sir 45:13).[32] Ben Sira does not even miss an explicit reference to "Dathan and Abiram and their followers and the company of Korah" as an eternal warning that God's "wrath" protects the sons of Aaron against whoever, priests or laypeople, dare challenge their authority (45:18).

Ben Sira also rejects a knowledge acquired by the unveiling of heavenly secrets apart from the authoritative teaching of the Zadokite Torah. Once again, his vocabulary brings Enochic Judaism to mind. In a passionate speech, Ben Sira dismisses the reliability of dreams, "for dreams have deceived many, and those who put their hope in them have perished. Without such deceptions the law will be fulfilled, and wisdom is complete in the mouth of the faithful" (Sir 34:1-8).

Ben Sira warns against those who claim the human ability to understand the secrets of heaven. "For the works of the Lord are wonderful, and his works are concealed from humankind" (Sir 11:4b). What is necessary for humans to know has already been revealed. The search for "hidden things" is superfluous and unnecessary; besides, it is a sinful presumption. "Neither seek what is too difficult for you, nor investigate what is beyond your power. Reflect upon what you have been commanded, for what is hidden [Gk. *krypta*] is not your concern. Do not meddle in matters that are beyond you, for more than you can understand has been shown you. For their conceit has led many astray, and wrong opinion has impaired their judgment" (Sir 3:21-24).

With the same decisiveness, Ben Sira rejects any theory of corruption.

32. On Ben Sira as an anti-Enochic document, see Gabriele Boccaccini, "Ben Sira, Qohelet, and Apocalyptic: A Turning Point in the History of Jewish Thought," *Middle Judaism*, 77-125; "Origine del male, libertà dell'uomo e retribuzione nella Sapienza di Ben Sira," *Hen* 8 (1986): 1-37; Randal A. Argall, *1 Enoch and Sirach: A Comparative Literary and Conceptual Analysis of the Themes of Revelation, Creation, and Judgment* (Atlanta: Scholars, 1995); Wright.

In line with the Priestly writing, he describes creation as a process of setting boundaries that produces a series of opposites. This is the reason why "all the works of the Most High . . . come in pairs, one the opposite of the other" (Sir 33:15). Sacred days and ordinary days, priests and laypeople, Jews and Gentiles, sinners and just (33:7-14), "good things and bad, life and death, poverty and wealth, come from the Lord" (11:14; cf. 33:14-15; 42:24).

The presence of opposites does not disrupt the goodness and unity of God's creation. "All things come in pairs, one opposite the other; and he has made nothing incomplete" (Sir 42:24). Everything is ultimately good, as everything has been made for a purpose. "All the works of the Lord are good, and he will supply every need in its time. No one can say, 'This is not as good as that,' for everything proves good in its appointed time" (39:33-34). Good for the good and evil for the wicked, is Ben Sira's general rule. "From the beginning good things were created for the good" (39:25). Evil things "were created for the wicked" (40:10), and for them even "good [things] . . . turn into evils" (39:27).

Ben Sira makes a strong case that the supreme authority of God is not challenged by any rebellious power. Even the most destructive forces of nature, such as "winds . . . fire and hail and famine and pestilence . . . the fangs of wild animals and scorpions and vipers, and the sword that punishes. . ." were created to meet a need — punishment for the wicked — and are unleashed according to God's will: "They delight in doing [God's] bidding . . . and when their time comes they never disobey his commands" (Sir 39:28-35).

The immutability and obedience of creation are underscored with particular emphasis in reference to the heavenly beings God created before humankind. "When the Lord created his works from the beginning, and, in making them, determined their boundaries, he arranged his works in an eternal order, and their dominion for all generations. . . . They do not crowd one another, and they never disobey his word" (Sir 16:26-28). The insistence is anything but random. Ben Sira is not ready to provide any pretext for the Enochic claim that evil is a consequence of any disorder that generated in the heavenly domain among the angels. In referring to Gen 6:1-4, Ben Sira consciously avoids any mythological overtone; the "giants" are princes of old "who revolted in their might" (Sir 16:7) and were punished by God as all other sinners. In Ben Sira's worldview there is no room for devils, fallen angels, or evil spirits, nor even for a mischievous officer of the divine court as the satan of Job, or for a domesticated demon as the Asmodeus of Tobit. The only reference to "the satan" in Sirach is in a context (21:1–22:18) that emphasizes personal responsibility and the capability of "whoever keeps the law [to control] his thoughts" (21:11). The satan of Sir 21:27 is primarily the personal adversary, but the skillful ambiguity of the saying is intended also to stigmatize the "impious" belief in the existence of the heavenly enemy. "When an ungodly person curses the satan, he [really] curses himself" (21:27).

Ben Sira is aware of the ambivalence of human nature, even of people's apparent attitude to sin: "Flesh and blood devise evil. . . the Lord alone is just" (Sir 17:31–18:2). Yet, he excludes the idea that evil should be attributed to an agent external to human beings, either to an angelic rebellion in heaven or even to God. Sirach is an unshakable champion of human free will and responsibility: "It was [God] who created humankind in the beginning, and he left them the power of their own free choice. If you choose, you can keep the commandments. . . . Before each person are life and death, and whichever one chooses will be given" (15:11-20).[33]

Since this is (and always will be) the good and uncorrupted universe created by God, Ben Sira rejects any hypothesis of an afterlife retribution; from death "there is no coming back . . . when [the] spirit has departed" (Sir 38:21-23). After death, there is only Sheol, the netherworld, the common destiny of all and the eternal and joyless resting place of the dead, righteous and sinners alike (14:16; 17:27-28; 21:10; 22:11; cf. Ps 88:4-7).

For the same reasons, God's creation will not be overthrown to make room for a new creation; a perfect work does not need to be redone. Rather, Ben Sira shares the primary concern of Zadokite Judaism that humans must cooperate to preserve the stability of this world, as it has been promised from God's part of the covenant with Noah: "A lasting sign sealed the assurance to him that never should all flesh be destroyed" (Sir 44:18).

Worship is the major guarantee of stability of the universe, as people continuously remind their Maker and Ruler of the obligations and responsibilities of the covenant. This is the goal of the "pleasing odor" of perpetual sacrifices (Sir 35:8) and the ultimate function of worship. Ben Sira singles out three cultic elements as "a reminder before the Most High," and all

33. Jean Hadot, *Penchant mauvais et volonté libre dans la Sagesse de Ben Sira* (Brussels: Presses universitaires, 1970); Gerhard Maier, *Mensch und freier Wille, nach den jüdischen Religionsparteien zwischen Ben Sira und Paulus* (Tübingen: Mohr, 1971).

of them are associated with the Jerusalem priesthood: the ringing of the golden bells of Aaron's robe (45:9), the precious stones with seal engraving in golden settings on the ephod (45:11), and the sounding of the trumpets (50:16).

The cycle is now complete. This world, and this world only, is the good and uncorrupted universe created by God, and the place of God's retribution. This priesthood, and this priesthood only, is the guarantee of the stability of the universe. As the world will last forever, so will the priesthood.

It has been argued that Ben Sira himself was a priest or levite; and he might well have been.[34] He takes pride in being an honored member of the ruling class, not a farmer or artisan who has to work (Sir 38:24-34). Being a priest or levite, however, is not Ben Sira's primary self-identity. He portrays himself as a scribe (39:1-11) who imparts wisdom in his school (51:23).

The Zadokite Torah has a place of honor in his teaching; he pronounces "woe to . . . the ungodly, who have forsaken the law of the Most High God" (Sir 41:8). Yet, "Ben Sira remains a wisdom teacher, not an exegete or expositor of the Torah."[35] The teachings of Ben Sira are largely those traditional of Sapiential Judaism, based on Proverbs in particular and on the popular wisdom of the Near East. Using the usual formula of wisdom literature, Ben Sira addresses his readers as "my son" (2:1; passim) or "my children" (3:1; passim). With great emphasis, he praises the role and teaching of the wise. "Do not slight the discourse of the sages, but busy yourself with their maxims; because from them you will learn discipline and how to serve princes. Do not ignore the discourse of the aged, for they themselves learned from their parents; from them you learn how to understand and to give an answer when the need arises" (8:8-9). Despite the emphasis of the priesthood and cultic obligations, Ben Sira's primary concerns are those of Sapiential Judaism — "agreement among brothers and sisters, friendship among neighbors, and a wife and a husband who live in harmony" (25:1).

As in the case of Tobit, we meet in Ben Sira a representative of a new generation of sages, who openly support the priesthood and the Zadokite order. The greater sophistication of Sirach's thought gives to the rap-

34. See Helge Stadelmann, *Ben Sira als Schriftgelehrte,* WUNT 6 (Tübingen: Mohr, 1980).

35. Collins, *Jewish Wisdom in the Hellenistic Age,* 56.

prochement between Zadokite and Sapiential Judaism more profound ramifications.

On the one hand, Zadokite Judaism, while maintaining the importance of cultic obligations, had to accept a special emphasis on the moral obligations of the covenant. As in Tobit, "almsgiving" is at the center of Jewish piety (Sir 29:8-13). Charity is described as the highest form of sacrifice and worship to God, having the power to atone for sins (35:1-5). Ben Sira goes even further than Tobit, as he makes moral laws a prerequisite to the effectiveness of sacrifices. God does not accept bribes (35:14) and rejects worship without charity. "The gifts of the lawless are not acceptable. The Most High is not pleased with the offerings of the ungodly, nor for a multitude of sacrifices does he forgive sins" (34:21-23).

There is no reason, however, to make the moral and cultic obligations clash in Ben Sira. In the same context in which he reclaims the superiority of moral obligations, he also emphasizes the duty for cultic obligations: "Do not appear before the Lord empty-handed, for all that you offer is in fulfillment of the commandment. The offering of the righteous enriches the altar, and its pleasing odor rises before the Most High. The sacrifice of the righteous is acceptable, and it will never be forgotten" (Sir 35:6-9). Moral obligations serve to strengthen the necessity and validity of worship, and are not a surrogate of it.

On the other hand, Sapiential Judaism, while maintaining its ideals of free inquiry for creation, had to go even further in tempering its most secular and cosmopolitan aspects and in retracting the arguments of the skeptical wisdom of Job, Jonah, and Qoheleth.

Religious egalitarianism between Jews and Gentiles, even Jonah's trust in the conversion of Gentiles, is overshadowed by the perspective of future punishment, when "The Lord . . . like a warrior . . . will [crush] the loins of the unmerciful and [repay] vengeance on the nations . . . [and] crush the heads of hostile rulers" (Sir 35:22–36:22). This is what the Mosaic covenant requires to happen in order to validate God's authority and promises: "Lift up your hand against foreign nations and let them see your might. . . . Then they will know, as we have known, that there is no God but you. . . . Bear witness to those whom you created in the beginning, and fulfill the prophecies spoken in your name. Reward those who wait for you and let your prophets be found trustworthy. . . . And all who are on earth will know that you are the Lord, the God of the ages" (36:3-5, 20-22).

The image that scholars such as Alexander A. Di Lella and Martin

Hengel have given of Ben Sira as the champion of traditional Judaism against advancing Hellenism is largely exaggerated, however, and must be balanced by his interest and curiosity in Hellenistic culture and his loyalty to foreign rulers.[36] The teaching of Ben Sira continues largely to be inspired by foreign wisdom and by exposure to nonpriestly environments. Nowhere in Sirach do we find an explicit rejection of Hellenism; the effort is rather at borrowing and adapting Hellenistic categories. Ben Sira emphasizes how important it is "to [serve] among the great, and [appear] before rulers" (Sir 39:4a), and by contrasting the scribe to the craftsman, makes it clear that the rightful place for the wise is "among the rulers" (38:33). He also highly recommends "travel[ing] in foreign lands and learn[ing] what is good and evil in the human lot" (39:4b; cf. 34:9-11) and recalls how beneficial this experience was to himself, how much he saw "in [his] travels" and how much he "learned" in spite of any "danger" (34:12-13). If the theology of Ben Sira is far less cosmopolitan than that of his predecessors of Sapiential Judaism, it is because he has a concern they did not have; he must oppose any compromise or syncretism that would soften the uniqueness and exclusiveness of the Mosaic covenant and the truth of its promises to Israel.

The same determination in defending the Mosaic covenant is apparent in Ben Sira's revisionist approach to skeptical wisdom. Sirach tries hard to react to any sense of despair and frustration and make people cope with the manifest absence of justice in this world. He will neither deny the evidence, nor the appropriateness of submitting reality to the scrutiny of experience, but is ready to fight back. Unlike Job, Jonah, and Qoheleth, he accepts that the answer comes before the inquiry and is the one given by the covenant: "The sinner will not escape with [his] plunder, and the patience of the godly will not be frustrated. [The Lord] makes room for every act of mercy; everyone receives in accordance with one's deeds" (Sir 16:13-14; cf. 2:8-10; 16:6-23; 35:10-23).

36. See Alexander A. Di Lella, "Conservative and Progressive Theology: Sirach and Wisdom," *CBQ* 28 (1966): 139-54; Hengel, 138-153. That, on the contrary, Ben Sira was not isolated from the Hellenistic world has been convincingly argued by scholars such as Theophil Middendorp, *Die Stellung Jesu ben Sira zwischen Judentum und Hellenismus* (Leiden: Brill, 1973); Jack T. Sanders, *Ben Sira and Demotic Wisdom,* SBLMS 28 (Chico: Scholars, 1983); and Reinhold Bohlen, *Die Ehrung der Eltern bei Ben Sira: Studien zur Motivation und Interpretation eines familien-ethischen Grundwertes in frühhellenistischer Zeit,* TThS 51 (Trier: Paulinus, 1991).

Ben Sira is not open to the possibility of a different answer; his search is only for the rationale. Human skill and the sophisticated techniques of sapiential inquiry are employed not to criticize but to prove the soundness of the Mosaic revelation. There must be some explanation, even when humans are unable to find it immediately and when all evidence seems to point to a different conclusion.

God's patience can explain the delay in punishing sinners and silence, at least for a while, those who doubt the validity of the covenant: "Do not say, 'I sinned, yet what has happened to me?' for the Lord is slow to anger" (Sir 5:4). God knows how frail humans are, and continually renews the offer of salvation, delaying the moment of punishment and giving more and more opportunities for repentance. "That is why the Lord is patient with [human beings] and pours out his mercy upon them" (18:11).

The testing of the righteous, which in Job was an (occasional) act of obstinacy by a heavenly adversary, "the satan," and in Tobit an (occasional) delay in the unfolding of God's retribution, is now a providential, almost ordinary aspect of the divine pedagogy. Just as God corrects and admonishes sinners, so God also tests the righteous to reinforce and confirm their righteousness. "When you come to serve the Lord, prepare yourself for trial. . . . Accept whatever befalls you, and in times of humiliation be patient. For gold is tested in the fire, and those found acceptable, in the furnace of humiliation" (Sir 2:1-5).

These arguments cannot be stretched too far, however, to the point that God's mercy nullifies God's justice. Ben Sira has to warn "[not to] be so confident of forgiveness that you add sin to sin" and not to "say, 'His mercy is great, he will forgive the multitude of my sins'" (Sir 5:5-6). Certainly, the God of Israel is "compassionate and merciful; he forgives sins and saves in time of distress" (2:11). This aspect of God, however, does not cancel the reality of judgment and the covenant. God's merciful and parental affection is reserved to "those who accept his discipline and who are eager for his precepts" (18:14). In the end, God's mercy cannot prevail over God's justice, which remains the measure of God's mercy. "Mercy and wrath are with the Lord; he is mighty to forgive — but he also pours out wrath. Great as his mercy, so also is his chastisement; he judges a person according to one's deeds" (16:11-12; cf. 5:6).

After some barrage fire, Ben Sira is back to the initial front of defense. The covenant requires God to reward the righteous and punish the sinners in this world. How does this happen? Ben Sira believes in what the covenant promises, yet he is also a wise man who, enlightened by experience, knows how things go in this world. He feels dramatically that the boundaries of individual existence, so uncertain and fleeting, have become too narrow for divine retribution to fulfill. He retreats to the day of death as the decisive, mysterious, and only remaining time in which the individual may meet God and fully experience the power of God's judgment. That "only when man's life comes to its end in prosperity can one call that man happy" was a widespread experience of popular wisdom.[37] In the religious world of Ben Sira, it is turned into a theological statement about God's retribution. "For it is easy for the Lord on the day of death to reward individuals according to their conduct. . . . An hour's misery makes one forget past delights, and at the close of one's life, one's deeds are revealed. Call no one happy before his death; by how he ends, a person becomes known" (Sir 11:26-28; cf. 9:11-12). The *memento mori* — the recurring reminder, "You must die!" — becomes one of the most characteristic elements in Ben Sira's parenesis, placing him at the beginning of a long and successful tradition of preaching. "In all you do, remember the end of your life, and then you will never sin" (7:36; cf. 14:12; 18:24; 28:6).

As strong as they may be, these arguments also are far from being conclusive against the burden of evidence. Ben Sira keeps promising a happy life and a good death (Sir 1:13) to the righteous, but at the very end, the only thing that he can plausibly offer, besides an uncertain experience of happy life and an equally uncertain hope of good death, is the perspective of everlasting memory. In this way, in his discussion of retribution, he can go decidedly beyond the boundaries of death, while remaining anchored to a system that excludes any hypothesis of afterlife.

The conservation of one's name for the righteous, corresponding to the *damnatio memoriae* for the wicked, is certainly not a new theme in Jewish thought (and in foreign wisdom).[38] However, in Sirach it receives singular emphasis, being affirmed as the truest and most authentic reward for the righteous, better than any riches or even a long and happy life.

37. See Aeschylus *Ag.* 928; Herodotus *Hist.* 1:32; Sophocles *Oed. tyr.* 1529.

38. P. A. H. de Boer, *Gedenken und Gedachtnis in der Welt des Alten Testament* (Stuttgart: Kohlhammer, 1962); Brevard S. Childs, *Memory and Tradition in Israel;* Willy Schottroff, *Gedenken im Alten Orient und im Alten Testament;* Gabriele Boccaccini, "Il tema della memoria nell'ebraismo e nel giudaismo antico," *Hen* 7 (1985): 164-92.

"Have regard for your name, since it will outlive you longer than a thousand hoards of gold. The days of a good life are numbered, but a good name lasts forever" (Sir 41:12-13).

In his criticism, Qoheleth had not spared even this traditional assumption: "There is no enduring remembrance of the wise or of fools, seeing that in the days to come all will have been long forgotten" (Eccl 2:16). Among the objections put forward by skeptical wisdom in the name of experience, this is the only one for which Ben Sira denies all evidence. He is aware that the memory of the righteous is the last trench, which cannot be lost, and his only remaining chance to shake off the skeptical inquiry of experience.

It was not an easy task, indeed. The righteous count on the blessing of children (Sir 30:4-5; 40:19); however, experience shows that their birth and righteousness are not at all guaranteed, so much so that "to die childless [is] better than to have ungodly children" (Sir 16:1-3). Ben Sira had to hold the name of the righteous to a more solid and less volatile anchorage, which could be provided only by the collective memory of Israel. "The days of a person's life are numbered, but the days of Israel are without number. One who is wise among his people will inherit honor, and his name will live forever" (37:25-26). The "praise of the fathers" that ends the book of Sirach (chs. 44–49) is a grandiose celebration of the collective memory of Israel, of its capability of keeping alive the name and legacy of the righteous, generation after generation. The wide-angle picture has the effect of putting out of focus the details of individual life and removing reward and punishment from the experience's critical eye. As evil fades and comes to nothing in the divine economy of the cosmos (42:15–43:33), so does any contradiction to the principle of covenantal retribution in the larger historical perspective of the history of Israel.

The link that Tobit had established between Zadokite and Sapiential tradition expands in Sirach into a synthesis of cosmic proportions.

First of all, Ben Sira emphasizes that there is no contradiction between the wise and the priest. On the one hand, "the one who devotes himself to the study of the law of the Most High . . . seeks out the wisdom of all the ancients, and is concerned with prophecies . . ." (Sir 38:34b–39:11). On the other hand, "the wise will not hate the law [Heb: He that hates the Law is not wise]" (33:2). Both traditions are necessary in order to achieve wisdom. "If you are willing, my child, you can be disciplined, and if you apply yourself you will become clever. . . . Stand in the company of the elders.

Who is wise? Attach yourself to such a one . . . . Reflect on the statutes of the Lord, and meditate at all times on his commandments. It is [God] who will give insight to your mind, and your desire for wisdom will be granted" (6:32-37). As John J. Collins comments on this passage, "it appears then that the student has two sources to study, at least initially: the discourse of the elders and the book of the Torah."[39]

Ben Sira acknowledges a dual revelation; God spoke at creation and on Sinai. With creation, "[God] put the fear of him into [human] hearts, to show them the majesty of his works," while with the Mosaic revelation "established with them an eternal covenant, and revealed to them his decrees" (Sir 17:8, 12). Both the fear of God and obedience to the Torah belong to the divine plan, and so do the Sapiential and Zadokite traditions.

Ben Sira, however, does not limit himself to claiming a harmony between wisdom and law; he is engaged in a bold and unprecedented attempt at showing the relationship between the two revelations, the deep reason why they are not contradictory.

The starting point is provided by the Sapiential tradition: wisdom is inaccessible to human beings. "The sand of the sea, the drops of rain, and the days of eternity — who can count them? The height of heaven, the breadth of the earth, [the depth of] the abyss, who can search them out? . . . The root of wisdom — to whom has it been revealed? Her subtleties — who knows them?" (Sir 1:2-3, 6-7). Only God knows her, and God made her the underlying order of the universe: "There is but one who is wise, greatly to be feared, seated upon his throne — the Lord. . . . He saw her and took her measure; he poured her out upon all his works, upon all the living according to his gift" (1:1-10).

Wisdom is God's possession only: "all wisdom is from the Lord, and with him it remains forever" (Sir 1:1). Yet, in a passionate speech, wisdom herself reveals how eager she was to find "a resting place" and how happily she obeyed "the command of God . . . to pitch her tent in Jacob . . . and put down roots in Jerusalem." There, "in an honored people," wisdom produced abundant fruit (24:1-22).

The author's comment immediately follows wisdom's speech: "All this is the book of the covenant of the Most High God, the law that Moses commanded us as an inheritance for the congregations of Jacob" (24:23). The rapprochement between Sapiential and Zadokite Judaism has thus

39. Collins, *Jewish Wisdom in the Hellenistic Age,* 48.

reached its most daring step: the Torah of Moses is the historical embodiment of the heavenly wisdom.

However, this does not mean that wisdom and law are identical.[40] Identity is a transitive relationship, in which the two elements bear the same properties. In Sirach, wisdom and law are not interchangeable and their relationship is still conceived in strongly asymmetrical terms.

On one hand, as Roland E. Murphy noticed, the unity of wisdom and Torah is the result of a one-way process. "Wisdom dwelling among God's people is concretized in the Torah. It is not the other way around, as though the eternal pre-existent Torah is now identified with Wisdom."[41]

In the process, in order to make her touchdown more feasible, the heavenly wisdom has lost some of her autonomy. Wisdom is "eternal" (Sir 1:1b; 24:9b) and pre-existent (1:4a; 24:9a), but no longer coexistent with God, as a goddess, or an attribute of God, could be. Sirach clarifies that there was a time in which God was alone; God is "the only one [who] exists before the times and forever" (42:21). Wisdom is now clearly defined as a creature of God: "it is he who created her" (1:4, 9). Wisdom herself confirms: "before the ages, in the beginning, he created me" (24:9).

Yet, wisdom remains a heavenly being who lives among the angels ("in the assembly of the Most High she opens her mouth," 24:2). To humankind, she is inaccessible. Only upon "those who love him" (1:10) and are "godly" (43:33), God lavished her. Wisdom is a gift sought after but not granted to all, indeed denied to the majority of people.

On the other hand, by virtue of its connection with wisdom, the Torah does not gain either the autonomy or the cosmic functions of the heavenly and pre-existent wisdom. "Sirach does not develop the notion of the law as a cosmic principle. There are no poems describing how Torah came forth from the mouth of God or circled the heavens before creation. The point of the identification is to accredit the Torah as the valid concretization (even as the ultimate concretization) of universal wisdom, not to attribute a cosmic role to the Torah itself."[42] Laws and covenants belong to history,

40. *Pace* Echard J. Schnabel, *Law and Wisdom from Ben Sira to Paul,* WUNT 2/16 (Tübingen: Mohr, 1985).

41. Roland E. Murphy, "The Personification of Wisdom," in *Wisdom in Ancient Israel,* ed. John Day, Robert P. Gordon, and H. G. M. Williamson (Cambridge: Cambridge University Press, 1995), 227.

42. Collins, *Jewish Wisdom in the Hellenistic Age,* 61.

to the relations between God and humankind. Since the creation, God in his wisdom established covenants and gave humans precepts about their peers (Sir 17:1-14).

As the definitive law and covenant, the Mosaic Torah is no exception; it has neither autonomy nor function beyond the limits of the relationship between God and humans. It exists to be observed; and to be observed it had to be made accessible. Unlike wisdom, the Torah is an already-given gift, the application of which depends on the free will of the individual.

It would take a long time before in Rabbinic Judaism the law superseded wisdom as "the precious tool by which the world was made" (*m. 'Abot* 3:14; cf. *Sifre* on Deut 11:10; *'Eqeb.* 37; *Gen. Rab.* 8:2) and all the biblical references to the heavenly wisdom would eventually be taken as references to the heavenly Torah. The asymmetrical relationship between wisdom and Torah still has an echo in Rabbinic literature in a saying (beautiful in its concision and effectiveness) which Genesis Rabbah attributed to the Amora R. Abin: "The incomplete form of the heavenly light is the orb of the sun; the incomplete form of the heavenly wisdom is the Torah" (*Gen. Rab.* 17:5; 44:7). This is no more than the last, inert relict of what had been the prevalent view. The Rabbinic notion of the preexistence of Torah has in Sirach its roots, not its first evidence.[43]

Regardless of its future developments, Ben Sira's view of the Torah as the historical embodiment of the heavenly wisdom has monumental ramifications on both Zadokite and Sapiential theology.

First, there is no wisdom without fear of God and obedience to the Torah. "The whole of wisdom is fear of the Lord, and in all wisdom there is the fulfillment of the law" (Sir 19:20). The two definitions of the righteous elaborated autonomously by Sapiential and Zadokite Judaism have become so interrelated as to be virtually interchangeable. "Those who fear the Lord do not disobey his words, and those who love him keep his ways. Those who fear the Lord seek to please him, and those who love him are filled with his law" (2:15-16). In Sirach's vocabulary, "transgressing the commandments" and "fearing the Lord" are antonyms (10:19; cf. 41:8), and "keeping the law" is synonymous with "fulfilling the fear of the Lord" (21:11).

Second, not only is there no wisdom without the practice of the Torah, but observance of the Torah is the propaedeutically indispensable condi-

43. Gabriele Boccaccini, *Hen* 17 (1995): 329-50.

tion by which people become worthy of receiving the gift of wisdom. Wisdom is the divine reward for meritorious conduct according to the Torah. "If you desire wisdom, keep the commandments, and the Lord will lavish her upon you" (Sir 1:26; cf. 6:37; 15:1)

Finally, for the individual obeying the law is morally more important than achieving wisdom. Sirach argues that the wise deserve a superior social status to that of workers. "The wisdom of the scribe depends upon the opportunity of leisure; only the one who has little business can became wise. . . . [Those] who labor by night as well as by day . . . [do not] attain eminence in the public assembly" (Sir 38:24-34). However, the logic of the covenant imposes the law as the sole and self-sufficient condition to salvation. Accordingly, Ben Sira acknowledges that the "fear of God" does not necessarily imply the awareness of knowledge. Workers cannot be wise, but they also "maintain the fabric of the world, and their concern is for the exercise of their trade" (38:34b). In this sense, Ben Sira can state that the fear of God is superior not only to all earthly goods (10:24; 40:26-27) and to all human knowledge (19:24), but also to the divine gift of wisdom. "How great is the one who finds wisdom! But none is superior to the one who fears the Lord. Fear of the Lord surpasses everything; to whom can we compare the one who has it?" (25:10-11; cf. 40:18-27).

In sum, wisdom is greater than the Torah, and the wise are greater than the ordinary righteous, yet obeying the Torah is ultimately more essential than having wisdom, because the stability of the universe and individual salvation depend on this. "Better are the God-fearing who lack understanding than the highly intelligent who transgress the law" (Sir 19:24).

Had the Zadokites kept their leadership over the Jewish society, the merging of Sapiential and Zadokite traditions would have ultimately resulted in the strengthening of the priestly power with an acknowledged role for the wise subordinate to the priest. While building up a fine reputation for himself as a scribe and teacher of wisdom, there cannot be doubts that Ben Sira served the priest as well. He confirmed the centrality of the covenant and the retributive principle, opposing the challenge of Enochic Judaism and putting an end to the doubts of skeptical wisdom. Furthermore, Ben Sira offered to Zadokite Judaism a sophisticated theological system in which there was a harmony between the order of the universe (Wisdom) and the priestly order (Torah), as well as a balance between revelation and experience — notions that Job, Jonah, and Qoheleth had deemed contradictory and Tobit had only juxtaposed. Everything, however, would have a different meaning after the sudden collapse of Zadokite power and the Maccabean crisis. Then, new opportunities would open in the increasingly diverse society of middle Judaism, and the wise would soon find a new, more autonomous role for themselves.

CHAPTER FOUR

Daniel: A Third Way between Zadokite and Enochic Judaism

1. The End of the Zadokite Power

The golden age of Zadokite Judaism ended abruptly under Simon's successor, Onias III.[1] Ironically, his term could not have begun under better auspices. In the words of 2 Maccabees, "the holy city was inhabited in unbroken peace and the laws were strictly observed" and "the kings themselves honored the place and glorified the temple with the finest presents" (2 Macc 3:1-2).

Eventually, it would be this accumulation of wealth and political power that would determine the crisis and then the end of the Zadokite priesthood. After the disastrous battle of Magnesia in 189 B.C.E. the Seleucid monarchy desperately needed money to pay the tribute to Rome. The situation came to a head when a much weaker King Seleucus IV (187-175) was seated on the Syrian throne. Ancient sources describe him as a crippled and unresourceful king. "Inactive and weak because of his father's defeat" (Appianus *Syriaca* 11), "despicable and unworthy of regal dignity" (Dan [Greek and Latin], 11:21), he "had an inglorious death without making any war" (Jerome *Expl. Dan.* 11). At a time when war was for a king the key to success and the principal means for making money, the inactivity of

1. On the events that led to the Maccabean crisis, see Paolo Sacchi, *The History of the Second Temple Period,* 214-49; John H. Hayes and Sara R. Mandell, *The Jewish People in Classical Antiquity,* 38-76; Henk Jagersma, *A History of Israel from Alexander the Great to Bar Kochba,* 36-67.

Seleucus IV meant lack of personal prestige and, for the royal administration, bankruptcy.

In Seleucid Jerusalem, the intermingling of religious and political functions meant that no economic project could be accomplished without controlling the temple. Among the Jewish upper class, the temptation of trading some confidential information about the treasury of the temple for the king's support to their political and economic ambitions had to be strong. 2 Maccabees narrates that Simon, an Aaronite priest of the tribe of Bilgah "who has been made captain of the temple, had a disagreement with the high priest about the administration of the city market . . . and reported to [the governor of Coelesyria] that the treasury in Jerusalem was full of untold sums of money . . . [which] did not belong to the account of the sacrifices, but that it was possible for them to fall under the control of the king" (2 Macc 3:4-6). Economic controversy began gnawing at the stability of Zadokite society from within.

Seleucus IV immediately sent an officer to inquire. The story of Heliodorus's mission (2 Macc 3:7-40), behind its legendary traits, confirms that the Zadokites' power was based on their fiscal alliance with the Tobiads. The high priest himself candidly admits that the bulk of the temple treasure is made of "some money of Hyrcanus son of Tobias, a man of very prominent position" (2 Macc 3:11). The story of Heliodorus also confirms the higher political status and power achieved by the Zadokite priesthood in the Seleucid period. Onias's predecessors in Persian times were largely at the mercy of the king's officers, who, as the episode of Bagoses shows, could "impose tributes . . . from the public treasury" (Josephus *Ant* 11:297-301). In Ptolemaic times, Zenon, the king's official, could ignore the priesthood of Jerusalem as politically and economically insignificant. Now, facing the king's attempt to confiscate some money from the treasury of the temple, Onias III had the power to withhold payment and even took the liberty of beating, humiliating, and finally bribing the king's officer without fear of punishment.

The mission, poorly prepared, was a complete failure. Seleucus IV had no legal basis to claim more money from one of his tax collectors than had been agreed upon. His patent underestimation of Onias's power led to comic results, with Heliodorus carrying back not the money the king hoped for, but a sarcastic piece of advice: "If you have any enemy or plotter against your government, send him there, for you will get him thoroughly flogged, if he survives at all" (2 Macc 3:38). The outcome did not stop Simon's complaints, however. He escalated the confrontation by accusing Onias of being "a plotter against the government" (4:2). The high priest "appealed to the king" (4:5) and decided to go to Antioch to defend his cause. He was never to return to Jerusalem.

The Seleucid monarchy learned the lesson. It took only a more cunning and stronger king to devise the right scheme for putting his hands on the temple treasure. While Onias was still on his way to Antioch, Seleucus IV was murdered and his brother, Antiochus IV, took power. The new king (175-164) may have been "contemptible" (Dan 11:21; 1 Macc 1:10) or even "mad" (Polybius *Hist.* 26:1); certainly he was much more ambitious and energetic than his brother. Pressed by the same need of confiscating funds from the Jerusalem temple in addition to those legally raised through taxation, and faced with the same difficulty of convincing by fair means the ruling high priest, Antiochus IV would not object to allowing somebody more complaisant to take control of the office. After all, although according to Jewish tradition the office of high priest was hereditary and held for life, according to the Greek administration the office of tax-collector was periodically reviewed and given to the highest bidder. As the Zadokites were also the tax-collectors, the appointment of the high priest could no longer be seen as an internal affair of Jewish religion. The king could lawfully claim his right to intervene and pick the best candidate. As soon as it became clear that the position was open, there was no lack of ambitious candidates among the priestly families of Judah.

A brother of Onias III, Joshua (Jason), immediately seized the opportunity to "[obtain] the high priesthood by corruption" (2 Macc 4:7). With Onias still in Antioch seeking a hearing at the Seleucid court, he petitioned the new king, "promising [him] . . . three hundred sixty talents of silver, and from another source of revenue eighty talents. In addition to this he promised to pay one hundred fifty more if permission were given to establish by his authority a gymnasium and a body of youth for it, and to enroll the people of Jerusalem as citizens of Antioch" (4:8-9).

Antiochus "assented" (2 Macc 4:10); Jason was in fact a very compelling candidate. First, he had the best credentials, being a member of the ruling house of Zadok and a relative of the Tobiads. His appointment was a serious blow to the Zadokite tradition, as he was made high priest before his brother's death. Yet, his pedigree and family connections guaranteed a smooth transition of power without raising too strong theological objections. One could still contend that Jason was simply acting in Jerusalem as deputy for his brother, while the legitimate high priest, Onias, was kept by the king in Antioch.

Also, the terms of Jason's offer prove that it was not simply out of personal ambition that he came before the king, but as the leader of a close-knit party of social climbers who aimed to stimulate economic growth by overcoming the economic and social limitations caused by the Zadokite laws. Jason did not promise the king only a sum of money from the treasury of the temple but also additional funds, some of them subordinate to the concession of economic privileges by the king. The economic interests of the king thus merged with the economic interests of the new high priest and his Jewish supporters to promote a closer integration of the Jewish upper class within the Hellenistic economy and culture.

The first step was to "set aside the existing royal concessions [decreed by King Antiochus III] to the Jews" (2 Macc 4:11), which were the major obstacle for the upper class of Jerusalem to enjoying the same privileges "as those in Antioch." The process of Hellenization under Jason was not coercive; Jerusalem was not turned overnight into a Hellenistic polis, and no persecution was unleashed against those who wanted to keep living under the traditional laws. Significantly, none of the ancient sources, even the most unsympathetic ones, accuse Jason either of transgressing the Zadokite law and adopting the Greek way of life or of any cultic misconduct in the management of the temple. Jason's culpability in the eyes of his adversaries was that of being "vile" (2 Macc 4:19), as he granted the Jews freedom of choice and so "shifted his compatriots over to the Greek way of life" (4:10). Zadokite law was no longer enforced as the law of the king for "all the members of the nation" (*Ant* 12:142), as it had been since Persian times, when even in the language of official documents the Zadokite law was defined as "the law of your God and the law of the king" (Ezra 7:26).

Many people in Judah welcomed the change. Even the Maccabean historiography would have to admit that the process of Hellenization was not imposed from the outside but began within Jewish society itself. "In those days certain renegades came out from Israel and misled many, saying, 'Let us go and make a covenant with the Gentiles around us, for since we separated from them many disasters have come upon us'" (1 Macc 1:11). The "priests" in particular seem to have benefited the most from the new situation: "despising the sanctuary and neglecting the sacrifices . . . [they disdained] the honors prized by their ancestors and [put] the highest value upon Greek forms of prestige" (2 Macc 4:14-15). There were some doubts and qualms when "Jason sent envoys, chosen as being Antiochian citizens from Jerusalem, to carry three hundred silver drachmas for the sacrifice to Hercules" (2 Macc 4:19). In line with the principles of inclusive monotheism, the sacrifice could be interpreted not as an act of idolatry but as a token of friendship in honor of the ancient hero and patron of Antioch. However, once they arrived in Antioch, the Jewish emissaries "thought best" to ask that the money be used not "for sacrifice" but for "the construction of triremes" (2 Macc 4:19-20). The incident did not arouse indignation or any public demonstration of outrage and discontent, either among the Jews or the Greeks. When shortly afterward Antiochus visited Jerusalem, "he was welcomed magnificently by Jason and the city, and ushered in with a blaze of torches and with shouts" (2 Macc 4:22).

Only three years after his appointment as high priest, however, Jason fell victim of his own schemes. Menelaus, the brother of the previously mentioned Simon, "secured the high priesthood for himself, outbidding Jason by three hundred talents of silver" (2 Macc 4:24). Pressed by economic needs and, according to Josephus, personally "angered with Jason" for reasons that remain unknown to us (*Ant* 12:238), Antiochus miscalculated the impact of his decision on the religious balance in Jerusalem. This time the transition of power did not go so smoothly. Not being a member of the house of Zadok, the Aaronite Menelaus "had no qualification for the high priesthood" (2 Macc 4:25). Jason fled to "the land of Ammon" (4:26), where he could count on the protection of the Tobiads of Transjordan. With Onias III still alive in his exile in Antioch, the new high priest faced two dangerous rivals; each of them could legitimately challenge his power.

In spite of all these easily foretold difficulties, the Hellenistic party shifted their support and money from Jason to Menelaus. Those who had benefited most from Jason's reforms, among them the Tobiads of Jerusalem, felt that they were strong enough to take the situation into their own hands and that the mediation of a "supporting" Zadokite was no longer necessary. However, for the first time they had to face a strong opposition that they were unable to overcome without applying to the king. "The multitude were divided between [Jason and Menelaus]. . . . The sons of Tobias took the part of Menelaus, but the greater part of the people assisted Jason; and by that means Menelaus and the sons of Tobias were distressed and retired to Antiochus and informed him that they were desirous to leave the laws of their country" (*Ant* 12:239-40). With even the high priest and his entourage now embracing the Greek way of life, the process of Hellenization went on, stronger than ever, but the Hellenistic party was more and more dependent on the support of Antiochus, and more and more identifiable as the pro-Seleucid party.

Further problems arose because of the patent inability of Menelaus to keep his promises to Antiochus IV. He had offered the Seleucid king a higher bid, but it was the people, and the poorest among the people, who had to pay for it. As the burden of taxation increased, so did the popular discontent. Menelaus realized this and tried to find alternative sources of income by selling "some of the gold vessels of the temple" (2 Macc 4:32). This did not help; the only apparent result was to add religious outrage to an already explosive situation. Onias III voiced the discontent: "when Onias became fully aware of these acts, he publicly exposed them" (4:33). Menelaus's bloody vengeance reached him in the sanctuary to Apollo and Artemis at Daphne near Antioch where Onias had sought refuge (4:33-34). Onias's complaint and subsequent murder in 170 would grant him a lasting fame among the enemies of Menelaus, but also proved that the former high priest, in spite of his personal prestige, was a figure of the past, unable to build a militant opposition. To Antiochus, Onias III was certainly more useful alive than dead. His forced inactivity in Antioch, which the king could publicly praise as "moderation and good conduct," made him a precious element of stability, in particular against the claims of Jason. Onias's murder was politically "unreasonable"; Antiochus could not openly denounce his man in Jerusalem, but made it clear that he was "inflamed with anger" (4:35-38).

Popular resentment against Menelaus grew. It was significant enough that in 169 "a false rumor arose that Antiochus was dead" (2 Macc 5:5), prompting a major crisis. Jason made an attempt to regain power. Confident of popular discontent, and reinforced by the fact that after his brother's death he was now by all means the legitimate high priest, he entered Jerusalem by force and, with Menelaus besieged in the citadel, began slaughtering his enemies (5:5-6). As Antiochus was not dead, Jason's attempt was doomed to fail. This time, the country of the Ammonites could no longer offer protection from the king's wrath: Jason fled "from city to city," until he "died in exile, having embarked to go to the Lacedaemonians in hope of finding protection because of their kinship" (5:7-10).

The reaction of the *redivivus* Antiochus was ruthless. He "went up against Israel and came to Jerusalem with a strong force" (1 Macc 1:20).

According to Josephus, "he took the city without fighting, those of his own party opening the gates to him" (*Ant* 12:246). By interpreting the "news of what had happened . . . to mean that Judea was in revolt" (2 Macc 5:11), the king finally had the legal excuse he needed to loot the temple: "he took the silver and the gold, and the costly vessels; he took also the hidden treasures that he found" (1 Macc 1:23; cf. *Ant* 12:247) — "eighteen hundred talents from the temple" (2 Macc 5:21). "Many of the opposite party" were slaughtered (*Ant* 12:247). Military governors were appointed to keep order and peace in Judea and Samaria, and the authority of Menelaus was restored, who "lorded over his compatriots worse than the others did" (2 Macc 5:23).

"Two years later [in 167, Antiochus] sent . . . [Apollonius] a chief collector of tribute . . . to Jerusalem with a large force" (1 Macc 1:29; 2 Macc 5:24; cf. *Ant* 12:248). The city was taken "by treachery . . . pretending peace" (*Ant* 12:248; 1 Macc 1:30), and then taking advantage of "the holy sabbath day" (2 Macc 5:25-26). "Great numbers of people" were killed, the temple was emptied of its secret treasures (*Ant* 2:250).

For the first time since the Hellenistic party took power in Jerusalem, the worship in the temple underwent radical changes: the daily sacrifices were interrupted (Dan 9:27; 1 Macc 1:45), the altar was defiled by "an abomination that desolates" (Dan 9:27; 11:31; 12:11; 1 Macc 1:54), and a new calendar was introduced (Dan 7:25) — a change from the Zadokite sabbatical calendar to the Macedonian lunar calendar that would have lasting and monumental consequences in the development of Jewish thought even after the Maccabean crisis.[2]

A large-scale religious persecution struck those who followed the Zadokite laws. The Jews were compelled "to forsake the laws of their ancestors and no longer to live by the laws of God" (2 Macc 6:1). As both the Seleucid and the Jewish priesthood agreed that the Zadokite law was no longer either the law of the king or the law of God, there was no justification in following it, nor pity for the transgressors: "Whoever does not obey the command of the king shall die" (1 Macc 1:50). Acceptance of the Greek way of life, which up to this time had been purely voluntary, was now enforced by the king's law (1 Macc 1:41-64; 2 Macc 6:1-11). Those who dared

2. Annie Jaubert, *VT* 3 (1953): 263; James C. VanderKam, *JSJ* 12 (1981): 60. See also Ernst Vogt, "Antiquum kalendarium sacerdotale," *Bib* 36 (1955): 403-8; VanderKam, *CBQ* 41 (1979): 390-411.

resist were seen as political enemies and treated as such. "Many Jews complied with the king's command, either voluntarily, or out of fear of the penalty that was announced; but the best men, and those of the noblest souls, did not regard him . . . on which account they every day underwent great miseries and bitter torments" (*Ant* 12:255-56; cf. 1 Macc 1:62-64). More than three centuries of Zadokite order came to an end amid bloodshed and persecution.

It is not easy to explain such a dramatic development. Neither Antiochus nor the Hellenistic party had ever before forced the inhabitants of Judea to abandon the Zadokite law. The major goal of Antiochus had been to put his hands on the temple treasure; the Hellenistic party sought exclusively their own freedom not to be bound by Zadokite law and the opportunity to join Hellenistic society. What suddenly turned an economic quest into a religious crisis?

According to Jewish post-Maccabean sources, the villain was Antiochus, who issued a general decree "to his whole kingdom that all should be one people, and that all should give up their particular customs" (1 Macc 1:41-42; cf. 2 Macc 6:1). At the beginning of the 2nd century C.E., the Roman Tacitus would reverse the blame by commending Antiochus for his eagerness to eradicate the "base and abominable customs of the Jews" (*Hist.* 5.4-7). The absence of any supporting evidence and the bias of an irreconcilable opposition between Judaism and Hellenism make both reports historically unreliable; modern historians agree that Antiochus pursued a policy of tolerance for local cults and that the religious persecution was limited to Jerusalem and Judah.[3]

The circumstances of the death of Menelaus, who was ultimately executed as a traitor by Antiochus V, betray a different story. The Greeks apparently thought that Menelaus "was to blame for all the trouble" (2 Macc 13:4) and specifically for having "persuaded [Antiochus IV] to compel the Jews to leave the religion of their fathers" (*Ant* 12:384), thus dragging the Seleucid monarchy through an unfortunate experience. The report sounds genuine, as it contradicts the view that the same Jewish authors previously offered of the Maccabean crisis as a religious persecution promoted by the Greeks. However, nothing is said about the motivations of Menelaus and, in particular, about what happened in the two critical years, between 169 and 167 B.C.E., which separate the two interventions of Antiochus IV in Je-

3. See Jagersma, 50-53.

rusalem. The only text that seems to apply to this period is the very confused beginning of Josephus's *Jewish War* (*B.J.* 1:31-33). We read that just before Antiochus "spoiled the temple and put a stop to the constant practice of offering a daily sacrifice," i.e., immediately before Antiochus's second intervention in 167, there was turmoil in Jerusalem. "A great sedition fell among the men of power in Judea and they had a contention about obtaining the government; while each of those who were of dignity could not endure to be subject to their equals." The authenticity of the passage is strengthened by the fact that it contradicts Josephus's own position that only after the beginning of the Maccabean Revolt was Alcimus the first "who was not of the high priest stock" (*Ant* 12:387) to take the office. In order to save the continuity of the priesthood, Josephus would like his readers to believe that Menelaus was the "younger brother" of Onias and Jason (*Ant* 12:238-39; 15:41; 19:298; 20:235), not an Aaronite priest from the tribe of Bilgah. Here, on the contrary, we have evidence that the issue of being ruled by "equals" arose before and not after the Maccabean Revolt. It happened when the non-Zadokite Menelaus took power, and more specifically between 169 and 167, after the death of both Onias III and Jason. Any other setting would be anachronistic.

Josephus's text contains some additional, important pieces of information, all of them consistent with the same historical setting. At that time "Antiochus had a quarrel with the sixth Ptolemy about his right to the whole country of Syria" (*B.J.* 1:31). In 168, Ptolemy VI broke the treaty to which he had been subjected after Antiochus's first campaign in Egypt. The Roman support stopped Antiochus's military reaction abruptly and forced him to a humiliating withdrawal (cf. Polybius *Hist.* 29.27.8; Livy *Urb. cond.* 45.12.4ff.). The defeat reopened the argument about the possession of Syria-Palestina and increased the military importance of Jerusalem. In this difficult situation, something happened in Jerusalem that must have caused no little concern to Antiochus, as it affected his major allies and leaders of the pro-Seleucid party: "the sons of Tobias [including Menelaus?] were cast out of the city and fled to Antiochus and besought him . . . to make an expedition into Judea" (*B.J.* 1:31-32). The Seleucid power in the region was at stake. The king would not forget to take advantage of the war laws which allowed him to loot the temple treasury again, but his intervention was primarily a punitive expedition against "a great multitude of those that favored Ptolemy" (*B.J.* 30–31).

The only major problem in such a reconstruction is the reference to the Zadokite "Onias, one of the high priests" (*B.J.* 1:31), who is said to have caused the sedition against the sons of the Tobiads and then "fled to Ptolemy" when Antiochus prevailed. In Josephus's *Jewish War,* the same Onias is later called "the son of Simon" (*B.J.* 7:423). This is usually taken as a puzzling and anachronistic reference to Onias III, which throws discredit on the historical reliability of the entire passage. In *Jewish Antiquities,* however, after apologizing for having provided in his previous work only brief and not very accurate information on the subject (*Ant* 12:245), Josephus corrects himself by clarifying that the Onias who fled to Egypt was not Onias III but his son, Onias IV (*Ant* 12:237, 387-88; 13:62-73).

When the reference to Onias at the beginning of the *Jewish War* is also taken as a reference to Onias IV, then the text becomes clear. At that time Onias IV was still a child (cf. *Ant* 12:237), yet after the murder of his father and the death in exile of his uncle Jason, he was *in pectore* the legitimate high priest according to the Zadokite succession. His coming to age brought up for discussion again the future of the Jerusalem priesthood. More than securing Menelaus's loyalty and consensus, the common Aaronite descent stirred up the jealousy of many of his fellow priests or "equals," who would have rather seen the Zadokite line restored. When the party that supported "Onias [IV] got the better" (*B.J.* 1:31), Menelaus and the sons of Tobias sought Antiochus's support, accusing their enemies of siding with the Ptolemies. After the failure of his second Egyptian campaign, Antiochus had a strategic interest in strengthening his military presence in Jerusalem and avoiding the coalescence of any opposition that could be used by the Ptolemies as a fifth column ready to rise and betray. Menelaus needed a sign of discontinuity that would definitively affirm his power and the legitimacy of his priesthood over the Zadokites from the religious point of view as well. As the author of the Letter to the Hebrews would say in a different historical context but addressing a similar theological problem: "When there is a change in the priesthood, there is necessarily a change in the law as well" (Heb 7:12). The abolishment of the Zadokite law served well both the interests of Menelaus and the king.

Even in this outbreak of violence, the goal of Menelaus and Antiochus was not to abolish Judaism, but only the Zadokite form of Judaism. As Paolo Sacchi points out, "no one wants to become the high priest to a god in liquidation."[4] Menelaus had succeeded in becoming the high priest of a

4. Sacchi, *The History of the Second Temple Period,* 226.

well-established sanctuary of a well-established religion. He had neither any intention of nor any interest in undermining the roots of his power and wealth. Given the economic and political importance of sanctuaries in the Hellenistic world, the king's goal was to take control of the Jerusalem temple and certainly not to destroy it. The religious persecution was limited in time and in space; it aimed not to fight the Jews and the Jewish religion but only to strike at the king's political enemies in Jerusalem. "From the perspective of hindsight . . . it is clear that the debate was not between Judaism and Hellenism as opposed forces, but really over the degree to which an already hellenized Judaism would self-consciously conform even further to international cultural norms."[5]

Within this context, it is likely that Menelaus himself directed the king by suggesting to him those measures that in a very simple and effective way could identify their enemies and lead to their punishment. "The very fact that Antiochus was able to individuate precisely which Jewish practices to abolish demonstrates that the person advising him on the matter knew the Judaism of the period very well and wanted to destroy *that particular Judaism*, not *all* Judaism."[6]

Without a hint from the high priest in Jerusalem, Antiochus would have never so ferociously banned circumcision as the mark of separation between Jews and Gentiles (2 Macc 6:10) or introduced pigs as sacrificial animals and forced Jews to consume them (1 Macc 1:47; 2 Macc 6:21; 7:1), which was not customary even among the Greeks and was an abomination for most of the peoples of the region.[7]

Without a hint from the high priest in Jerusalem, Antiochus would have never "[defiled] the sanctuary and the priests" (1 Macc 1:46) by actually erecting a new altar and offering magnificent sacrifices on it (1:54; 2 Macc 6:7; Dan 11:31; 12:11), or "[building] altars in the surrounding towns of Judah and [offering] incense at the doors of the houses and in the streets" (1 Macc 1:54-55). Only in the eyes of the Zadokite law were these measures an abomination as they challenged the holiness and uniqueness of the Jerusalem temple. In every other context the same measures of benevolent patronage would have appeared as a sign of the king's favor and

5. Martin S. Jaffee, *Early Judaism*, 40.

6. Sacchi, *The History of the Second Temple Period*, 226.

7. Elias J. Bickerman, *The God of the Maccabees: Studies on the Meaning and Origin of the Maccabean Revolt*, SJLA 32 (Leiden: Brill, 1979), 88-89.

respect to the temple of Jerusalem, which Antiochus did not destroy but honored, and to its priesthood, which Antiochus did not persecute but supported.

Without a hint from the high priest in Jerusalem, Antiochus would never have commanded "to profane sabbaths and festivals" (1 Macc 1:45) or "to change the sacred seasons" by introducing a new calendar in the temple (Dan 7:25), which altered the holiness of times which in the Zadokite worldview was no less crucial than that of people and places.

All these measures implied an inside knowledge of the Zadokite law and a conscious and well-meditated plan aimed not to eradicate the religion of the Jews but, on the contrary, to affirm the importance of the Jerusalem cult under the new priesthood of Menelaus, while targeting the boundaries of separation within people and animals, places, and times as established by the Zadokite purity laws. Antiochus had vital political and military interests in Jerusalem; Menelaus knew that only the support of the king could give legitimacy to the new priesthood. Both wanted to get rid of their enemies. Antiochus had the power, but only Menelaus could articulate a plan of religious reforms that would serve both well. Antiochus trusted and supported him.

What Antiochus and Menelaus did not foretell, however, was that the punishment of their enemies would ignite the flames of a ruinous civil war. The unexpected opposition came not from the nostalgia of the Zadokite or Ptolemaic power but from those who, mostly in the countryside outside Jerusalem, more heavily had to bear the burden of taxation while being excluded from the benefits of Hellenistic economy and culture. The catalysts were "a priestly family of Joarib," the Hasmoneans or Maccabees as they were soon called out of admiration for the military skill of Judah. Soon, the conflict escalated into a large-scale civil war.

The genius of the Maccabees was to present themselves not as the leaders of just another rival priestly family seeking power, as they were, but as the champions of the national tradition against the Greeks, and to turn the civil war into a war of liberation against the foreign oppressors. The Maccabean propaganda presents Antiochus's measures in Judah not as the result of intra-Jewish conflicts but as the last chapter and inevitable outcome of the opposition between Hellenism and Judaism (1 Macc 1:1-10).

Around the military and political leadership of the Maccabees a varied coalition of groups arose, with different religious or political agendas, but united in their opposition to Menelaus.[8] Their victory would mark the restoration of the Mosaic law and its transformation from the law of the house of Zadok into the national law of all Jews. Their victory also meant the defeat of any hypothesis of inclusive monotheism; from now on, any form of Judaism would have to define itself as exclusive monotheism.[9] Religious conflicts, however, did not cease, even when the Maccabees reached complete independence as the new high priests and kings of Judah. Competitive interpretations of the crisis emerged and clashed. Judaism would remain a profoundly divided society.[10]

2. The Emergence of a "Third Way" between Zadokite and Enochic Judaism

With the religious persecution, the crisis of Zadokite Judaism became not only political but theological. Politically, the ties that the house of Zadok had established for one century through the Tobiads with either the Ptolemies or the Seleucids disqualified them as leaders of a nationalistic movement. The last descendants of the Zadokites fled Jerusalem to Egypt where they built a military colony under the Ptolemies and a temple (Josephus *C. Ap.* 2:50-52).[11]

Theologically, the misery the house of Zadok experienced could only mean that God had revoked support to the ruling priesthood because of their personal sins. Once they lost their power, the Zadokites found themselves condemned by the same theology that justified their power as long as they were in power.

However, nothing prevented the Zadokite ideology from surviving the end of the house of Zadok. The Maccabees presented themselves at the same time as the defenders of the Zadokite Torah against the Gentiles, and the new house of high priests that God had chosen instead of the evil house of Zadok.

8. Joseph Sievers, *The Hasmoneans and Their Supporters* (Atlanta: Scholars, 1990).

9. Diana Vikander Edelman, ed., *The Triumph of Elohim;* Gabriele Boccaccini, "Il Dio unico, Padre e Creatore, nel giudaismo di etá ellenistico-romana," *DSBP* 13 (Rome: Borla, 1996), 102-21.

10. Albert I. Baumgarten, *The Flourishing of Jewish Sects in the Maccabean Era: An Interpretation,* JSJSup 55 (Leiden: Brill, 1997).

11. Collins, *Between Athens and Jerusalem,* 71-76.

It was not only a matter of leadership, however. Before a collective catastrophe of such magnitude, the logic of the Zadokite covenant required the entire people to recognize that they were justly punished by God for their own transgressions. The sin of the nation was identified by the Maccabean propaganda with the passive attitude of those "renegades from Israel" who instead of fighting against gentile influence after Alexander the Great, accepted Greek rule and law and "misled many" (1 Macc 1:1-11). The Hasmoneans boasted themselves not only as the new high priests of the Zadokite covenant but also as the leaders of a new generation of righteous rising from the ashes of a previous generation of sinners.

Yet, there was a problem that the Zadokite tradition was not equipped to cope with — martyrdom. Zadokite Judaism had already experienced trouble explaining the meaning of the suffering of the righteous and defending the integrity of the covenant from the attack of skeptical wisdom, by showing that at the end there is always some reward for the righteous in this world. The religious persecution under Antiochus and Menelaus transformed the perspective of martyrdom from an exceptional individual choice into a concrete collective experience and a theological paradox. In order to remain faithful to Zadokite law, the righteous had to deny themselves the very goals of Zadokite law — the promised blessings — and with conscious and passive resignation facilitate their own annihilation and oblivion as individuals and as a people. Counting on their obedience, the enemies could easily identify them by their own "good deeds" and then defeat and exterminate them "on the sabbath day."

The Maccabees had to address the point of vulnerability for the survival of the Jews as the people of the covenant and defuse the potentially explosive theological problem. Martyrdom may be a forcible option and a last resort for the individual, but it becomes an irresponsible act when it jeopardizes the very existence of the Jewish people. "When Mattathias and his friends learned" that "a thousand persons" had chosen to be killed "unjustly" rather than defend themselves on the sabbath day (1 Macc 2:29-38; cf. 2 Macc 6:11), they "mourned for them deeply," but also made clear their disagreement. "If we all do as our kindred have done and refuse to fight with the Gentiles for our lives and for our ordinances, they will quickly destroy us from the earth" (1 Macc 2:39-40). The decision to fight back on sabbath days was a landmark in the Maccabean Revolt, the only teaching that the Maccabees could not help portraying as innovative, and, theologically, probably their most lasting legacy. "Mattathias taught them to fight even on the sabbath day . . . and this rule continues among us to this day, that if there be a necessity, we may fight on sabbath days" (*Ant* 12:76-277; cf. 1 Macc 2:39-41). The Maccabees advocated fighting instead of martyrdom, open insurrection instead of passive resistance. "Arm yourself and be courageous. . . . It is better for us to die in battle than to see the misfortunes of our nation and of the sanctuary" (1 Macc 3:58-59).

By shifting the emphasis from martyrdom to death in battle, the Maccabees recovered a more familiar and solid ground. Unlike martyrdom, death in battle brought not only a perspective of eternal memory for the individual, but also had meaning for the sake of the entire people. The response was enthusiastic: "All who became fugitives to escape their troubles joined them and reinforced them. They organized an army, and struck down sinners in their anger and renegades in their wrath" (1 Macc 2:42-44). In their army the Maccabees took care to enroll also the ancestors of Israel, including some who could have better been seen as examples of passive resistance. "Remember the deeds of the ancestors, which they did in their generations; and you will receive great honor and an everlasting name . . . Abraham . . . Joseph . . . Phinehas . . . Joshua . . . Caleb . . . David . . . Elijah . . . Hananiah, Azariah, and Mishael . . . Daniel" (2:51-60). They all showed both "trust in [God]" and "strength." (2:61). Their example was an invitation to "pay back the Gentiles in full, and obey the commands of the law" (2:68).

The Aaronite Hasmoneans were very careful to link any innovation to the previous Zadokite tradition, from which only they could receive legitimacy. The perspective they consistently offered was one of continuity with Zadokite theology, with only one major exception: they put themselves in place of the house of Zadok.

Even among those who joined the struggle against Antiochus and Menelaus, not everyone agreed on the theological premises of the Maccabees. In the eyes of Enochic Judaism, the crisis was something deeper than the consequence of human sin. Dream Visions (1 En 83–90) presents the war as the inevitable outcome of the degeneration of history caused by the angelic sin, and the beginning of a time in which God would restore the goodness of the universe.

In a first vision (1 En 83–84), Enoch repeats the sense of history according to the Enochic point of view. The order of creation has been disrupted by the angelic sin, and the earth has become the victim of chaotic forces. "I saw in a vision the sky being hurled down and snatched and falling upon the earth. . . . I saw the earth being swallowed into the great abyss, the mountains being suspended upon mountains, the hills sinking down upon the hills, and tall trees being uprooted and thrown and sinking into the deep abyss" (83:3-4). There is no remedy in history for this unfortunate state of things: the world is condemned to be under God's wrath until its end would come. "The angels of your heavens are now committing sin (upon the earth), and your wrath shall rest upon the flesh of the people until (the arrival of) the great day of judgment" (84:4). Enoch can only pray that God would not "destroy . . . the flesh that has angered you from upon the earth, but sustain the flesh of righteousness and uprightness as a plant of eternal seed" (84:6).

The evil that tears apart the world is historically spelled out in its various stages in a second and much longer vision, the so-called Animal Apocalypse (1 En 85–90).[12] Humans were created as "snow-white cows" (85:3), but then "a star fell down from heaven but (managed) to rise and eat and to be pastured among those cows" (86:1). The fall of the devil was followed by a large rebellion of angels: "many stars descending and casting themselves down from the sky upon that first star; and they became bovids among those calves and were pastured together with them" (86:2). The angelic sin of trespassing and mingling is the origin of what the vision presents as the spread of a genetic disease that changes the nature of humankind, subsequently producing inferior species of animals. "I kept observing, and behold, I saw all of them extending their sexual organs like horses and commencing to mount upon the heifers, the bovids; and they (the latter) all became pregnant and bore elephants, camels, and donkeys" (86:4).

The insistence on the modality of the angelic sin, which is so graphically described (see also 1 En 87:3; 90:21), is not without meaning: through sexual union evil not only penetrated into human nature and contaminated it but also continues to be transmitted from generation to generation. Neither the intervention of the good angels, who reduce the rebels to impotence (1 En 87-88), nor the flood (see 89:2-8) can eradicate evil from the earth. Evil descendants are bound to arise, even from the holy survivors. From Noah, "the snow-white cow which became a man" (i.e., like the angels), are born "three cows," but "one of those three cows was

12. See Patrick A. Tiller, *A Commentary on the Animal Apocalypse of 1 Enoch* (Atlanta: Scholars, 1993).

snow-white, similar to that (first) cow [Shem], and one red like blood [Japheth] . . . and one black [Ham]. . . . They began to bear the beasts of the fields and the birds. There arose out of them all classes of [species]" (89:9-10).

History thus witnesses a continuous expansion of evil, with no way for human beings to oppose its spread. Nobody is spared: in the metaphorical world of the Animal Apocalypse, even the Jews, who are the noblest segment of humankind, bear the evil gene of degeneration; by the generation of Jacob, from "cows" they have become "sheep." Abraham, "the snow-white cow which was born in their midst begat a wild ass [Ishmael], and a snow-white cow with it [Isaac]; and the wild asses multiplied. And that cow which was born from him bore a black wild boar [Esau] and a snow-white sheep [Jacob]; the former then bore many wild boars and the latter bore twelve sheep" (1 En 89:11-12).

The vision continues by describing the various episodes of biblical history in great detail: slavery in Egypt, the exodus, the conquest of the promised land, and the monarchy. After the Babylonian exile the situation collapses; God entrusts God's people to "seventy shepherds" (the angels of the nations), who show themselves to be evil, trespassing upon their assigned tasks in such a way that the entire history of Israel in the postexilic period unfolds under a demonic influence (see 1 En 89:59ff.). God's response is limited to watching the dramatic succession of events and assigning the task of checking the work of the "seventy shepherds" — to write down and to relate to God their actions — to one of God's angels (who has the characteristics of Michael, although not mentioned by name). The task, however, excludes any direct intervention: "Do not reveal [what they should do] to them, neither admonish them, but write down every destruction caused by the shepherds — for each and every one in his appointed time — and elevate all of it to me" (89:64).

However, at the climax of evil and destruction, people will start seeing the light. Some "sheep" will open their eyes and begin fighting against their oppressors (90:1-12). The "great sword . . . given to the sheep" (93:19) is the sign that the end is close, that the good angels have abandoned their passive role (90:14), and the time of God's vengeance has finally come (90:15). God's judgment eliminates the guilty and offers to the elect of every nation and time, including "those which have been destroyed" (90:33), the prospect of eternal salvation in a new world totally purified of evil. God's wrath is laid down (90:34) and all the elect, "sheep . . . beasts of the field and birds of the sky," undergo their final mutation (90:37). "I went on seeing until all their kindred were transformed, and became snow-white cows" (90:38). The circle closes: by restoring the original integrity of human nature, the new creation recovers the goals of the first creation that the angelic sin had disrupted.

The Enochic answer proved to be quite attractive. Enochic Judaism promised the elect not only a militant perspective of battle at the end of this world (that is, in the author's present), but also a time of vindication for the martyrs in the world to come. The end of the Zadokite priesthood gave confidence to the group, while the harshness of the struggle seemed to confirm the soundness of their ideas about the spread of evil and the degeneration of history. What was before a minority movement of a few priestly families, during the Maccabean crisis spread and won adherents and became a larger popular movement. Yet, the Enochic answer did not satisfy many, as many were not convinced by the Zadokite solution, even in its revised Maccabean version. During the Maccabean Revolt, the book of Daniel testifies to the emergence of a "third way" between Zadokite and Enochic Judaism, which would open new horizons in Jewish thought and signal a decisive step toward the building of the foundations of what would develop into the rabbinic system of thought.

Daniel has been often, and sometimes improperly, associated with Dream Visions. The two documents are very nearly contemporary, both being dated to the first years of the Maccabean Revolt, between the murder of Onias III, the last legitimate Zadokite high priest (170 B.C.E.), and the death of Antiochus Epiphanes (164). Both documents are apocalyptic; they share the same literary genre (apocalypse) and the same worldview (apocalypticism), and — what is even more significant — substantially address the same questions. Yet, as I have been highlighting since 1987 in a series of studies, Stephen Breck Reid independently confirmed in a monograph in 1989, and is now commonly accepted by commentators, a comparison between Daniel and the Book of Dream Visions (1 En 83–90) shows that the two apocalyptic documents cannot be ascribed to a single movement or party. The apocalyptic Daniel is a non-Enochic or even anti-Enochic document.[13]

13. See Gabriele Boccaccini, "É Daniele un testo apocalittico? Una (ri)definizione del pensiero del Libro di Daniele in rapporto al Libro dei Sogni e all'apocalittica," *Hen* 9 (1987): 267-302; "*Daniel* and the *Dream Visions:* The Genre of Apocalyptic and the

The difficulty can be overcome by claiming with John J. Collins that "the Jewish apocalypses were not produced by a single 'apocalyptic movement' but constituted a genre that could be utilized by different groups in various situations."[14] For example, the two parties that produced Daniel and Dream Visions, respectively. The sharing of the same worldview neither is necessarily evidence of ideological continuity, nor can overshadow theological differences. A holistic comparison of systems of thought shows that the ties between Daniel and Zadokite Judaism, in spite of any innovations, remain no less important and are even more substantial than those that relate Daniel to Dream Visions.

3. The Danielic Revolution

Daniel is a complex document that presents a unique structure, a composite both in language (partly in Hebrew [Dan 1:1-2:4a; 8–12] and partly in Aramaic [2:4b–7:28]) and in literary genre (third person edifying stories about Daniel and his friends [Dan 1–6] alternate with first person apocalyptic visions [Dan 7–12]).

Unlike the Aramaic parts of Ezra (Ezra 4:8–6:18 and 7:12-26), which are reserved to official documents, there is no self-explanatory rationale for Daniel's bilingualism. The text tries somehow to smooth the transition from the Hebrew to the Aramaic at the beginning of Dan 2 by introducing a direct discourse by the Chaldean sages, but there is no reason why the entire narrative should at this point turn into Aramaic and then revert again to Hebrew at the beginning of Dan 8.

The problem is made even more puzzling by the fact that the division by genre does not coincide with the transition between the Hebrew and the Aramaic. What is the logic for Dan 1 to be in Hebrew, when the other

---

Apocalyptic Tradition," *Middle Judaism,* 126-60; cf. Stephen Breck Reid, *Enoch and Daniel: A Form Critical and Sociological Study of Historical Apocalypses* (Berkeley: BIBAL, 1989). "Boccaccini has quite correctly pointed out that Daniel does not belong to the same ideological tradition as Enoch"; John J. Collins, *Seers, Sybils and Sages in Hellenistic-Roman Judaism,* JSJSup 54 (Leiden: Brill, 1997), 295. "Daniel and the *Book of Dreams* are on two sides of Jewish thought that are more opposed than distinct. . . . [Boccaccini's] argumentation is broad and conclusive"; Paolo Sacchi, *Jewish Apocalyptic and Its History,* 23 and n.

14. Collins, *The Apocalyptic Imagination,* 280.

court tales are in Aramaic, and for Dan 7 to be in Aramaic when the other apocalyptic visions are in Hebrew?

It is apparent, and commonly accepted by scholars, that the court tales of Dan 1–6, which are remarkably free of insertions referring to the persecution of Antiochus Epiphanes, have a lengthy prehistory and originated as independent stories. The so-called apocryphal additions to the Greek Daniel, the Old Greek version, and cognate texts like the Prayer of Nabonidus (4QPrNab) confirm that we face an old literary tradition which, over the early Second Temple period, brought a vast wealth of material, more than is actually collected in the book of Daniel. As for the apocalyptic parts of Daniel (Dan 7–12), the general sense is that they were composed during the Maccabean Revolt, by "authors [who] belonged to the same circle and wrote within a very short time of each other," if not by "a single author."[15]

The distinction between Dan 1–6 and 7–12, therefore, makes sense on a formal and chronological level, but does not at all resolve the problem of their having been placed together. Too sharp a distinction between court tales and apocalyptic visions tends to exclude any reciprocal relationship aside from the reference to the same protagonist. If the theology of the document depended solely on the chronology, the ideology of Daniel would be resolved, or better dissolved, in the ideologies of its two separate parts.

The presentation of Daniel as a collection of passages written in different periods with changing ideological intentions appears inadequate. The prehistory of the document does not explain why both parts were retained and were given a final shape that included both court tales and apocalyptic visions. Furthermore, there is something that makes Daniel a profoundly unitary work; the juxtaposition of the parts to form a whole is too coherent to be due to chance. Whoever gave the book its final shape during the Maccabean Revolt was much more than a mere copyist and passive collector of old and new stories about Daniel; he was a creative author. He inherited material from an old tradition and certainly did not write all the parts of the book; nonetheless, he was the creator of an original work. It is to him whom I will refer here as the author of Daniel. To no one else does this title fit more properly.

In this respect, the case of Daniel is different from that of the Enochic literature, where tradition grew by addition, with each book maintaining

15. Collins, *The Apocalyptic Imagination*, 107.

its own autonomy and original form. The choice of the final redactor of Daniel was not to write a new Danielic book to be added to previous stories, but to reshape into a single work the tradition he inherited.

The hand of the author can be traced in the presence of recurring themes, in the unity of character given to the protagonist Daniel even when he faces the most diverse situations, and in what André Lacocque calls "the omnipresent shadow of Antiochus Epiphanes."[16] But first of all, the intervention of the author is apparent in the linguistic arrangement of the parts of the book. That Dan 1 was likely translated from Aramaic into Hebrew means that the aim was to separate it from the following Aramaic chapters and make it function as a general introduction to the work when the Hebrew parts were added. That Dan 7, unlike the following chapters from the Maccabean period, was written in Aramaic instead of Hebrew means that the final author wanted it to be read as the conclusion of the Aramaic section and not as the beginning of the Hebrew section. In other words, Daniel's bilingualism was, at least in part, the result of a chronological literary process in the composition of its parts, but the actual linguistic structure of the book was the consequence of a skillful choice by the final author. The aim was to give the book a threefold structure so that, after the introduction (Dan 1, now in Hebrew), two distinct parts, one in Aramaic (Dan 2–7) and one in Hebrew (Dan 8–12), would follow.

An analysis of the internal structure of these two parts confirms the unity given to the book of Daniel by its author, and shows the identity between the book's scheme of composition and its actual linguistic structure, making sense of the unresolved problem of its bilingualism. There are precise thematic connections between Dan 2 and 7 (the succession of the four kingdoms), Dan 3 and 6 (Daniel's experience in the lions' den repeats that of his three friends in the fiery furnace), Dan 4 and 5 (God punishes the kings' pride) and Dan 8 and 10–12 (the characteristics and duration of the fourth kingdom). Thus, the constituent parts of each section are disposed concentrically around their respective nuclei (Dan 4–5 and 9).

The concentric arrangement of the chapters is not a mere matter of style; it is perfectly functional for the unitary ideological project carried out by its author, who organized his thought, as well as the literary structure of the book, around two fundamental ideas. First, sovereignty belongs to God, who grants it and revokes it according to God's will and establishes

16. André Lacocque, *The Book of Daniel* (Atlanta: John Knox, 1979), 15.

the times of history, the time of increasing suffering under foreign rule as well as the final time of glorious restoration of the kingdom of Israel (Dan 2–7). Second, the cause of history's degeneration is the breaking of the Mosaic covenant, which, starting from the Babylonian exile, has brought down upon the people the curse contained therein, yet leaves the individuals free to determine their own destiny even in the darkest age of persecution and in the face of martyrdom (Dan 8–12). The framework is provided by the reference to the seer Daniel, whom Dan 1 introduces as the one who has received wisdom by his faithfulness to the covenant and the conclusion (12:5-13) praises as the model figure for the righteous of Israel.

The coherent structure of the book requires the accent to be shifted from the prehistory of the single parts to the unity of the composite project, the setting of persecution that brought the parts together and gave new meaning to the old tales. In its very structure, the book is an invitation to a journey that from the tenets of Zadokite Judaism moves towards the principles of Enochic Judaism, to land midway, in a new, unexplored land between and beyond the two traditions.

A. *Daniel and Enoch: Two Different Kinds of Apocalyptic Seers (Daniel 1)*

The story of the food test (Dan 1) belongs to the same setting as the other court tales of Dan 2–6, to which it provides a sort of historical prologue. Here we find a reference not only to Daniel but also to his three friends, who are the protagonists in Dan 3, and to the "vessels of the temple" which would gain central stage in Dan 5. As Collins correctly points out, the story had originally "a specific practical aim: to encourage Jews of the diaspora to avoid defilement in their food while participating actively in the cultural life of their environment," and to show them that "fidelity to Jewish religion is the best way to success in the gentile world."[17] However, in the context of the book of Daniel as a whole, the story has now a new function, which the translation into Hebrew only makes more obvious. By artificially creating a linguistic gap between the story and its most immediate context of Aramaic tales, the author of Daniel transforms the narrative into a general introduction to the entire document, apocalyptic parts in-

17. John J. Collins, *Daniel,* Herm (Minneapolis: Fortress, 1993), 144-45.

cluded. The focus inevitably shifts from the story itself to the person of Daniel. It was Daniel who took the leadership in keeping the dietary laws. It was Daniel whom God rewarded with a special gift of interpreting dreams. And, at the very end, it is Daniel who is singled out as the protagonist of a story that it is said would continue until "the first year of King Cyrus" (1:21). The structure of the entire book is consistent with these premises; it provides a narrative that looks like a biography, beginning with the youth of Daniel at the Babylonian court and ending with the announcement of his death and reward in the world to come (12:5-13). Daniel is the hero who is to be introduced; he is the one of whom the reader wants to hear. What kind of apocalyptic seer is he?

Enochic Judaism had its own established hero, Enoch, the ancient patriarch and apocalyptic seer who was shown the secrets of heaven and revealed them to his sons and did not die because God took him away. With Dream Visions, the character shows a certain evolution. In the previous Enochic tradition, Enoch is said to derive his wisdom from his ascent to heaven, while in Dream Visions Enoch is essentially a dreamer. In the Danielic tradition, Daniel bears a similar evolution, from an interpreter of dreams in Dan 1–6 to a dreamer himself in Dan 7–12. The two characters of Enoch and Daniel, originally very different from each other, have now very similar functions and features. Even the content of their revelation is similar; Enoch's dreams have acquired a historical dimension that was unknown in the previous Enochic tradition, and Daniel's dreams have now a cosmological dimension that was unknown in the previous Danielic tradition. Yet an essential distinction remains.

Dream Visions continues to show the utmost indifference to the personal righteousness of Enoch. The book adds practically nothing to our knowledge of the character except that, when he saw the dreams God sent him, he knew how to write (this concerns his ability to receive and transmit the revelation; 1 En 83:2) and that he was not yet married (this regards his status of purity in a context that, as we have seen, assigns a fundamental role to sexual activity in the spread of evil; 83:2; 85:3). Enoch lived long before Moses, and Enochic Judaism is consistent in dismissing the implications that, even retroactively, the Mosaic covenant has for human righteousness according to the covenantal theology of Zadokite Judaism. In the theological understanding of Enochic Judaism, the apocalyptic seer is not chosen for his merits; the knowledge imparted to him is a gracious act of enlightenment on God's part.

Dan 1, on the other hand, presents its hero as a wise man who has received the gift of divine wisdom in virtue of his faithfulness to the Mosaic covenant. Daniel lived long after Moses; he is a Jewish youth in the court of Nebuchadnezzar, the king of Babylonia, and, unlike most of his companions, he refuses to "defile himself with the royal rations of food and wine" (Dan 1:8), requesting "vegetables to eat and water to drink" (1:12) in order to avoid breaking the Zadokite dietary laws. The concern for purity of food is attested with increasing frequency in the Hellenistic period (see Tob 1:10-11), but the new Maccabean context of persecution, when "many in Israel chose to die rather than to be defiled by food" (1 Macc 1:63), undoubtedly shed new light on Daniel's case. Vegetarianism is an ancient (and modern) way to follow the Jewish dietary laws. With admiration Flavius Josephus would tell us of some priests conducted in captivity to Rome, who "had not forgotten the piety owed to God, and supported themselves on figs and nuts" (*Vita* 14). Dan 1:8 singles out the leadership of Daniel as the one who took the initiative on the matter of food. To him, and to the three youths who followed his example (Hananiah, Mishael, Azariah), as a reward "God gave . . . knowledge and skill in every aspect of literature and wisdom (Heb. *hkmh*)," but only Daniel "had insight into all visions and dreams" (1:17). In short, in the theological understanding of the book's author, Daniel is not made an apocalyptic seer because he is of the elect, but because he is righteous according to the criteria of Zadokite Judaism.

Thematically, this is the meaning of the episode placed as the introduction to the book of Daniel. One can continue to read it as an edifying story directed at the Jews of the Diaspora. However, in the ecology of the final redaction it now plays a more specific role: to present the figure of Daniel as righteous and to clarify the limits of his knowledge, bringing the apocalyptic enlightenment into the sphere of a covenantal theology. The first chapter provides, in substance, the key to reading the book, the frame of reference for both Daniel's cognitive experiences and the continuous reminders that wisdom is the property and gift of God.

While the biblical precedents are clearly provided by the patriarch Joseph (Gen 37–50) and King Solomon (1 Kgs 3:1–8:66), the relationship between obedience to the covenant and knowledge is resolved according to the more sophisticated scheme explicated in the book of Sirach after the encounter between Zadokite and Sapiential Judaism. The author of Daniel acknowledges the value of education and common wisdom. Daniel and his companions are "young men without physical defect and handsome, versed in every branch of wisdom, endowed with knowledge and insight," chosen to be educated and "serve in the king's palace" (Dan 1:4). Human wisdom is only the first step, however. Knowledge of the "hidden things" is a gift from God, and such enlightenment is granted only to the worthy, those who merit it through faithfulness to the Mosaic covenant ("If you desire wisdom, keep the commandments, and the Lord will lavish her upon you," Sir 1:26; cf. 6:37; 21:11).

The final redaction made the entire book consistent with this view. The most obvious example is given by the insertion of the doxology in Dan 2 (2:14-23) in which Daniel blesses God as the one who gives wisdom to the wise: "Wisdom . . . [is] his. He gives wisdom to the wise and knowledge to those who have understanding . . . [and] reveals deep and hidden things" (2:14-23). The link with Sirach is evident also by the vocabulary. The phrase *gl' mstrt'*, "[God] reveals the hidden things," is the Aramaic equivalent of the formula found in the Hebrew text of Sir 4:18 (*glyty mstry,* "I [wisdom] reveal [my] secrets"; cf. 3:22). The terminological coincidence is all the more significant inasmuch as in Daniel the formula constitutes a hapax, interrupting the context of the original story in which another similar Aramaic expression (*gl' rzyn,* "God reveals the mysteries [the enigmas]"; Dan 2:19, 28, 29, 30, 47[bis]; cf. 2:17, 27; 4:6) was repeated constantly. The latter is a formula of Persian origin, much less pregnant with meaning and certainly much nearer to the popular tradition.[18]

However, in his desire for understanding Daniel goes beyond Sirach. Against Enochic Judaism, Ben Sira had condemned (Sir 34:1-8) any kind of knowledge based on visions and dreams, unless it be a vision specially "sent by intervention from the Most High" (34:6a).[19] After reassuring its readers that Daniel's knowledge is not in spite (but because) of the covenant, the book can open wide the small window left half-closed by Ben Sira. Daniel does not distinguish among a "dream," a "vision," a miraculous apparition, a written word, or a prophetic word; God's revelation may come in different modalities and may even be addressed to a gentile king like Nebuchadnezzar, or to his son Belshazzar. What every revelation has in

18. See Franz Rosenthal, *A Grammar of Biblical Aramaic,* rev. ed. (Wiesbaden: Harrassowitz, 1974), 59.

19. On the relationship between Sirach and Enochic Judaism, see the previous chapter.

common, however, is that it remains obscure if God does not also provide its interpretation and reveal its hidden meaning to one who is worthy of it. The passage from the phase of revelation to that of interpretation is emphasized in the narrative by a time of disturbance and fear, a time in which Daniel turns to prayer and penitence (Dan 2:16-18; 4:19[Aram. 16]; 7:15-16; 8:15; 9:3; 10:2-3; 12:8). The reader is alerted that there is in fact something new to be revealed and understood, but this is not contradictory to the covenant. Daniel's success in interpreting God's revelation is due neither to his own skill only, nor to a gracious revelation of God only, but to a synergy of the human and the divine, when God's gift of wisdom meets the prayers of a righteous individual.

Daniel's personal story also does not end with his election as the interpreter of God's revelation. Enochic Judaism does not report about the final destiny of Enoch. It does not have to: Enoch's reward is in his being chosen. Nothing needs be added to the story of his election. On the contrary, we must wait until the very end of the narrative to know Daniel's final destiny. "You shall rise for your reward at the end of the days" (Dan 12:13). Daniel will be rewarded not because of God's gift of wisdom but because of his perseverance and righteousness in making good use of that gift, according to the rules of the covenant. Once again, the author sends a clear message to his readers: Daniel's experience stands out against Enoch's. Daniel is not the same kind of unlawful apocalyptic seer as Enoch.

B. *God's Power over the Kingdoms (Daniel 2–7)*

Some of the old stories from the Diaspora proved to be equally effective in delivering the author's message. In Dan 4–5 (the nucleus of the first section, Dan 2–7), the affirmation of God's absolute sovereignty ("His sovereignty is an everlasting sovereignty, and his kingdom endures from generation to generation"; 4:34[Aram. 31]; cf. 4:3[3:33]; 4:26[23]) runs parallel to the affirmation of God's supreme control in granting sovereignty to kings, even gentile kings ("the Most High is sovereign over the kingdom of mortals; he gives it to whom he will"; 4:17, 25, 32[14, 22, 29]; cf. 5:21). The power exercised by God is absolute and unquestionable: no one can oppose it. "All the inhabitants of the earth are accounted as nothing, and . . . there is no one who can stay his hand or say to him, 'What are you doing?'" (4:35[32]).

This idea is exemplified in the individual destinies of King Nebuchadnezzar and his son Belshazzar. God has granted them sovereignty, but is always ready to revoke it whenever they show themselves to be unworthy. In one case, Nebuchadnezzar is punished for having dared to proclaim himself the origin of his sovereignty: "Is this not magnificent Babylon, which I have built as a royal capital by my mighty power and for my glorious majesty?" (Dan 4:30[Aram. 27]). The consequences are immediate. The king is condemned to madness and is deprived of sovereignty (4:31-32[28-29]) for as long as he refuses to recognize that it does not belong to him, "until he learned that the Most High God has sovereignty over the kingdom of mortals, and sets over it whomever he will" (5:21; cf. 4:32[29]). God is the absolute protagonist of history; the sovereignty of kings is only a reflection of God's sovereignty.

As for King Belshazzar, guilty of having profaned the vessels of the temple by using them at his table (Dan 5:2-4, 23), Daniel accuses him of having committed an act of idolatry, instead of glorifying "God in whose power is your very breath, and to whom belong all your ways" (5:23). Through the mysterious and terrifying apparition of a hand writing incomprehensible words on the wall, God once again expresses judgment and reconfirms God's power over the king (5:24-28). In this case the withdrawal of sovereignty is irrevocable. "That very night Belshazzar, the Chaldean king, was killed. And Darius the Mede received the kingdom" (5:26–6:1).

God, therefore, possessor of an eternal and absolute power, is the source of the sovereignty of gentile kings who govern by God's will and within the limits set by God's judgment. It follows that a dual fidelity is required of the Jews because they are subject to a sovereignty exercised by two authorities: God and, through God, the gentile king. The possibility of a conflict of fidelity between that owed to God and that owed to the king is addressed in Dan 3 and 6, the first frame around Dan 4–5.

The same story is told in these two chapters, although with different nuances. Daniel and his companions are presented as faithful subjects, placed in charge of the very administration of the kingdom, honored and esteemed by the gentile king for their services (Dan 3:12; 6:2-4). Taking advantage of a royal decree that goes against the Jewish religious obligations, imposing an act of idolatry (3:4-6) or denying certain religious practices (6:7), some "envious men" denounce Daniel (6:4ff.) and his companions (3:8-12). God miraculously intervenes, sparing them from punishment and allowing them to emerge unharmed from the furnace (3:25, 28) and from the lions' den (6:23). The "envious men" pay for their deeds with their lives. The fire devours those who threw Shadrach, Meshach, and Abednego (the Babylonian names of Hananiah, Mishael, and Azariah, according to 1:7) into the furnace. As for those who denounced Daniel, they and their families end up as food for the lions in place of Daniel (6:24). The king recognizes God's power and the privileges of the Jews, making himself guardian of their diversity. Nebuchadnezzar orders that, under penalty of death and the loss of belongings, no one in his kingdom "utters blasphemy against the God of Shadrach, Meshach, and Abednego; . . . for there is no other god who is able to deliver in this way" (3:29). Darius puts out an edict that "in all [his] royal dominion people should tremble and fear before the God of Daniel. . . . His kingdom shall never be destroyed, and his dominion has no end" (6:26-28). Daniel and his companions are eventually restored to their court responsibilities (cf. 3:30; 6:28).

As disconcerting as it may seem, even though the order to perform idolatry came from the king, he is not at all blamed for it. The king can be benevolent like Darius, who saw himself "forced" to punish Daniel against his will and "[spent] the night fasting," begging God for salvation (Dan 6:15-19); or he can be malevolent like Nebuchadnezzar, who "was so filled with rage" when faced with the unexpected rebellion of the three young functionaries (3:19). Only those who maintain that the king's edict should also be valid for the Jews are guilty, those "envious men" who do not consent to the particular status of Israel. Kings pass away; they are good or bad: the pious Jew follows the same course with both. Daniel and his companions show no difficulty in continuing to serve faithfully the gentile king whose orders they have broken with such determination.

This is not a contradiction. The king's power is not so holy that it should not be contradicted, because it originates in and is limited by a "jealous" God; however, for the same reason its legitimacy remains unquestionable, even when it is wielded in opposition to the law of God, and the Jew, in the name of fidelity to the covenant, is led to disobedience. In Daniel's view, Jewish particularism contests the idolatrous pretenses of the royal authority, not its essence; sovereignty is from God, is granted by God, and only subsists by God's will.

The outer frame (Dan 2 and 7) is an announcement that this situation is destined to change, however, because at the end of time "the kingship and dominion and the greatness of the kingdoms under the whole heaven shall be given to the people of the holy ones of the Most High" (Dan 7:27; cf. 2:44; 7:14). First, however, "four kingdoms" must pass, represented in the two visions by a "great statue" made of various materials (Dan 2) and by "four beasts" (Dan 7). Sovereignty is granted to these four kingdoms, but not forever; only the eschatological kingdom that "the God of heaven will set up . . . shall never be destroyed, nor shall this kingdom be left to another people" (2:44), so mirroring the characteristics of divine sovereignty: "[God's] dominion is an everlasting dominion, that shall not pass away, and his kingship is one that shall never be destroyed" (Dan 7:14; cf. 7:18, 27).

The author again insists on God's absolute freedom to grant and revoke sovereignty; even the eschatological kingdom will be exclusively God's work ("not by [human] hands"; Dan 2:45; cf. 7:9-14, 26-27). Just as Daniel derived the idea that all knowledge is a gift of God from the idea that wisdom is from God, from the idea that sovereignty belongs to God it follows that every kingdom is God's gift. In the prayer of blessing that Daniel offers to God in Dan 2, the two themes are closely linked: "Wisdom and power are his. He . . . deposes kings and sets up kings; he gives wisdom to the wise" (2:20-21).

The religious conception of the origin of sovereignty that emerges in Dan 2–7 contrasts with the more secular vision with which Ben Sira confronted the same subject only a few decades earlier (cf. Sir 10:4-18). Of course, for Ben Sira too, "the government of the earth is in the hand of the Lord, and over it he will raise up the right leader for the time," and kings are subject to God's judgment, who "overthrows the thrones of rulers, and enthrones the lowly in their place" (10:4, 14). However, God's interest is turned exclusively to the ethical qualities of the kings whose pride is reproached (10:7, 12, 13, 18), not to the origin or foundation of their power. The succession of kingdoms is the work of human beings, of their ambitions and strength; "sovereignty passes from nation to nation on account of injustice and insolence and wealth" (10:8).

This is one of the elements that most clearly distinguish Daniel from Sirach, two documents linked by many deep ties. It is not by chance that the same element also characterizes the Dream Visions with respect to its own tradition. For Sirach, as for the early Enochic tradition, the unfolding of history holds not much interest. In both traditions the problem of evil, as well as salvation, is played out on the cosmic and anthropological levels, certainly not on the historical level. History is autonomous simply because it has no value. In this respect Daniel and Dream Visions signal a change of perspective. The Maccabean crisis brought the problem of history to the center of Jewish thought.

The ideas expressed in the court tales (Dan 1–6), which the author of Daniel inherited from the early Second Temple period, were largely reassuring and consistent with the Zadokite viewpoint. Despite any difficulty and crisis, the world is firmly under God's control, and God's faithful people under gentile rule may expect a happy and prosperous life if they remain loyal to their God. To the old court tales, however, the author of Daniel adds the story of an apocalyptic vision (Dan 7) — a story born in a completely different context. From the literary point of view, the addition was necessary, not only to create a double to Dan 2 and complete the first section, but also to prepare the transition to the second section of the document. Not accidentally, the beginning of Dan 8 would explicitly refer to the previous chapter: "a vision appeared to me, Daniel, after the one that had appeared to me at first" (8:1).

The conscious insertion of Dan 7 at the conclusion of the first section of the document has dramatic consequences on the theological level. The narrative breaks abruptly with the too idyllic descriptions of the previous chapters, the dream taking on the disturbing traits of a nightmare. Dan 7 delivers something that seems to fracture the very universality of the stated principle of God's unchallenged sovereignty. It is prophesied that an "iniquitous" king will come who "shall speak words against the Most High" and "wear out the holy ones of the Most High" (7:25; cf. 7:8). At that time, however brief it may be, God will not intervene.

Collins rightly notes that "in the context of the Book of Daniel as a whole, it is natural enough that chap. 2 should have been read in the light of chap. 7."[20] Dan 7 corrects the "deferred eschatology" of Dan 2 and introduces a sense of urgency and drama. However, the opposite is also true: the concentric arrangement requires also that Dan 7 be read in the light of Dan 2 and of its reassuring tone. Furthermore, the structure of the document demands that Dan 7 also be read in the context of the previous chapters (in particular of Dan 4–5, of which Dan 7 constitutes half of the outer frame), not vice versa, as if the final redaction of Daniel preserved some ancient stories of the Diaspora only to pay respect to an old and outdated tradition.

In other words, Dan 7 corrects but does not invalidate the Zadokite principles that God wields supreme power over the kingdoms of the earth

20. Collins, *Daniel,* 174.

and that nothing happens outside of God's will. What is to be understood, then, is not so much why God in freedom will grant sovereignty to a gentile king, but why God will permit a power subject to God to "afflict" God's people and even show itself rebellious to God without immediately being punished. This was the challenge of the author's own times, and to meet the challenge, he would not hesitate to use the same language and the same worldview as the Enochic tradition and to nearly accept the ideas of degeneration developed by Dream Visions. Beginning with Dan 7, the reader is advised that the traditional Zadokite categories are still valid, yet need implementation. They are not sufficient to explain the new situation of Israel during the Maccabean crisis. The unshaken certainties of Zadokite Judaism, their too simplistic interpretation of the covenant, must leave room for a more sophisticated and complex analysis.

C. *The Meaning of History (Daniel 9)*

Dan 9 is the nucleus of the second section of the book (Dan 8–12), and at the center of ch. 9 is Daniel's prayer to God (9:4-19). Daniel is reflecting upon Jeremiah's prophecy regarding the time of exile (cf. Jer 25:11-12; 29:10). In the prayer Daniel lucidly shows that he knows the cause of what is happening. He confesses the transgressions of the people before a "great and awesome God, keeping covenant and steadfast love with those who love [him] and keep [his] commandments" (Dan 9:4). The people have sinned; they did not listen to the appeals of the prophets and brought down a just punishment. "The curse and the oath written in the law of Moses, the servant of God, have been poured out upon us, because we have sinned against [him]" (9:11). This explains the history that awaits Israel; God is "right" (9:14) and therefore punishes the people who have revealed themselves to be unfaithful.

The smooth style of the Hebrew text, full of traditional phrases and free of Aramaisms, makes likely that the prayer was not composed by the author of the rest of the chapter. However, evidence against the hypothesis of a secondary addition is quite strong. The fragments from Qumran have shown that the prayer belongs to a very early stage in the history of the Hebrew text.[21] Besides, the linguistic connections between the prayer and its

21. The Hebrew text of ch. 9 is attested in 4Q116 (4Qdan^{e}), which has survived in

actual context in Dan 9 are too many and too circumstantial to be merely accidental.[22] The best we can say is, with Collins, that "although the prayer was not composed for the present context, it was included purposefully by the author of Daniel 9 and was not a secondary addition."[23] The real problem therefore is not the authenticity of the prayer but its relation with the overall ideology of the document. Daniel's prayer takes texts like Neh 1:4-11; 9:6-37 or Ezra 9:5-15 as its models; it is "a communal prayer of confession, of a type widely used in the postexilic period."[24] Why was this piece of Zadokite covenantal theology included?

Among those scholars who recognize that the prayer belongs to the original composition, there is no agreement about its actual meaning. With W. Sibley Towner, Collins claims that "the content of the prayer does not represent the theology . . . of the author of the book."[25] Furthermore, Collins sees a "[sharp contrast] with the apocalyptic framework of Daniel," the Zadokite idea that "the affliction of Jerusalem is a punishment for sin and will be removed if the people repent and pray" being irreconcilable with the apocalyptic view that "the course of events is predetermined . . . and people . . . cannot change the course of events."[26] According to this interpretation, the prayer would be no more than a literary topos, "an act of piety, which is appropriate as the prayer of the one who failed to understand at the end of chap. 8," or as Lacocque says, "a sort of initiation rite" with no real significance for the theology of the book as a whole.[27]

The centrality of the prayer and its theological implications cannot be so easily dismissed, however. If the prayer of confession was such an inert topos in the Jewish literature of the Second Temple, why do we not find anything similar at the beginning of Dream Visions, where Enoch is experiencing an identical situation of dismay yet his prayer is so markedly dif-

five tiny fragments, all from Daniel's prayer. See Eugene C. Ulrich et al., *Qumran Cave 4.XI: Psalms to Chronicles,* DJD 16 (Oxford: Clarendon, 2001).

22. Bruce William Jones, "The Prayer in Daniel IX," *VT* 18 (1968): 488-93; Maurice Gilbert, "La prière de Daniel: Dn 9,4-19," *RTL* 3 (1972): 284-310.

23. Collins, *Daniel,* 348.

24. Collins, *The Apocalyptic Imagination,* 108; cf. André Lacocque, "The Liturgical Prayer in Daniel 9," *HUCA* 47 (1976): 119-42.

25. Collins, *Daniel,* 360; cf. W. Sibley Towner, "Retributional Theology in the Apocalyptic Setting," *USQR* 26 (1971): 213.

26. Collins, *The Apocalyptic Imagination,* 108-9.

27. Collins, *Daniel,* 360; and Lacocque, *The Book of Daniel,* 177.

ferent (1 En 83–84)? Furthermore, Daniel's prayer occupies a key position at the core of the second section of the book. Why should the author of Daniel have wanted to waste such an important spot to accommodate a literary topos, one that was not even consistent with his own thought?

In Dan 7 and now in Dan 9, the author of Daniel has made his point; he shares the apocalyptic worldview and accepts the Enochic idea that history is condemned to inexorable degeneration — an idea that is indeed in sharp contrast with Zadokite Judaism. Yet, in spite of any similarities, a fundamental difference makes Daniel representative of yet a different party. Daniel opposes the Enochic doctrine of superhuman origin of evil, and strenuously defends the tenets of Zadokite covenantal theology.

To Enoch, the entire course of history is revealed, from the creation until the eschatological reign. History is a drama that unfolds with humankind as both protagonist and victim. "The deeds of the people were also shown to me, each according to its type" (1 En 90:41), says Enoch at the book's conclusion. The explanation of everything that has happened, is happening, and will happen is contained in Dream Visions, which declares the superhuman origin of evil, sets the limits of human freedom, and indicates the characteristics of future salvation. The idea of causality within the unfolding of history corresponds to the Enochic idea of a world corrupted by an original sin of angels. For Dream Visions this sin effects its degenerative action in the succession of increasingly iniquitous kingdoms up until the cathartic intervention of God.

This concept appears completely extraneous to the author of Daniel. The vision of history in Daniel does not have the same comprehensive character seen in Dream Visions. The entire course of history is not revealed to Daniel, only the events that await Israel in the period immediately following the breaking of the covenant, that is, since the time in which revelation is imagined to have taken place. Nothing is said of the preceding history. Daniel's apocalyptic visions do not set themselves up as a tool for a universal and self-sufficient interpretation of reality. The events described do not make sense in themselves; their cause must be found elsewhere. We are told what is going to happen, not why.

Norman W. Porteous writes: "Without this prayer there would be something essential missing from the Book of Daniel."[28] Martin McNamara explains the role of the prayer within Dan 9: "The prayer introduces the vision

28. Norman W. Porteous, *Daniel,* OTL (Philadelphia: Westminster, 1965), 136.

of [Dan 9:]24-27 as it gives the theological reason why Israel is punished, and why the period of tribulation spoken of by Jeremiah has now been prolonged sevenfold."[29] I would say even more: without the prayer of Dan 9, the book of Daniel as a whole would lack any internal logic. The consistency of the theological message of the book depends entirely on the establishing of cause-and-effect between the Zadokite idea of covenant and the Enochic theory of degeneration of history.

We can speak, then, of historical determinism in Daniel, even though we are dealing with a *sui generis* determinism, limited to a single historical season and not to the entire course of history, the consequence of a misused opportunity to observe the covenant on the part of humankind, not of angelic sin. Despite all challenges, God's order stands firm; no rebellion in heaven has destroyed it. The evil of this world, including the evil of the "iniquitous king," has cosmic implications, but is not the result of corruption and chaotic disorder.

Nowhere in Daniel do the angels appear as rebellious against God, whose dominion they cannot challenge: "His sovereignty is an everlasting sovereignty. . . . He does what he wills with the host of heaven and . . . there is no one who can stay his hand or say to him, 'What are you doing?'" (Dan 4:34-35[31-32]). The angels protect Israel, free Daniel and his companions from every mortal danger (cf. 3:25, 28; 6:23), and above all they are the messengers of divine knowledge (Dan 4:13[10]; 7:16, 23; 8:13, 15-19; 9:21-22; 10:5-6, 9-11, 21; 12:5-9). Strikingly, in the significant context of Dan 4–5, the message of God's absolute sovereignty over creatures is entrusted to one of the "Watchers" (4:13-17, 23-27[10-14, 20-24]). Daniel obviously intends to restore the reputation of those angels, which the Enochic tradition had made protagonists of the rebellion against God.

Only on one occasion (Dan 10) does the vision present a conflict among angels. The conflict pits the guardian angel of Israel against the "prince of the kingdom of Persia" (that is, the guardian angel of Persia; 10:12-14) and then the "prince of the kingdom of Jawan" (the guardian angel of Greece; 10:20-21). But here the argument already discussed about the kingdoms is still valid; the battle among the angels corresponds to the struggle among the kingdoms, which, as we have seen, takes place by the will and under the direct control of God. The conflict is real, yet is

29. Martin McNamara, "Daniel," in *A New Catholic Commentary on Holy Scripture,* ed. Reginald C. Fuller (London: Nelson, 1969), 667.

not the result of a rebellion in heaven. The active presence of Michael ("the great prince, the protector of your people"; 12:1; cf. 10:21) guarantees that the final results will conform to God's plan. When the vision is made explicit, as always in Daniel the apocalyptic conflict dissolves as a symbolic image, and if the angels are granted an active role, it is in no way in opposition to God. The total absence of angels to be punished in the last judgment is the ultimate proof of their innocence, whereas in Dream Visions God takes revenge primarily against the rebellious angels (1 En 90:21-25) and, only by association, against human beings and their institutions (90:26-28).

We have already stressed how the author of Daniel retained from the ancient Danielic tradition the idea that sovereignty belongs to God and God has full control over the foreign nations. References to the Zadokite covenantal theology are not limited to the court tales or to Dan 9. In Dan 10–12 the conflict is between those who are loyal to the holy covenant and those who forsake it (11:22, 28, 30, 32). In Dan 8 the last days are described as the time of "wrath [Heb. *zʿm*]" (8:19), a term that in the Zadokite tradition is normally associated with "God's wrath" for the sins of Israel (see Ezek 22:24). From Deut 28:50 the reader also knows that when the prophet foretells that an iniquitous king "will arise [*ʿz pnym*]" (Dan 8:23), this applies to the nation that God will send against Israel for breaking the covenant. This understanding is strengthened by the remark that Antiochus will not act "with his [own] power" (Dan 8:24), his success depending only on the permission of God.

Not only Daniel's prayer but the overall theology of the book of Daniel is far removed from the positions of Dream Visions, in which the angelic world is seen as gone out of control and no reference whatsoever is made to the covenant, even when it would have been obvious to do so in describing Moses' ascent of Mount Sinai (1 En 89:29-33). Enoch reveals that Israel is caught by demonic forces and without divine protection, and Michael appears relegated to the passive position of onlooker — all until the time established by God for definitive intervention.

Unlike his apocalyptic colleague and competitor, the author of Daniel does not blame angels, nor does he dismiss the validity of the covenant, as the old sages of Sapiental Judaism had done before. What Daniel seeks in Jeremiah's prophecy is not the cause of the degenerative process of history, which, he already knows, is the sin of the people against the covenant, but the consequences the realization of the divine curse has on history and the individual. To pose the question about the duration of the exile means to question the possibility of a redemption of history once the punitive mechanism has been set in motion. It is to question the enduring effects of the covenant on the collective and the individual levels in the new situation in which the people find themselves — subject to the divine curse.

The angel responds to Daniel's doubts and reveals that the seventy years of Jeremiah's prophecy should in reality be understood as "seventy weeks of years" and that this span of time corresponds to the time necessary "to finish the transgression, to put an end to sin, and to atone for iniquity" (Dan 9:24).

Once again, as in Daniel's prayer, the reference is to Leviticus (Lev 26:3-45 [P]). Daniel's prayer is not the only point at which the present crisis is seen as God's punishment for the sins of Israel. The angel's answer also is consistent with the principles of Zadokite covenantal theology. According to Lev 26, "peace in the land" is one of the blessings of the covenant (26:3-13), but "if you will not obey me . . . I will set my face against you, and you shall be struck down by your enemies; your foes shall rule over you" (26:14-17). The length of the punishment is subordinated to Israel's repentance: "If in spite of these punishments you have not turned back to me, but continue hostile to me, then I too will continue hostile to you: I myself will strike you sevenfold for your sins" (Lev 26:23-24; cf. 26:18, 21, 27-28). This is exactly what happened according to Daniel. Israel "broke the covenant" (Lev 26:15) and was punished by God with 70 years of exile, as announced by the prophet Jeremiah, but then Israel in spite of this did not turn back to God but continued hostile. As a result, God multiplied the punishment "sevenfold" and the 70 years became "seventy weeks of years" (Dan 9:24). God's punishment will culminate in the coming, in the last week, of a king, who "shall make a strong covenant with many for one week, and for half of the week he shall make sacrifice and offering cease; and in their place shall be an abomination that desolates, until the decreed end is poured out upon the desolator" (Dan 9:26-27). In the present of the author of Daniel, the last "week" (spring 170 to spring 163 B.C.E.) is that inaugurated by the death of Onias III, the "anointed one [who] shall be cut off and have nothing [to help him]" (Dan 9:26). The middle of the week (around the fall equinox 167) marks the beginning of persecution of the righteous and defilement of the temple when the daily offerings were interrupted and sacrifices were offered monthly to celebrate the king's birthday (2 Macc 6:7; 1 Macc 1:59). Daniel expected the end to occur on the spring equinox of 163, after the completion of the "three and a half years," with the death of the "desolator" Antiochus (Dan 9:27).

The iniquitous king who in Dan 9 signals the climax of God's punishment is undoubtedly the same figure already introduced in Dan 7. His actions against God and God's people are identical ("he shall speak words against the Most High . . . and shall attempt to change the sacred seasons and the law"; 7:25; cf. 8:9-12, 24-26; 9:26-27; 11:28-39), as well as the duration of his apparent success ("a time, two times, and half a time"; 7:25 = 12:7; cf. 9:27) and his end (he shall "be consumed and totally destroyed"; 7:26; cf. 8:25; 9:27; 11:45). The emphasis is significant. In the two sections of Daniel two different periodizations are used: history seen phenomenologically by humankind as a succession of kingdoms ("the four kingdoms") and history seen by God as the instrument of God's punishment ("the seventy weeks"). The common figure of the "iniquitous king" allows the two periodizations to be synchronized just as the visual and aural presence of clapboards allows the image and sound of a film to be synchronized exactly. The unity of the two sections is further strengthened by the role of the number "four" as the number for punishment. Four are the times God repeats the curse in Leviticus (Lev 26:18, 21, 23-24, 27-28); four are the subdivisions of the 70 weeks (7 + 62 + half a week + half a week); four are the times of the iniquitous king's persecution ("one time, two times, half a time"); four are the kingdoms.

The connection so established between Dan 2–7 and 8–12 explains the apparent contradiction between God's supreme control over the kingdoms (emphasized in Dan 2–7, but also confirmed in Dan 9) and their iniquity (emphasized in Dan 8–12, but also announced in Dan 7). The kings are not "stray bullets," but instruments of divine punishment. Even Antiochus, whose sacrilegious actions would seem to challenge God, acts "not with his power . . . but he shall be broken, and not by human hands" (8:24-25). The death of Antiochus will mean the end of God's punishment, as well as the beginning of the everlasting kingdom of Israel.

From Lev 26 Daniel also learned that the righteous will suffer, and understood the reason of their suffering. "You shall have no power to stand against your enemies. . . . And those of you who survive shall languish in the land of your enemies . . . because of the iniquities of their ancestors" (Lev 26:37-39). The punishment will in fact have an end, but only after the 70 weeks have passed. The period is necessary to expiate the guilt, and not even a righteous generation can change the course of the events.

Lev 26, however, ended with a word of hope. If the people would recognize not only that they had broken the covenant but that they also continued to sin afterwards, at the end God will deliver them from their enemies. "If they confess their iniquity and the iniquity of their ancestors, in that they committed treachery against me and, moreover, that they continued hostile to me . . . then will I remember my covenant with Jacob . . . Isaac . . . and Abraham . . . and I will remember the land" (Lev 26:40-45). This is what Daniel says will happen at the end of the 70 weeks (Dan 9:27).

We began our discussion of Dan 9 defending the authenticity of Daniel's prayer as part of the original composition. We stressed the far-reaching implications of the passage for the overall theology of the book, as well as the consistency of the doctrine of the origin of evil as expressed both in the prayer and in the rest of the book. We can now end celebrating the unity of the entire ch. 9 of Daniel that is provided by the reference of all its parts (Daniel's prayer and the angel's interpretation included) to the same text of Lev 26. Daniel's prayer can be no longer artificially separated from the rest of Dan 9, and Dan 9 from the rest of the document. Structurally and theologically, Dan 9 plays a central role in the book of Daniel. It answers the call for meaning in history, and it does so, not referring to the Enochic myth of the fallen angels, but recalling a foundational text of the Zadokite tradition and a foundational concept of Zadokite covenantal theology — "the curse and the oath written in the law of Moses" against those who would break the covenant (9:11; Lev 26:3-45; cf. Deut 28:15-68; Exod 24:3-8).

However, identifying the time of history ("the four kingdoms") with the time of divine punishment ("the seventy weeks") also means making the end of history coincide with the end of punishment. In both periodizations the "iniquitous king" represents the last link in the chain; after that there are only the eschatological kingdom and God's forgiveness (cf. Dan 7:26-27; 12:1-3). Daniel discovers that for the people of Israel there is no redemption in history. As they broke the covenant and continued to sin even after the Babylonian exile, history is destined to be the time of God's wrath. After the divine punishment, which multiplied the 70 years of Jeremiah sevenfold, there is no more history; God's forgiveness marks the end of history.

D. *For the Sake of the Temple and the Priesthood (Daniel 8)*

Although the same story is told in Dan 8 and 10–12, it is seen from a different point of view. By John J. Collins we are reminded that "repetition of a structural pattern with variations of specific detail is a basic means of communication, well attested in myth and folklore as well as in modern communication."[30] Providing two "revelatory units" around Dan 9, the final author not only gave to Dan 8–12 the same concentric structure as Dan 2–7, but also provided a different emphasis. In Dan 8 "the primary focus of the end is the restoration of the temple cult," while Dan 10–12 "focus their hopes . . . on the resurrection of the dead."[31]

As we have seen, in Dream Visions the entire postexilic history of Israel unfolds under a demonic influence, and even the temple is not spared. The temple, whose Mosaic origins and construction by Solomon are emphatically evoked (cf. 1 En 89:36, 50), after the Babylonian destruction is also involved in the common ruin. Reconstructed "under the seventy shepherds," it can only be a contaminated temple. "They again began to build as before; and they raised up that tower which is called the high tower. But they started to place a table before the tower, with all the bread which is upon it being polluted and impure" (1 En 89:73).

The argument is drawn from an episode narrated in Mal 1:6ff. In the context of Dream Visions, however, it is raised to the level of a paradigm of the condition into which the entire worship activity of the temple has fallen. The profaning action of Antiochus IV adds nothing to an already compromised situation, and as a result, it is not even mentioned.

Daniel also looks at the postexilic period with critical eyes. The glorious age of the return from exile and of the Second Temple is not as glorious for Daniel, but "a troubled time" (Dan 9:25). The temple has been rebuilt, but as we have seen, Dan 9 rejects the Zadokite view of the restoration as the fulfillment of Jeremiah's prophecy (Ezra 1:1; 2 Chr 36:22). The Second Temple period is still a time of punishment; the exile has not yet completely ended. The author of Daniel cannot be enlisted among the supporters of the house of Zadok.

The criticism of Zadokite Judaism did not prevent Dream Visions, nor does it prevent Daniel, from acknowledging, without elaboration, the piety

30. Collins, *The Apocalyptic Imagination,* 107.

31. Collins, *Seers, Sybils and Sages,* 163.

of the murdered high priest Onias III (1 En 90:8; Dan 9:26; 11:22), in sharp contrast with the Maccabean propaganda which would ignore him entirely. Daniel sees Onias as a righteous and innocent martyr, and Dream Visions speaks of him as one of "the sheep that opened its eyes," while from the Maccabean vantage point, being righteous and losing power was an insurmontable contradiction. In order to legitimate their own power, the Maccabees had to portray themselves as righteous and winners over against the last Zadokite high priests who were losers and sinners. Neither Daniel nor Dream Visions shares this concern.

What distinguishes Daniel from Dream Visions, too, is a contrasting attitude toward the temple. In the eyes of Daniel, the cult in the temple of Jerusalem is absolutely legitimate and no religious or political event seems to have tarnished this legitimacy, either the crisis of the Zadokite priesthood or the philo-Hellenistic politics of the high priests Jason and Menelaus. The break comes only when the perpetual sacrifice is interrupted and the temple is profaned by the "abomination that desolates" (cf. Dan 8:13; 9:27; 11:31; 12:11), that is, when the very raison d'être of the Aaronite priesthood is challenged. Antiochus's intervention is presented as a sacrilegious action against God. "[He] grew as high as the host of heaven. [He] threw down to the earth some of the host and some of the stars, and trampled on them. Even against the prince of the host [he] acted arrogantly; [he] took the regular burnt offering away from him, and [overthrew their place. The sanctuary was made desert.] Because of wickedness, the host was given over to it together with the regular burnt offering; it cast truth to the ground, and kept prospering in what it did" (8:10-12; cf. 11:36-39).[32]

The interruption of the continuity of the cult and the introduction of idolatrous practices in the temple, therefore, create a qualitatively new situation. History itself is indelibly stained. From Dan 9 we learned that from the historical-political point of view these events signal the beginning of the "half week" when the "iniquitous king" will appear to triumph over the righteous (9:27). Now we see that from the perspective of the cult also these events are the beginning of a time in which the cult in the Jerusalem temple is delegitimated. "For how long is this vision concerning the continual burnt offering [to be taken away], the transgression that makes des-

32. The Masoretic text, at some points corrupted, has been reconstructed based on the Greek version of the Septuagint.

olate [to be substituted], and the giving over of the sanctuary and host to be trampled? . . . For two thousand three hundred evenings and mornings; then the sanctuary shall be restored to its rightful state" (8:13-14; cf. 8:26).

Whatever calendar, solar or lunar, Daniel may have used to calculate the length of the year, the figure of "two thousand three hundred evenings and mornings" (= 1150 days) falls short of either the "three and a half years" of Antiochus's persecution (Dan 9:27; cf. 7:25; 12:7) or the "1290–1335 days" of 12:11-12. Scholars have struggled to reconcile the data, in vain. Collins recognized the difficulty: the "figure [of 1150 days] . . . is specified as the time until the sanctuary is set right, which is not necessarily identical with the end as envisaged [elsewhere]."[33] The discrepancy is in fact intentional. In Daniel's view, the profanation of the temple is only an episode of the divine punishment. The seer expects God to restore the temple sometime before the end of times as an act of justice owed to its legitimate cult.

It is generally accepted that Dan 8 was written before the rededication of the temple, even though the figure of "2300 evenings and mornings," as Lacocque already noticed, looks too precise to be symbolic and seems to correspond to an actual time counted *post eventum*.[34] What has mostly puzzled scholars is the difficulty of relating this time to the date of the rededication of the temple, the 25th of Chislev (the ninth month of the lunar calendar), and the information given in 1 Macc 4:52-54 and in Josephus (*Ant* 12:320) that the cult was restored after "three years."

Daniel, however, was most likely using a different calendar — the 360+4-day Zadokite sabbatical calendar. In Daniel's calculation, the fall equinox of 167 B.C.E. marks the division of time at the middle of the last week of years and the beginning of Antiochus's persecution. From that time, the text asks us to count 2300 evenings and mornings. If we add such a number of "evenings and mornings" (not "days," which in the Zadokite calendar would not have included the additional times between seasons), we reach a precise day: the 27th of the eighth month of 164.[35] This is shortly before the winter equinox of 164, in the same year and in the same season in which according to the books of Maccabees and Josephus the rededication of the temple took place.

33. Collins, *Daniel*, 400.

34. Lacocque, *The Book of Daniel*, 250.

35. See Gabriele Boccaccini, "The Solar Calendars of Daniel and Enoch."

The *Megillat Ta'anit,* a list of auspicious days composed "in the first, or at the latest at the beginning of the second century A.D." between the two Jewish Wars,[36] shows that the Jewish people had preserved the memory of a happy event on the 27th of the eighth month. We read: "On the 27th (of Marchesvan, the eighth month) thereof they began again to bring the offerings of fine flour upon the altar."

The comment of the *Scholiast* does not help; it interprets the event as an episode in the conflict between the Sadducees and the Pharisees, as it usually does when it cannot understand the historical references of the *Megillat.* The only thing we learn from the *Scholiast* is that in Talmudic times the memory of the event associated with the 27th of the eighth month had been completely lost.

In his commentary on the *Megillat Ta'anit,* Solomon Zeitlin recognized that the event had to be related to "the period of the Hasmoneans," and struggled to refer it to something that may have occurred before the feast of Hanukkah. "From 1 Macc 4:42-3 we learn that after Judas cleansed the temple he chose for the temple service such priests as were qualified to officiate. According to Lev 6:13, the priests who were thus anointed had to offer the meal-offering of fine flour. . . . This, we may assume, was the cause of the holiday of the 27th of Heshvan."[37]

What Zeitlin did not contemplate was the difference between the solar calendar of Daniel and the lunar calendar of 1 and 2 Maccabees and Josephus. The date of the 27th of the eighth month appears to be a double of the 25th of Chislev. After all, this is the only occasion on which we know that the daily sacrifices were discontinued and then restored during the Second Temple period. The recognition that Daniel used the solar calendar gives strength to an intriguing possibility, that the 25th of Chislev, the ninth month of the Hellenistic calendar, was the same day as the 27th of the eighth month of the Zadokite calendar. The closeness of the dates is striking, and the fact that the lunar calendar tends to go short of the solar only reinforces this possibility.

If Daniel and the books of Maccabees likely refer to the same event, what is certainly different is the starting point of their calculations. Daniel

36. Schürer (rev. Vermes), *The History of the Jewish People,* 1:114-15.

37. Solomon Zeitlin, *Megillat Taanit as a Source for Jewish Chronology and History in the Hellenistic and Roman Periods* (Philadelphia: Jewish Publication Society of America, 1922), 78-79.

counts "2300 evenings and mornings" (1150 days) since when the daily sacrifices were interrupted. The books of Maccabees instead counted a shorter period of time, "three years" of the lunar calendar (1062 days), since when, shortly after the daily sacrifices were discontinued, on the 25th of Chislev of the newly introduced Hellenistic calendar, for the first time "the monthly celebration of the king's birthday" was observed (2 Macc 6:7) and "they offered sacrifice on the altar that was on top of the altar of burnt offering" (1 Macc 1:59).[38] Not inconsistently, Josephus agrees with the chronology of the books of Maccabees ("after three years' time, on the very same day on which their divine worship had fallen off, and was reduced to a profane and common use; for so it was, that the temple was made desolate by Antiochus, and so continued for three years"; *Ant* 12:320), and at the same time takes the day of the rededication of the temple also as the fulfillment of the "three and a half years" prophesied by Daniel (*B.J.* 1:32: "[Antiochus] spoiled the temple, and put a stop to the constant practice of offering a daily sacrifice of expiation for three years and six months").

In truth, Daniel expected the end of the final week to happen only later, around the spring equinox of 163. The book predicts a successful campaign of Antiochus in Egypt, which actually did not take place, and is very vague about the place and circumstances of the king's death, which it ignores. Daniel must have reached its present form shortly after the reestablishment of the daily sacrifices.

E. *Individual Freedom and Responsibility (Daniel 10–12)*

In Dream Visions, corruption is brought about in creation because the angels' sin directly influences the very possibility of human resistance to evil. Human freedom of choice and responsibility are not denied, yet drastically limited. Humankind is more the victim of than the doer of evil. The degeneration of history is the collective manifestation of a corruption at work against individuals on the ontological level.

Dan 9, on the contrary, has made clear that history degenerates because God has made it the instrument of punishment for the people of Israel who,

38. That 2 Macc 6:7 and 1 Macc 1:59 refer to the same event on the 25th of Chislev has been convincingly argued by VanderKam, *JSJ* 12 (1981): 52-74.

fully exercising their freedom, failed to meet the commitments of the covenant. Nothing intervened to modify human ability to choose; human beings were and remain free. However, if the times of history are now fixed, if every possibility to modify them has been denied, and if salvation depends solely on an act of God's mercy at the end of the 70 weeks of punishment, it is worth asking what sense there is to the notion that human beings continue to enjoy a state of freedom. Breaking the link between freedom and salvation means denying the very presuppositions of a covenantal theology. Does unleashing the divine curse signal the end of the covenant itself?

Daniel confronts this problem in the last part of the book (Dan 10–12). The author brings into operation a clear distinction between the corporate and the individual dimensions of guilt and salvation. In condemning history, God has collectively punished the people for a sin committed collectively. Historical determinism makes the individual powerless. Everything is in the hands of God, there is nothing that at this point humans can do; neither prayer nor repentance is effective to change the course of history which is determined by forces totally beyond human control.

However, judgment of the individual has not yet been pronounced, and will not be pronounced until the end of time, when everyone living and dead will be called individually to answer for their own actions before the divine tribunal. The collective guilt does not condemn the individual, nor will the individual be saved by God's forgiveness. Individual salvation will not necessarily correspond to collective salvation; the time that history and the people are redeemed will be also the time of judgment for the individual. Coherently, at the announcement of God's collective forgiveness ("at that time your people shall be delivered"; Dan 12:1a), Daniel follows immediately with a proposition that limits the effects of the divine intervention on the individual level ("everyone who is found written in the book [shall be delivered]"; 12:1b). The various destinies to which each person is brought by the resurrection are then indicated: "Many of those who sleep in the dust of the earth shall awake, some to everlasting life, and some to shame and everlasting contempt" (12:2).

The idea of resurrection certainly emerges within the Zadokite tradition from the process of progressive deduction from human verification of God's retributory work, as it appears already carried to its (pen)ultimate consequences by Ben Sira.[39] This is made even more necessary,

39. Ben Sira pointedly denies any possibility of life after death, but his discourse

however, by the ecology of Daniel's thought. In this way our author can restore meaning to individual freedom as well as saving value to the covenant.

The distinction brought about between the collective and individual dimensions of salvation and guilt also allows a different meaning to be given to the suffering that inevitably comes with a history seen as punishment. On the collective level this suffering is the expiation of a collectively committed sin. On the individual level it becomes the context within which human beings are called to demonstrate their faithfulness to the covenant. Those who succumb will be damned; those who persevere will be rewarded.

The idea of suffering as a test was already a part of the heritage of Zadokite Judaism; Ben Sira made it an element of the pedagogical design of wisdom (cf. Sir 4:11-19). In Daniel suffering returns to being primarily a consequence of guilt. Even though individuals are innocent because they did not personally commit the sin, as part of an unfaithful collective they must suffer the consequences of collective guilt. The time of wrath and punishment is, therefore, also the time of expiation and testing. The protests of Job and the skepticism of Qoheleth by now belong to a distant past. From contradiction and scandal, the suffering of the righteous has become the norm of existence.

Every space for earthly retribution will progressively be reduced until, with the coming of the "iniquitous king," only "sword and flame . . . captivity and plunder" await the righteous (Dan 11:33). The only choice will be between apostasy and obedience to the covenant, a heroic obedience carried even to self-sacrifice. The iniquitous king "shall seduce with intrigue those who violate the covenant; but the people who are loyal to their God shall stand firm and take action" (11:32).

Politically, Daniel voices the persecuted "sages" of Israel (Dan 11:33-35; 12:3) and shows the utmost contempt against "those who forsake the holy covenant" (11:30), the apostates who make themselves accomplices to the "iniquitous king" Antiochus IV (cf. 1 En 90:7, 16; Dan 11:30). In this

---

on retribution already prevents humankind from verifying God's action because it makes a "good death" and an everlasting memory the true compensation for the righteous. See the previous chapter. Cf. G. W. E. Nickelsburg, *Resurrection, Immortality, and Eternal Life in Intertestamental Judaism,* HTS 26 (Cambridge, Mass.: Harvard University Press, 1972).

respect, the attitude of Daniel is objectively coincident with that of the Hasmoneans (cf. 1 Macc 2:15-26). Daniel's commitment to the Maccabean Revolt had to be conditioned, however, by the distrust that it felt toward the possibility of a human intervention capable of modifying the course of events from within. Because of the unleashing of the divine curse, human responsibility toward history has been suspended; opposing it means opposing divine punishment. The only alternative is that of passive resistance, followed and suffered by each individual. The "iniquitous king," as we have seen, "shall be broken, and not by human hands" (Dan 8:25; cf. 2:34).

This position is difficult to reconcile with the activism (the zeal for the Law) of the Maccabees, whose political action is, in effect, completely disregarded. "Without any doubt," writes Gerhard von Rad, "the writer of Daniel sides with those who endure persecution rather than those who take up arms against it, and in so doing he is only being true to his own basic conviction that what must be will be. He is far removed from the Maccabees and their policy of active resistance; their large following is actually suspect in his eyes."[40]

In many ways Daniel's position is closer to that of Dream Visions. Both agree that the eschatological kingdom will be exclusively God's work and that any messianic claim on the part of human beings is to be excluded. This insight is significant; it is most likely that the first Hasmoneans were not entirely insensitive to describing their actions in messianic terms.[41] In Dream Visions a sort of messiah appears only after the establishment of the eschatological kingdom and divine judgment — events in which he does not appear to be involved (cf. 1 En 90:37-38). In Daniel there is no individual messiah; the "son of man" is "the angelic or supernatural counterpart" of the people of Israel, to whom God has entrusted sovereignty (cf. Dan 7:13-14, 18, 27).[42] In any case, the "son of man" is present only after judgment and is limited to receiving that which God has prepared as a gift.

40. Gerhard von Rad, *Old Testament Theology* (New York: Harper & Row, 1965), 2:315.

41. It is not difficult, for example, to make out messianic traits in the eulogy of Simon (1 Macc 14:4-15), although within the framework of an eschatology fulfilled within the confines of history.

42. Collins, *The Apocalyptic Imagination,* 103.

However, the judgment Daniel and Dream Visions express on the political life of their time remains radically different. Unlike Daniel, Dream Visions' perspective is more disposed to allow room for the elect to act as instruments of social change. As a result, the figure of Judas Maccabeus (the "sheep" on which "one great horn sprouted"; 1 En 90:9) acquires a certain relevance. His coming appears to be a fundamental step in the process of preparing God's intervention, and his success is a sure sign of election. The angel Michael has finally abandoned his passive role to deploy himself at Judas's side (cf. 1 En 90:14). Judas Maccabeus is, therefore, an instrument of God's wrath, used by God to rout the impious just before the erection of the thrones and the final judgment.

In the words of Reid, Daniel represents "the revolutionist/nonresistant apocalypticism, which understands that social change must be exclusively the work of God. . . . On the other hand, there is a utopian/activist apocalypticism which also acknowledges that social change must originate with God, but goes on to stress that the community of faith must help implement God's eschatological promises, such as found in the apocalypses of Enoch." Whereas for Dream Visions "God and the community are instruments of social change," for Daniel God "is the sole instrument of social change."[43]

It is significant that in the context of Dan 10–12, Daniel returns explicitly and repeatedly to speaking about the "covenant," or the "holy covenant" (Heb. *bryt; bryt qwds;* Dan 11:22, 28, 30[bis], 32). The reference in Dan 9 was to the covenant as the remote and irrevocable source of the curse for the entire community; Dan 10–12 restates its enduring validity as a "measure" of human responsibility. The covenant marks the boundaries of apostasy and obedience. In the concrete choice between the two ways, human beings put their freedom into action and construct their own salvation.

Consistent in its distinction between the collective and individual dimensions of guilt and salvation, Daniel speaks of the judgment on two occasions (Dan 7 and 12). In Dan 7 the judgment is seen in its collective dimension of salvation; sovereignty has been taken away from the kingdoms and entrusted forever to Israel. In this dimension, the judgment signals God's last intervention in history, signifying the manifestation of God's forgiveness and the end of punishment, as is clarified in the second section of Daniel. The definitiveness of the divine decision is emphasized: "the

43. Reid, 133-34.

[fourth] beast was put to death, and its body destroyed and given over to be burned with fire," in contrast to the three preceding beasts, whose "lives were prolonged for a season and a time" (7:11-12).[44]

In Dan 12:1-3, on the other hand, the judgment is presented in its ambivalent individual dimension: salvation for the righteous and condemnation for the unrighteous. Recompense and punishment give meaning to the individual's attitude in facing history. This well explains the insistence on individual resurrection and on the personal nature of the judgment: each person will be called to answer for his or her own actions. At judgment day, the sufferings of the righteous will be redeemed and their perseverance rewarded by resurrection, "those who are wise shall shine like the brightness of the firmament . . . like the stars forever and ever" (Dan 12:3). The wicked instead will be condemned to annihilation, "to shame and everlasting contempt" (12:2).

Perseverance in the test is affirmed as the principal virtue, decisive for salvation. In light of the hope of resurrection, even martyrdom has a rationale, and the death of the righteous in the persecution is no longer a scandal. The book, in fact, ends with a general invitation to persevere and the promise of resurrection and future recompense for the "righteous" Daniel. In a brief appendix (Dan 12:5-13), which concludes both the second section and the entire book, the predetermined duration of history is confirmed. The persecution of the "iniquitous king" will last, as announced in 7:25 and 9:27, three and a half years, "a time, two times, and half a time" (12:7). The moment that the difference in individual destiny is noted ("Many shall be purified, cleansed, and refined, but the wicked shall continue to act wickedly"; 12:10), the times are unexpectedly lengthened, passing in rapid succession, first to 1290 days ("From the time that the regular burnt offering is taken away and the abomination that desolates is set up, there shall be one thousand two hundred ninety days"; 12:11), then to 1335 days ("Happy are those who persevere and attain the thousand three hundred thirty-five days!"; 12:12).

This dissonance of times has never failed to trouble the commentators. Some have maintained that these are two variant calculations of the

44. The text indicates an imprecise yet historically defined period when the "beasts" (the reigns), although deprived of any power over Israel, continue to exist before disappearing completely from history. No "prolongation of life" will be granted, however, to the "fourth beast" because its end marks the end of history itself.

three and a half years — a thesis that Collins dismisses as unconvincing, "as if the author were doing multiple calculations for their own sake."[45] Since Hermann Gunkel, it has become a sort of commonplace to talk of later additions that were inserted with the intention of justifying the "delay of the end," when the end did not come at the time originally expected but faith rose above disappointment.[46] Collins agrees: "When one predicted number of days had elapsed, a glossator revised the prediction with a higher number."[47]

The hypothesis, which is not supported by any ancient variants or versions, rests on the presupposition that the figure of 1290 days must be a first attempt to calculate the three and a half years, while it so obviously exceeds any possible calculation by any known ancient calendar, solar or lunar. If the issue was in fact the delay of the end, we must face the paradox of a book that over the span of no more than three or four months was updated not once but twice, the second time certainly less than 45 days after the first updating, and yet left an amazingly homogeneous literary tradition in the history of its transmission. For Porteous, the case is plagued with perplexities: "There is, it must be confessed, some difficulty in seeing how urgent corrections, such as these would be, could have been added to a book that had just been issued, even though in a limited number of copies."[48] The glossator then was such a bungler: contrary to all rules of decency and discretion that would have required a correction by emendation, he did his best to make his disappointment as manifest as possible to his readers. "That both vv. 11 and 12 should be permitted to remain in the text is sufficient commentary on this rather unadroit explanation."[49] It is time to give back the notion of the delay of the end to New Testament theology, from where it comes and to which it more properly belongs.

There is no reason to speak of later additions. Every time Daniel refers to the time of God's wrath between the desecration of the temple and the end of history, it gives the figure of "a time, two times, and half a time"

45. Collins, *Daniel,* 401.

46. Hermann Gunkel, *Schöpfung und Chaos in Urzeit und Endzeit: Eine religionsgeschichtliche Untersuchung über Gen 1 und Ap Joh 12* (Göttingen: Vandenhoeck & Ruprecht, 1895), 269.

47. Collins, *Daniel,* 401.

48. Porteous, *Daniel,* 172.

49. Robert A. Anderson, *Signs and Wonders: A Commentary on the Book of Daniel,* ITC (Grand Rapids: Wm. B. Eerdmans, 1984), 153.

(Dan 7:25; 12:7), which 9:27 makes explicit as "half of the week [of years]," that is, "three and a half years." In both halves of the outer frame around Dan 9, instead, we face slightly different chronological indications, one approximate by deficiency (the "2300 evenings and mornings" of 8:14) and the other by excess (the 1290–1335 days of 12:11-12). The harmonious distribution of chronological indications in the book of Daniel is evidence of a skillful plan; obviously, the author expected some events to happen immediately before and immediately after the end of history. As we have already noted, the time in Dan 8 makes sense as reference to the reestablishment of the temple sacrifices, which is a sign of the legitimacy of the temple's cult. The times in Dan 12 instead refer to the final judgment of the individual. The chronological setting of the event, exceeding the limits of history to include the beginning of the new times, only serves to reaffirm what we have highlighted as one of the central points of the author's theology, that is, the independence of the collective and individual dimensions of guilt and salvation. The goal is to emphasize the centrality of perseverance for the individual and the personal liability of the individual independent of the destiny of the people of Israel as a whole. The almost careless, yet ingenious mechanism of progressive lengthening of the times of the individual judgment fits well in the theology of the author more than in the concerns of any elusive glossator.

There may be an even more subtle explanation why in Dan 12 the author chose those apparently unrelated figures of 1290 and 1335 days. Evidence strongly suggests that Daniel must have used the old Zadokite sabbatical calendar of 360+4 days, in which solstices and equinoxes were not counted as "days" but as "intercalary times" between seasons.[50] At the end of the 1st century C.E., the Revelation of John still preserves memory of this calendar and consistently calculates the three and a half years of Daniel's prophecy as "1260 days" (Rev 11:3; 12:6).

The 360+4–day calendar allows us to establish a sensible correlation among the three calendrical references in Dan 12. If we add exactly one month (30 days) to the three and a half years (1260 days), we reach the 1290 days of 12:11, which in turn become 1335 days in 12:12 with the further addition of one and a half months (45 days). What modern interpreters have mistaken as evidence for the "delay of the end" might more likely refer to the desire to link the individual judgment to a meaningful day in

50. See Boccaccini, "The Solar Calendars of Daniel and Enoch."

the liturgical calendar. Daniel asks the individuals to look beyond the end of history, after the time in which God would set an end to the "70 weeks" of punishment and, with the first judgment, establish the everlasting kingdom of Israel. By skillfully exploiting the richness of the cultic calendar, the text depicts a sort of spiritual itinerary of preparation for the individual. First, one month is given, the month of Passover, so that 1290 days are completed. Then, one and a half more months are added (1335 days) to reach the third month, which according to the Zadokite calendar was the "month of the oaths" (2 Chr 15:10-15; cf. Jubilees). And after three and half months of celebration, with the 15th of the third month being the feast of Shevuot, what date could be more appropriate than the feast of the renewal of the covenant for the celebration of the final judgment?

The author of Daniel foretold that the end of the final week would happen around the spring equinox of 163 B.C.E. and the individual judgment would be fulfilled by the summer of the same year, in the first quarter of what we could call the first year of the new age. That the events went differently than he expected did not cause much trouble, nor did the delay of the end keep a restless glossator awake for months before he set his mind at peace. Daniel had accomplished its major goal: to give to history a meaningful sense for which people could live and die. Daniel was neither the first nor the last apocalyptic book to accomplish this task and then survive triumphantly over its failed predictions.

SUMMARY AND CONCLUSION

The search for the roots of Rabbinic Judaism in pre-Maccabean times is not a search for rabbis, rabbi-like leaders, pseudo-rabbis, or elusive and disembodied oral traditions. Extant documents from the Second Temple period do not support the ideological reconstruction the sages offered of their own origins in *'Abot.* Centuries-old bricks were indeed used in the construction of the rabbinic building, but Rabbinic Judaism was other than the old, uncompromisingly conservative movement it claimed to be. It was a reform and relatively young group of sages who creatively built up their fortunes upon the foundations others had laid before them. There were no rabbinic traditions or institutions in the early Second Temple period, and no rabbis to carry them out, but priests and wise, Aaronites and levites, Zadokites and Enochians. From extant sources a very different society emerges from that idealized in rabbinic literature: a society centered on the temple, not on the Torah; dominated by a priestly aristocracy, not by a lay institution of scholars; preoccupied with the stability and regularity of worship, not with the transmission of oral traditions.

The early Second Temple period had an undisputed protagonist whose role the sages struggled to downplay — the house of Zadok. Members of this priestly family controlled without interruption the Jerusalem temple up to the eve of the Maccabean revolt. They were the first editors, keepers, and interpreters of that Torah on which the sages would claim to have had exclusive control since its Mosaic inception.

Many centuries before the emergence of the rabbinic movement, the Zadokites had been themselves at the center of a similar revolution that reshaped the past of Israel in order to validate their rise to power. The Zadokite historiography presents the "reconstruction" of the Jerusalem temple after the Babylonian exile as the triumphant restoration of the preexilic order, or, better, of the Sinaitic order. Where ancient sources stress continuity, however, modern scholars see discontinuity and innovation, if not evidence of a coup d'etat.

The priest Joshua, who presided at the dedication of the new temple, was not the lucky scion of a noble dynasty of high priests to regain the position his family had been deprived of for some time. He was the first high priest to come to power in the history of Israel. His authority was not the natural result of an established tradition but the outcome of a ruthless struggle for supremacy that during the Babylonian exile and the early Persian period opposed the house of Zadok to the Davidic monarchy and to the other priestly families of Israel.

The balance of power within the Jewish people was dramatically altered. The returnees imposed their hegemony over the remainees, the peoples of the land and their leaders — the Tobiads of Ammon and the Sanballats of Samaria. With the fall of the last king of Judah, Zerubbabel, the house of David lost any political visibility and the Davidic prophets their religious authority; the priesthood of the Zadokites promptly preempted the monarchic and prophetic prerogatives. It took a much longer time to find a new balance within the priesthood that would enlarge the foundations of the Zadokite power without diminishing their supremacy. The hierarchy of high priests, priests, and levites was the result of struggle and ruthless exclusions, which the Priestly writing barely hides behind the Sinaitic view of a natural genealogical succession of "sons of Levi," "sons of Aaron," and "sons of Phinehas." Tensions gradually resulted in accommodation and compromise in which the majority of priestly groups found stability and mutual advantage.

Zadokite theology offered a framework of stability and order centered around the temple sacrificial system and the notion of personal responsibility and accountability. The Zadokites saw themselves as the faithful keepers of God's creative order, established through a coherent system of graded purity and maintained under God's omnipotent and unchallenged control.

In spite of its accomplishment and undeniable authority, however, the Zadokite hegemony was not without its critics. The Samaritan schism had tremendous and lasting consequences for the definition of Jewish identity.

The Tobiads, although temporarily alienated, remained a significant political power. The legacy of the prophets never died off. But more important for the future developments of Jewish thought as well as for our search of rabbinic origins is the challenge that two internal movements of opposition posited to the Zadokite order. Enochic Judaism and Sapiential Judaism are the modern names we give to these movements.

In the name of God's goodness, the priestly opposition of the Enochians challenged the idea that evil was a necessary component of God's order. They saw God's creative order being disrupted by a rebellion in heaven and the earth fall prey to the same chaotic forces God had struggled to contain. The idea of a superhuman origin of evil provided an explanation for the alienation they felt from the priestly society built by the Zadokites as well as satisfaction for their feelings of frustration and exclusion. The priestly order, of which the Zadokites boast themselves to be the holy keepers, was in their eyes nothing but a sinister parody of God's creative order.

Sapiential Judaism challenged the Zadokite idea of covenantal relationship between God and humankind. Experience showed the wise that there was no perfect harmony between the wisdom of God's creative order and the Mosaic covenant as interpreted by the Zadokites. While sharing the priestly idea of order and stability, the wise would rather emphasize God's unlimited freedom and omnipotence to act for the supreme good of the universe and not only to react to human behavior under the constraints of the covenant.

The tripartition of Jewish thought in the Persian period among Zadokites, Enochians, and the wise corresponds to the sociological structure of the Jewish society (or, better, of its upper class). The house of Zadok and their Aaronite allies dominated the temple but not without internal struggle and challenges by those who were excluded. The Zadokites controlled the religious life and institutions of Judah, but could not prevent an autonomous and cosmopolitan administration of educated laypeople from continuing to flourish and be nurtured under the protection of the foreign king.

In an assessment of the contribution given by these ancient Judaisms to the rise of the rabbinic movement, there can be no doubt that Rabbinic Judaism had its roots neither in the skeptical wisdom of Job, Jonah, and Qoheleth nor in the priestly opposition of the Enochians. It was the theology of Zadokite Judaism which offered to the sages the basic, covenantal framework of their system of thought and the idea that God's will was embodied in a book — the Mosaic Torah. It would take a long journey and many steps, however, before the rabbinic building would take its shape.

Zadokite, Enochic, and Sapiential Judaism maintained their distinct identities down to the early Hellenistic period, as long as the structure of Jewish society remained unaltered. While the opposition of the Enochians would never be reabsorbed, sources signal that a first, significant development occurred prior to the Maccabean revolt.

The Ptolemaic system of tax-farming broke the balance between the religious and the secular powers by giving actual political supremacy to those who were the quickest to take advantage of the new possibilities of Hellenistic economy. In the 3rd cent. B.C.E., the rising Tobiads forced the Zadokites to a compromise, which was political and economical but also ideological as it implied the acceptance by the priesthood of the basic demands of Sapiential Judaism. The twist had a lasting impact on the development of Zadokite Judaism, and from the perspective of hindsight it was a major step in the definition of what we now call Rabbinic Judaism. The works of Tobit and Ben Sira paved the path to a rapprochement between Wisdom and Torah, which made the traditions of the wise based on experience acquire a recognized status along with the book of Moses.

The Maccabean revolt sees a further, important step in the gradual evolution of a protorabbinic tradition. The book of Daniel signals the emergence of "a third way" between Enochic and Zadokite Judaism. Daniel freely assumed themes and forms of the Enochic tradition while inserting them in an ideological context that denies them many of their original characteristics and draws them into the sphere of a covenantal theology.

With the Enochic Dreams Visions, Daniel shares the same apocalyptic worldview and accepts the idea that history is condemned to inexorable degeneration and then must have an end and a new beginning — a perspective that was in sharp contrast with the Ẓadokite idea of order and stability. Daniel, however, opposed the Enochic doctrine of the superhuman origin of evil and strenuously defended the tenets of Zadokite Judaism: the covenant (based on the Mosaic Torah) and the legitimacy of the Second Temple.

The contribution of Daniel was certainly not without consequences for the principles of Zadokite Judaism. The centrality of the covenant was reconfirmed only through courageous choices and painful renunciations by making a sharp distinction between corporate and individual retribution. Humankind preserves its freedom and denies evil any autonomy, yet accepts life in a history condemned to inexorable degeneration ("the four kingdoms"). The idea of the resurrection, on the one hand, solves a problem that had tormented generations from Job to Sirach, by removing God's judgment from the scrutiny of human experience; on the other hand, it painfully distances the hope of seeing merit compensated and guilt punished from the horizons of human existence. The protests of Job and Jonah and the skepticism of Qoheleth belong to a distant past. From contradiction and scandal, the suffering of the righteous has become the norm of their existence.

It is certainly with great caution that one may label Daniel as the first protorabbinic text. The boundaries of the apocalyptic group that produced Daniel were not yet so well defined. The text itself was open to diametrically opposite interpretations.

Because of its covenantal theology and its anti-Enochic stance, Daniel could be easily reinterpreted in light of traditional Zadokite principles, as were Baruch or 1 Maccabees. It was enough to claim that a new righteous and successful generation was about to arise or had in fact arisen to replace the old, sinful generation. Degeneration of history and suffering belong to the past. Prompted by human righteousness and repentance, God's forgiveness has once again re-established the eternal order of the covenant, following the deserved time of punishment.

Because of its apocalyptic worldview and its anti-Zadokite stance, Daniel easily lent itself to be reinterpreted in light of the Enochic principles, as proved by the presence of an abundant pseudo-Danielic literature within the Dead Sea Scrolls. It was sufficient to add a few elements so that the "seventy weeks" and the "four kingdoms" were adapted from a special period of punishment for humans breaking the law into the final era in the comprehensive degeneration of history provoked by angelic forces.

Yet the attempt made by neo-Zadokite and neo-Enochic documents to bring Daniel back to their own traditions cannot obscure the profound originality of Daniel's thought.

The modifications introduced by Daniel into the Zadokite system were essential in initiating that trajectory of thought that would ultimately give birth to Rabbinic Judaism. The book of Daniel opened a breach between the Zadokite system (which had already been enriched by absorbing important elements from Sapiential Judaism) and the Enochic system. The confrontation between these two mutually exclusive forms of Judaism had characterized the history of Jewish thought in the early Second Temple period. A "third way" was now possible, and it is in this area that rabbinic origins must be located.

Behind the mythical construction of an unchangeable Judaism, the rabbinic tradition itself preserves reliable records of its roots. The Hebrew Bible is the highest tribute the rabbis could offer to the role of the ancient Jerusalem priesthood. The rabbinic canon accepted all the ancient documents of Zadokite Judaism while rejecting the literary products of their priestly adversaries, even erasing the memory of Enochic Judaism. The acceptance of texts from Sapiential Judaism also reflects the indirect and tortuous way in which the tradition of the wise came to join the Zadokite tradition. Proverbs, Job, and Jonah had already been well "digested" within the Zadokite theology and so would be in the rabbinic system. Not suprisingly, some discussions involved the text that since its appearence had been the most controversial, Qoheleth, at least until the sages provided the happy ending the Sapiential document never intended to have.

As for Tobit and Sirach, that is, the two documents that more directly were protagonists of the rapprochement between Wisdom and Torah, they would not find their way into the rabbinic canon, and so their role in rabbinic origins would not be openly acknowledged, even though they remained highly influential and esteemed among the sages. There is some rationale, however, even in this ironical and ambiguous destiny. The synthesis Tobit and Sirach provided opened the path to the rabbinic synthesis, yet from the perspective of hindsight their theologies appeared primitive and obsolete, completely superseded by the rabbinic synthesis. As often happens to the closest precursors, Tobit and Ben Sira would be dismissed for not having done enough, much more than praised for what they accomplished.

In contrast, the covenantal Daniel was accepted without reserve in the rabbinic canon of scriptures. The sages skilfully downplayed its most radical, apocalyptic views by denying Daniel the title and role of "prophet," but would never forget what they owed to this revolutionary text. By introducing the ideas of resurrection and the end time and final judgment, and stressing the distinction between collective and individual retribution, Daniel provided the necessary keys for reinterpreting creatively all the previous documents of Zadokite tradition and opening the Zadokite system to substantial implementation.

What followed Daniel was a long period of gestation, a troubled period of experimentation, out of which a new creature had to take its shape after experiencing all the formless stages of growth of the newborn. To none of these preliminary stages (which were, however, all crucial for the growth of the new system) would Rabbinic Judaism ever ascribe any dignity. They were dismissed as miscarriages, and the documents that were produced in the process were disregarded as marginal, sectarian, and apocryphal. The myth of the orality of the rabbinic tradition served to make the Mishnah shine in its unique relation with the old Scripture and hide the pains of a difficult gestation. Behind the four centuries of "silence" from Daniel to the Mishnah there was a time of greatest creativity, on both the intellectual and the literary levels — the glorious and yet so neglected period of rabbinic origins.

BIBLIOGRAPHY

A. Methodological Foundations of Intellectual History

Abbagnano, Nicola. "Il lavoro storiografico in filosofia." *Rivista di filosofia* 46 (1955): 4-16.

——— et al. *Verità e storia: Un dibattito sul metodo della storia della filosofia.* Asti: Arethusa, 1956.

Barker, Charles A. "Needs and Opportunities in American Social and Intellectual History." *PHR* 20 (1951): 1-9.

Baumer, Franklin L. "Intellectual History and Its Problems." *JMH* 21 (1949): 191-203.

Birkos, Alexander S., and Lewis A. Tambs. *Historiography, Method, History Teaching: A Bibliography of Books and Articles in English, 1965-1973.* Hamden: Linnet, 1975.

Boas, George. *The History of Ideas: An Introduction.* New York: Scribner, 1969.

———. "Bias and the History of Ideas." *JHI* 25 (1964): 451-57.

———, ed. *Studies in Intellectual History.* Baltimore: Johns Hopkins University Press, 1953.

———. "The History of Philosophy." In *Philosophic Thought in the United States and France,* ed. Marvin Farber. Buffalo: State University of New York Press, 1950, 389-404.

———. "The History of Philosophy." In *Naturalism and the Human Spirit,* ed. Yervant H. Krikorian. New York: Columbia University Press, 1944, 133-53.

Bréhier, Émile. *La philosophie et son passé.* Paris: Presses universitaires de France, 1940.

———. "La causalité en histoire de la philosophie." *Theoria* 4 (1938): 97-116.

———. "The Formation of Our History of Philosophy." In Raymond Klibansky and Herbert J. Paton, *Philosophy and History,* 159-72.

Calogero, Guido. "On the So-called Identity of History and Philosophy." In Raymond Klibansky and Herbert J. Paton, *Philosophy and History,* 35-52.

Castelli, Enrico, ed. *La philosophie de l'histoire de la philosophie.* Rome: Istituto di studi filosofici, 1956.

Cristofolini, Paolo, ed. *La storia della filosofia come problema.* Pisa: Scuola normale superiore, 1988.

Croce, Benedetto."Il concetto filosofico della storia della filosofia." *Il carattere della filosofia moderna.* Bari: Laterza, 1941, 52-71.

Danto, Arthur C. *Narration and Knowledge.* New York: Columbia University Press, 1985.

———. *Analytical Philosophy of History.* Cambridge: Cambridge University Press, 1965.

Dauenhauer, Bernard P., ed. *At the Nexus of Philosophy and History.* Athens: University of Georgia Press, 1987.

Derrida, Jacques. *Dissemination.* Chicago: University of Chicago Press, 1981.

———. *Of Grammatology.* Baltimore: Johns Hopkins University Press, 1976.

Dupré, Louis. "Is the History of Philosophy Philosophy?" *Review of Metaphysics* 42 (1989): 463-82.

Edel, Abraham, Paul Oskar Kristeller, and Philip P. Wiener. "A Symposium on the History of Thought." *JHI* 7 (1946): 355-73.

Foucault, Michel. *The Archaeology of Knowledge.* New York: Pantheon, 1972.

French, Peter A., Theodore E. Uehling, and Howard K. Wettstein, eds. *Contemporary Perspectives on the History of Philosophy.* Minneapolis: University of Minnesota Press, 1983.

Gadamer, Hans-Georg. *Truth and Method.* New York: Seabury, 1975.

Garin, Eugenio. "Filosofia e storia della storiografia filosofica." In *La storiografia filosofica e la sua storia,* ed. Giovanni Santinello. Padova: Antenore, 1982, 39-52.

———. "Questioni di storiografia filosofica." *RCSF* 29 (1974): 448-52.

———. "Discussioni di storiografia filosofica." *RCSF* 26 (1971): 340-42.

———. "Ancora sulla storia della filosofia e del suo metodo." *RCSF* 14 (1960): 373-90, 521-35.

———. *La filosofia come sapere storico.* Bari: Laterza, 1959.

———. "Osservazioni preliminari a una storia della filosofia. *GCFI* 38 (1959): 1-55.

———. "L'unità nella storiografia filosofica." *RCSF* 11 (1956): 206-17.

Gracia, J. J. E. *Philosophy and Its History: Issues in Philosophical Historiography.* Albany: State University of New York Press, 1992.

Greene, John C. "Objectives and Methods in Intellectual History."*MVHR* 44/1 (1957-58): 58-74.

Hare, Peter H., ed. *Doing Philosophy Historically.* Buffalo: Prometheus, 1988.

Harlan, David. "Intellectual History and the Return of Literature." *AHR* 94 (1989): 581-609.

———. "Reply to David Hollinger." *AHR* 94 (1989): 622-26.

Higham, John. "Intellectual History and Its Neighbors." *JHI* 15 (1954): 339-47.

———. "The Rise of American Intellectual History." *AHR* 56 (1951): 453-71.

——— and Paul K. Conkin, eds. *New Directions in American Intellectual History.* Baltimore: Johns Hopkins University Press, 1979.

Hollinger, David A. "Discourse about Discourse about Discourse? A Response to Dominick LaCapra." *IHN* 13 (1991): 15-18.

———. "The Return of the Prodigal: The Persistence of Historical Knowing." *AHR* 94 (1989): 610-21.

———. *In the American Province: Studies in the History and Historiography of Ideas.* Bloomington: Indiana University Press, 1985.

Jay, Martin. *Force Fields: Between Intellectual History and Cultural Critique.* London: Routledge, 1993.

Kelley, Donald R. *Faces of History: Historical Inquiry from Herodotus to Herder.* New Haven: Yale University Press, 1998.

———. *The History of Ideas: Canon and Variations.* Rochester: University of Rochester Press, 1990.

———. "What Is Happening to the History of Ideas?" *JHI* 51 (1990): 3-25.

———. "Horizons of Intellectual History: Retrospect, Circumspect, Prospect." *JHI* 48 (1987): 143-69.

King, Preston, ed. *The History of Ideas: An Introduction to Method.* London: Helm, 1984.

Klibansky, Raymond, and Herbert J. Paton, eds. *Philosophy and History: Essays Presented to Ernst Cassirer.* 1936; repr. New York: Harper & Row, 1963.

Kristeller, Paul Oskar. "Philosophy and Its Historiography." *JP* 82 (1985): 618-25.

———. "History of Philosophy and History of Ideas." *JHP* 2 (1964): 1-14.

———. "The Philosophical Significance of the History of Thought." *JHI* 7 (1946): 360-66.

LaCapra, Dominick. "Canons and Their Discontents." *IHN* 13 (1991): 3-14.

———. "A Review of a Review." *JHI* 49 (1988): 677-87.

———. "Intellectual History and Defining the Present as 'Postmodern.'" In *Innovation/Renovation: New Perspectives on the Humanities,* ed. Ihab Hassan and Sally Hassan. Madison: University of Wisconsin Press, 1983, 47-63.

———. *Rethinking Intellectual History: Texts, Contexts, Language.* Ithaca: Cornell University Press, 1983.

——— and Steven L. Kaplan, eds. *Modern European Intellectual History: Reappraisals and New Perspectives.* Ithaca: Cornell University Press, 1982.

Lamprecht, Sterling P. "Historiography of Philosophy." *JP* 36 (1939): 449-60.

Lavine, T. Z., and Victor Tejera, eds. *History and Anti-History in Philosophy.* Dordrecht: Kluwer Academic, 1989.

Lemon, Michael C. *The Discipline of History and the History of Thought.* London: Routledge, 1995.

Lovejoy, Arthur O. *Essays in the History of Ideas.* Baltimore: Johns Hopkins University Press, 1948.

———. "Reflections on the History of Ideas." *JHI* 1 (1940): 3-23.

———. "The Historiography of Ideas." *PAPS* 78 (1938): 529-43.

———. *The Great Chain of Being: The Study of the History of an Idea.* Cambridge, Mass.: Harvard University Press, 1936.

Mandelbaum, Maurice. *Philosophy, History, and the Sciences: Selected Critical Essays.* Baltimore: Johns Hopkins University Press, 1984.

———. "The History of Philosophy: Some Methodological Issues." *JP* 74 (1977): 561-72.

———. "The History of Ideas, Intellectual History, and the History of Philosophy." *History and Theory* Beiheft 5 (1965): 33-66.

Murphey, Murray G. *Philosophical Foundations of Historical Knowledge.* Albany: State University of New York Press, 1994.

———. *Our Knowledge of the Historical Past.* Indianapolis: Bobbs-Merrill, 1973.

Pacchi, Arrigo. *Definizione e problemi della storia della filosofia.* Milano: UNICOPLI, 1985.

Pagden, Anthony. "Rethinking the Linguistic Turn: Current Anxieties in Intellectual History." *JHI* 49 (1988): 519-29.

Pearce, Roy Henry. "A Note on Method in the History of Ideas." *JHI* 9 (1948): 372-79.

Piovani, Pietro. *Filosofia e storia delle idee.* Bari: Laterza, 1965.

Randall, John Herman. "On Understanding the History of Philosophy." *JP* 36 (1939): 460-74.

Ricoeur, Paul. *La mémoire, l'histoire, l'oubli.* Paris: Seuil, 2000.

———. *The Reality of the Historical Past.* Milwaukee: Marquette University Press, 1984.

———. *Time and Narrative.* 3 vols. Chicago: University of Chicago Press, 1984-88.

———. *History and Truth.* Evanston: Northwestern University Press, 1965.

Robin, Léon et al. "Sur la notion d'histoire de la philosophie." *Bulletin de la Société française de la philosophie* 36 (1936): 103-406. Discussion by J. Baruzi, I. Lévy, L. Brunschvicg, P. Étard, J. Wahl, P. Ducassé, P. Schrecker, D. Parodi, H. Berr, and A. Koyré (106-40).

———. "L'histoire et la légende de la philosophie." *Revue philosophique de la France et de l'Étranger* 120 (1935): 161-75.

Rossi, Paolo. *Storia e filosofia: Saggi sulla storiografia filosofica.* Turin: G. Einaudi, 1969.

———. "La fallacia del 'superamento' come categoria storiografica." *RCSF* 11 (1956): 460-67.

———. "Sulla storiografia filosofica italiana." *RCSF* 11 (1956): 68-99.

——— and Carlo A. Viano. "Storia della filosofia e storia della cultura." *Rivista di filosofia* 46 (1955): 327-41.

Santinello, Giovanni, ed. *La storiografia filosofica e la sua storia.* Padova: Antenore, 1982.

Smart, Harold Robert. *Philosophy and Its History.* La Salle: Open Court, 1962.

Teggart, Frederick J. *Prolegomena to History: The Relation of History to Literature, Philosophy, and Science.* 1916; repr. New York: Arno, 1974.

Tocco, Felice. "Pensieri sulla storia della filosofia." *Giornale napoletano di filosofia e letteratura* 5 (1877): 1-15.

Toews, John E. "Intellectual History after the Linguistic Turn: The Autonomy of Meaning and the Irreducibility of Experience." *AHR* 92 (1987): 879-907.

Wiener, Philip P., ed. *Dictionary of the History of Ideas.* 5 vols. New York: Scribner, 1973-74.

———. "Some Problems and Methods in the History of Ideas." *JHI* 22 (1961): 531-48.

——— and Aaron Noland, eds. *Ideas in Cultural Perspective.* New Brunswick: Rutgers University Press, 1962.

Yolton, John W. "Some Remarks on the Historiography of Philosophy." *JHP* 23 (1985): 571-78.

B. History and Religion in Early Second Temple Judaism

Abel, F. M. *Histoire de la Palestine depuis la conquête d'Alexandre jusqu'à l'invasion arabe.* 1: *De la conquête d'Alexandre jusqu'à la guerre juive.* Paris: J. Gabalda, 1952.

Ackroyd, Peter R. *The Chronicler in His Age.* JSOTSup 101. Sheffield: JSOT, 1991.

———. *I & II Chronicles, Ezra, Nehemiah.* TBC. London: SCM, 1973.

———. *Israel under Babylon and Persia.* New Clarendon Bible, Old Testament 4. Oxford: Oxford University Press, 1970.

———. *Exile and Restoration: A Study of Hebrew Thought of the Sixth Century* B.C. OTL. Philadelphia: Westminster, 1968.

Albani, Matthias. *Astronomie und Schöpfungsglaube: Untersuchungen zum astronomischen Henochbuch.* WMANT 68. Neukirchen-Vluyn: Neukirchener, 1994.

Albertz, Rainer *A History of Israelite Religion in the Old Testament Period.* 2: *From the Exile to the Maccabees.* OTL. Louisville: Westminster John Knox, 1994.

Albright, William F. *From the Stone Age to Christianity: Monotheism and the Historical Process.* 2nd ed. Garden City: Doubleday, 1957.

Allegro, John M. *The Chosen People: A Study of Jewish History from the Time of the Exile until the Revolt of Bar Kocheba.* Garden City: Doubleday, 1972.

Anderson, Bernhard. *Understanding the Old Testament.* 4th ed. Englewood Cliffs: Prentice-Hall, 1986.

Anderson, Gary A., and Saul M. Olyan, eds. *Priesthood and Cult in Ancient Israel.* JSOTSup 125. Sheffield: JSOT, 1991.

Argall, Randal A. *1 Enoch and Sirach: A Comparative Literary and Conceptual Analysis of the Themes of Revelation, Creation, and Judgment.* Atlanta: Scholars, 1995.

Avigad, Naḥman. *Bullae and Seals from a Post-Exilic Judean Archive.* Jerusalem: Hebrew University, 1976.

Avi-Yonah, Michael, and Zvi Baras, eds. *The World History of the Jewish People.* 8: *Society and Religion in the Second Temple Period.* Jerusalem: Massada, 1977.

Barclay, John M. G. *Jews in the Mediterranean Diaspora: From Alexander to Trajan (323* B.C.E.*-117* C.E.*).* Edinburgh: T. & T. Clark, 1996.

Barker, Margaret. *The Great Angel: A Study of Israel's Second God.* Louisville: Westminster John Knox, 1992.

———. *The Lost Prophet: The Book of Enoch and Its Influence on Christianity.* Nashville: Abingdon, 1988.

———. *The Older Testament: The Survival of Themes from the Ancient Royal Cult in Sectarian Judaism and Early Christianity.* London: SPCK, 1987.

Baron, Salo Wittmayer. *A Social and Religious History of the Jews.* 2nd ed. 18 vols. New York: Columbia University Press, 1952-1993.

Barstad, Hans M. *The Myth of the Empty Land: A Study in the History and Archaeology of Judah during the 'Exilic' Period.* Oslo: Scandinavian University Press, 1996.

Bartlett, John R. *The Jews in the Hellenistic World.* Cambridge: Cambridge University Press, 1985.

Baumgarten, Albert I. *The Flourishing of Jewish Sects in the Maccabean Era: An Interpretation.* JSJSup 55. Leiden: Brill, 1997.

Becking, Bob, and Marjo C. A. Korpel, eds. *The Crisis of Israelite Religion: Transformation of Religious Tradition in Exilic and Post-Exilic Times.* OtSt 41. Leiden: Brill, 1999.

Bedenbender, Andreas. *Der Gott der Welt tritt auf den Sinai: Entstehung, Entwicklung und Funktionsweise der frühjüdischen Apokalyptik.* Berlin: Institut Kirche und Judentum, 2000.

Beek, Martinus A. *A Short History of Israel from Abraham to the Bar Cochba Rebellion.* New York: Harper, 1963.

Beentjes, Pancratius C., ed. *The Book of Ben Sira in Modern Research: Proceedings of the First International Ben Sira Conference, 28-31 July 1996, Soesterberg, Netherlands.* Berlin: Walter de Gruyter, 1997.

Berquist, Jon L. *Judaism in Persia's Shadow: A Social and Historical Approach.* Minneapolis: Fortress, 1995.

Betlyon, John Wilson. "The Provincial Government of Persian Period Judea and the Yehud Coins." *JBL* 105 (1986): 633-42.

Bevan, Edwyn R. *Jerusalem under the High-Priests: Five Lectures on the Period between Nehemiah and the New Testament.* London: Arnold, 1904.

Bianchi, Francesco. "Zorobabele, re di Giuda." *Hen* 13 (1991): 133-50.

Bianchi-Giovini, Aurelio A. *Storia degli ebrei e delle loro sette e dottrine religiose durante il secondo tempio.* Milan, 1844.

Bickerman, Elias J. *The God of the Maccabees: Studies on the Meaning and Origin of the Maccabean Revolt.* SJLA 32. Leiden: Brill, 1979.

———. *From Ezra to the Last of the Maccabees: Foundations of Post-Biblical Judaism.* New York: Schocken, 1967.

Blenkinsopp, Joseph. "The Judaean Priesthood during the Neo-Babylonian and Achaemenid Periods: A Hypothetical Reconstruction." *CBQ* 60 (1998): 25-43.

———. *Sage, Priest, Prophet: Religious and Intellectual Leadership in Ancient Israel.* Louisville: Westminster John Knox, 1995.

———. "Temple and Society in Achaemenid Judah." In Philip R. Davies, ed., *Second Temple Studies,* 1:22-53.

Boccaccini, Gabriele. "The Solar Calendars of Daniel and Enoch." In *The Book of Dan-*

iel: Composition and Reception, ed. John J. Collins and Peter W. Flint. Leiden: Brill, 2001, 2:311-28.
———. "The Origins of Qumran in Light of the Enoch Groups." In *The Hebrew Bible and Qumran*, ed. James H. Charlesworth. N. Richland Hills: Bibal Press, 2000, 63-92.
———. "Esiste una letteratura farisaica del secondo tempio?" *RSB* 11/2 (1999): 23-41.
———. *Beyond the Essene Hypothesis: The Parting of the Ways between Qumran and Enochic Judaism*. Grand Rapids: Wm. B. Eerdmans, 1998.
———. "Middle Judaism and Its Contemporary Interpreters (1993-1997): What Makes Any Judaism a Judaism?" *Hen* 20 (1998): 349-56.
———. "E se l'essenismo fosse il movimento enochiano? Una nuova ipotesi circa il rapporto tra Qumran e gli esseni." *RSB* 9/2 (1997): 49-67.
———. "Il Dio unico, Padre e Creatore, nel giudaismo di età ellenistico-romana." *DSBP* 13 (1996): 102-21.
———. "Dallo straniero come categoria sociale allo straniero come problema religioso: alle radici dell'universalismo cristiano e rabbinico." *RSB* 8/1-2 (1996): 163-72.
———. "The Preexistence of the Torah: A Commonplace in Second Temple Judaism, or a Later Rabbinic Development?" *Hen* 17 (1995): 329-50.
———. "Multiple Judaisms." *BRev* 11/1 (1995): 38-41, 46.
———. "History of Judaism: Its Periods in Antiquity." In *Judaism in Late Antiquity*, ed. Jacob Neusner, 2:285-308.
———. "Testi apocalittici coevi all'Apocalisse di Giovanni." *RSB* 7/2 (1995): 151-61.
———. "Middle Judaism and Its Contemporary Interpreters (1986-1992): Methodological Foundations for the Study of Judaisms, 300 BCE to 200 CE." *Hen* 15 (1993): 207-33.
———. "Targum Neofiti as a Proto-Rabbinic Document: A Systemic Analysis." In *The Aramaic Bible: Targums in Their Historical Context*, ed. D. R. G. Beattie and Martin McNamara. Proceedings of the Dublin Conference in Targumic Studies, Held at the Irish National Academy (Dublin, July 1992). Sheffield: JSOT, 1994, 254-63.
———. *Portraits of Middle Judaism in Scholarship and Arts: A Multimedia Catalog from Flavius Josephus to 1991*. Turin: Zamorani, 1992.
———. *Middle Judaism: Jewish Thought, 300 B.C.E. to 200 C.E.* Minneapolis: Fortress, 1991.
———. "Jewish Apocalyptic Tradition: The Contribution of Italian Scholarship." In *Mysteries and Revelations: Apocalyptic Studies since the Uppsala Colloquium*, ed. John J. Collins and James H. Charlesworth. JSPSup 9. Sheffield: JSOT, 1991, 33-50.
———. "É Daniele un testo apocalittico? Una (ri)definizione del Libro di Daniele in rapporto al Libro dei Sogni e all'apocalittica." *Hen* 9 (1987): 267-302.
———. "Origine del male, libertà dell'uomo e retribuzione nella Sapienza di Ben Sira." *Hen* 8 (1986): 1-37.
———. "Il tema della memoria nell'ebraismo e nel giudaismo antico." *Hen* 7 (1985): 1-26.

Bohlen, Reinhold. *Die Ehrung der Eltern bei Ben Sira: Studien zur Motivation und Interpretation eines familien-ethischen Grundwertes in frühhellenistischer Zeit.* TThS 51. Trier: Paulinus, 1991.

Bolin, Thomas M. *Freedom Beyond Forgiveness: The Book of Jonah Re-Examined.* JSOTSup 236. Sheffield: JSOT, 1997.

Bonsirven, Joseph S. *Palestinian Judaism in the Time of Jesus Christ.* New York: Holt, Rinehalt and Winston, 1964.

Booth, Henry Kendall. *The Bridge Between the Testaments: A Survey of the Life and Literature of the Period of the Connections.* New York: Scribner's, 1929.

Bousset, Wilhelm. *Die Religion des Judentums im späthellenistichen Zeitalter.* Ed. Hugo Gressmann. Tübingen: Mohr, 1926.

———. *Die Religion des Judentums im neutestamentlichen Zeitalter.* 2nd ed. Berlin: Reuther & Reichard, 1906.

Bright, John. *A History of Israel.* 3rd ed. Philadelphia: Westminster, 1981.

Charles, R. H. *Religious Development between the Old and the New Testament.* London: Williams and Norgate, 1914.

———, ed. *The Apocrypha and Pseudepigrapha of the Old Testament.* 2 vols. Oxford: Clarendon, 1913.

Charlesworth, James H., ed. *The Old Testament Pseudepigrapha.* 2 vols. Garden City: Doubleday, 1983-85.

Cody, Aelred. *A History of the Old Testament Priesthood.* AnBib 35. Rome: Pontifical Biblical Institute, 1969.

Cohen, Shaye J. D. *The Beginnings of Jewishness: Boundaries, Varieties, Uncertainties.* Berkeley: University of California Press, 1999.

———. *From the Maccabees to the Mishnah.* Philadelphia: Westminster, 1987.

———. "The Significance of Yavneh: Pharisees, Rabbis, and the End of Jewish Sectarianism." *HUCA* 55 (1984): 27-53.

Collins, John J. *Between Athens and Jerusalem: Jewish Identity in the Hellenistic Diaspora.* 2nd ed. Grand Rapids: Wm. B. Eerdmans, 2000.

———. *The Apocalyptic Imagination: An Introduction to Jewish Apocalyptic Literature.* 2nd ed. Grand Rapids: Wm. B. Eerdmans, 1998.

———. *Apocalypticism in the Dead Sea Scrolls.* London: Routledge, 1997.

———. *Jewish Wisdom in the Hellenistic Age.* OTL. Louisville: Westminster John Knox, 1997.

———. *Seers, Sybils and Sages in Hellenistic-Roman Judaism.* JSJSup 54. Leiden: Brill, 1997.

———. *Daniel.* Herm. Minneapolis: Fortress, 1993.

———. *Daniel; with an Introduction to Apocalyptic Literature.* FOTL 20. Grand Rapids: Wm. B. Eerdmans, 1984.

———. *The Apocalyptic Vision of the Book of Daniel.* HSM 16. Missoula: Scholars, 1977.

Cook, Stephen L. *Prophecy and Apocalypticism: The Postexilic Social Setting.* Minneapolis: Fortress, 1995.

Crenshaw, James L. *Education in Ancient Israel: Across the Deadening Silence.* New York: Doubleday, 1998.

———. *Urgent Advice and Probing Questions: Collected Writings on Old Testament Wisdom.* Macon: Mercer University Press, 1995.

———. *Old Testament Wisdom: An Introduction.* Atlanta: John Knox, 1981.

———, ed. *Studies in Ancient Israelite Wisdom.* New York: Ktav, 1976.

Cross, Frank Moore. "A Reconstruction of the Judean Restoration." *JBL* 94 (1975): 4-18.

Davies, Philip R. *In Search of "Ancient Israel."* JSOTSup 248. Sheffield: JSOT, 1992.

———, ed. *Second Temple Studies.* 1: *The Persian Period.* JSOTSup 117. Sheffield: JSOT, 1991.

Davies, William D., and Louis Finkelstein, eds. *The Cambridge History of Judaism.* 1: *Introduction, The Persian Period.* Cambridge: Cambridge University Press, 1984.

———. 2: *The Hellenistic Age.* Cambridge: Cambridge University Press, 1989.

Davis, Moshe, ed. *Israel: Its Role in Civilization.* 1956; repr. New York: Arno, 1977.

Day, John, Robert P. Gordon, and H. G. M. Williamson, eds. *Wisdom in Ancient Israel.* Cambridge: Cambridge University Press, 1995.

Day, Peggy L. *An Adversary in Heaven:* sāṭān *in the Hebrew Bible.* HSM 43. Atlanta: Scholars, 1988.

Delcor, Matthias. "Le mythe de la chute des anges et de l'origine des géants comme explication du mal dans le monde dans l'apocalyptique juive: Histoire des traditions." *RHR* 190 (1976): 3-53.

Dimant, Devorah. "The Seventy Weeks Chronology (Dan 9,24-27) in the Light of New Qumranic Texts." In *The Book of Daniel,* ed. A. S. van der Woude. BETL 106. Leuven: Leuven University Press, 1993, 57-76.

———. "The Biography of Enoch and the Books of Enoch." *VT* 33 (1983): 14-29.

Dubnow, Simon. *History of the Jews.* 5 vols. South Brunswick: T. Yoseloff, 1967-1973.

Duguid, Iain M. *Ezekiel and the Leaders of Israel.* VTSup 56. Leiden: Brill, 1994.

Dyck, Jonathan E. *The Theocratic Ideology of the Chronicler.* Leiden: Brill, 1998.

Eddy, Samuel Kennedy. *The King Is Dead: Studies in the New Eastern Resistance to Hellenism, 334-31 B.C.* Lincoln: University of Nebraska Press, 1961.

Edelman, Diana Vikander. ed. *The Triumph of Elohim: From Yahwisms to Judaisms.* Grand Rapids: Wm. B. Eerdmans, 1995.

Eissfeldt, Otto. *The Old Testament: An Introduction.* New York: Harper & Row, 1965.

Elliott, Mark A. *The Survivors of Israel: A Reconsideration of the Theology of Pre-Christian Judaism.* Grand Rapids: Wm. B. Eerdmans, 2000.

Eskenazi, Tamara Cohn, and Kent Harold Richards, eds. *Second Temple Studies.* 2: *Temple and Community in the Persian Period.* JSOTSup 175. Sheffield: JSOT, 1994.

Fairweather, William. *The Background of the Gospels: Judaism in the Period between the Old and the New Testament.* 4th ed. Edinburgh: T. & T. Clark, 1926.

———. *From the Exile to the Advent.* Edinburgh: T. & T. Clark, 1895.

Feldman, Louis H. *Jew and Gentile in the Ancient World: Attitudes and Interactions from Alexander to Justinian.* Princeton: Princeton University Press, 1993.

Finkelstein, Louis. *Pharisaism in the Making: Selected Essays.* New York: Ktav, 1972.

Fretheim, Terence E. *The Message of Jonah: A Theological Commentary.* Minneapolis: Augsburg, 1977.

Galling, Kurt. *Studien zur Geschichte Israels im persischen Zeitalter.* Tübingen: Mohr, 1964.

Ganz, Timothy. *Early Greek Myth: A Guide to Literary and Artistic Sources.* Baltimore: John Hopkins University Press, 1993, 44-56.

Garbini, Giovanni. *History and Ideology in Ancient Israel.* New York: Crossroad, 1988.

García Martínez, Florentino. *Qumran and Apocalyptic: Studies on the Aramaic Texts from Qumran.* STDJ 9. Leiden: Brill, 1992.

Gera, Dov. *Judaea and Mediterranean Politics, 219 to 161* B.C.E. Leiden: Brill, 1998.

Gottwald, Norman K. *The Hebrew Bible: A Socio-Literary Introduction.* Philadelphia: Fortress, 1985.

Gowan, Donald E. *Bridge between the Testaments: A Reappraisal of Judaism from the Exile to the Birth of Christianity.* 3rd ed. Allison Park, Pa.: Pickwick, 1986.

Grabbe, Lester L. *Ezra-Nehemiah.* London: Routledge, 1998.

———. *Priests, Prophets, Diviners, Sages: A Socio-Historical Study of Religious Specialists in Ancient Israel.* Valley Forge: Trinity, 1995.

———. *Judaism from Cyrus to Hadrian.* 2 vols. Minneapolis: Fortress, 1992.

Graetz, Heinrich H. *History of the Jews.* 6 vols. Philadelphia: Jewish Publication Society of America, 1891-98.

Grant, Charles M. *Between the Testaments: A Study of the Four Hundred Years Separating the Old and New Testament.* New York: Revell, 1905.

Grelot, Pierre. "La légende d'Hénoch dans les apocryphes et dans la Bible: origine et signification." *RSR* 46 (1958): 5-26, 181-210.

Gruen, Erich S. *Heritage and Hellenism: The Reinvention of Jewish Tradition.* Berkeley: University of California Press, 1998.

Gruenwald, Ithamar. *From Apocalypticism to Gnosticism.* BEATAJ 14. Frankfurt: P. Lang, 1988.

———. *Apocalyptic and Merkavah Mysticism.* AGJU 14. Leiden: Brill, 1980.

Guttmann, Alexander. *Rabbinic Judaism in the Making: A Chapter in the History of the Halakhah from Ezra to Judah I.* Detroit: Wayne State University Press, 1970.

Hadas, Moses. *Hellenistic Culture: Fusion and Diffusion.* New York: Norton, 1972.

Hanson, Paul D. "Rebellion in Heaven, Azazel, and Euhemeristic Heroes in 1 Enoch 6–11." *JBL* 96 (1977): 195-233.

———. *The Dawn of Apocalyptic: The Historical and Sociological Roots of Jewish Apocalyptic Eschatology.* Rev. ed. Philadelphia: Fortress, 1979.

Harrington, Daniel J. *The Maccabean Revolt: Anatomy of a Biblical Revolution.* Wilmington: Michael Glazier, 1988.

Hayes, John H., and Sara R. Mandell. *The Jewish People in Classical Antiquity: From Alexander to Bar Kochba.* Louisville: Westminster John Knox, 1998.

Hayes, John H., and J. Maxwell Miller, eds. *Israelite and Judaean History.* Philadelphia: Westminster, 1977.

Hellholm, David, ed. *Apocalypticism in the Mediterranean World and the Near East.* Tübingen: Mohr, 1983.

Hengel, Martin. *Judaism and Hellenism: Studies in Their Encounter in Palestine during the Early Hellenistic Period.* 2 vols. Philadelphia: Fortress, 1974.

Himmelfarb, Martha. *Ascent to Heaven in Jewish and Christian Apocalypses.* New York: Oxford University Press, 1993.

———. *Tours of Hell: An Apocalyptic Form in Jewish and Christian Literature.* Philadelphia: Fortress, 1985.

Hoffmann, Heinrich. *Das Gesetz in der frühjüdischen Apokalyptik.* SUNT 23. Göttingen: Vanderhoeck & Ruprecht, 1999.

Hoglund, Kenneth G. *Achaemenid Imperial Administration in Syria-Palestine and the Missions of Ezra and Nehemiah.* SBLDS 125. Atlanta: Scholars, 1992.

Jaffee, Martin S. *Early Judaism.* Upper Saddle River, N.J.: Prentice-Hall, 1997.

Jagersma, Henk. *A History of Israel from Alexander the Great to Bar Kochba.* Philadelphia: Fortrress, 1985.

Jenson, Philip Peter. *Graded Holiness: A Key to the Priestly Conception of the World.* JSOTSup 106. Sheffield: Sheffield Academic, 1992.

Jeremias, Joachim. *Jerusalem in the time of Jesus: An Investigation into Economic and Social Conditions during the New Testament Period.* Philadelphia: Fortress, 1969.

Johnson, A. R. *Sacral Kingship in Ancient Israel.* 2nd ed. Cardiff: University of Wales Press, 1967.

Kelly, Brian E. *Retribution and Eschatology in Chronicles.* JSOTSup 211. Sheffield: Sheffield Academic, 1996.

Kent, Charles F. *The Makers and Teachers of Judaism from the Fall of Jerusalem to the Death of Herod the Great.* New York: Scribner's, 1911.

Klausner, Joseph G. *Bi-yeme bayit sheni.* Berlin: Aayanut, 1923.

Klein, Ralph W. *Israel in Exile: A Theological Interpretation.* OBT. Philadelphia: Fortress, 1979.

Knibb, Michael A. "The Exile in the Literature of the Intertestamental Period." *HeyJ* 17 (1976): 253-72.

Koch, Klaus. *The Rediscovery of Apocalyptic: A Polemical Work on a Neglected Area of Biblical Studies and Its Damaging Effects on Theology and Philosophy.* SBT, 2nd series, 22. Naperville: Allenson, 1972.

Kraft, Robert A., and George W. E. Nickelsburg, eds. *Early Judaism and Its Modern Interpreters.* Atlanta: Scholars, 1986.

Kugler, Robert A. *From Patriarch to Priest: The Levi-Priestly Tradition from Aramaic Levi to Testament of Levi.* Atlanta: Scholars, 1996.

Kvangig, Helge S. *Roots of Apocalyptic: The Mesopotamian Background of the Enoch Figure and of the Son of Man.* WMANT 61. Neukirchen-Vluyn: Neukirchener, 1988.

Lacocque, André. *Daniel in His Time.* Columbia: University of South Carolina Press, 1988.

———. *The Book of Daniel.* Atlanta: John Knox, 1979.

Laperrousaz, Ernst-Marie, and André Lemaire, eds. *La Palestine à l'époque perse.* Paris: Editions du Cerf, 1994.

Levenson, Jon D. *Theology of the Program of Restoration of Ezekiel 40–48.* HSM 10. Missoula: Scholars, 1976.

Liberman, Saul. *Hellenism in Jewish Palestine.* New York: Jewish Theological Seminary of America, 1950.

———. *Greek in Jewish Palestine.* New York: Jewish Theological Seminary of America, 1942.

McCullough, W. Stewart. *The History and Literature of the Palestinian Jews from Cyrus to Herod, 550 B.C. to 4 B.C.* Toronto: University of Toronto Press, 1975.

Maier, Johann. *Zwischen den Testamenten: Geschichte und Religion in der Zeit des zweiten Tempels.* Munich: Echter, 1990.

Martin, Luther H. *Hellenistic Religions: An Introduction.* Oxford: Oxford University Press, 1987.

Mendels, Doran. *The Rise and Fall of Jewish Nationalism.* 1992; repr. Grand Rapids: Wm. B. Eerdmans, 1997.

Middendorp, Theophil. *Die Stellung Jesu ben Sira zwischen Judentum und Hellenismus.* Leiden: Brill, 1973.

Milik, Josef T. *The Books of Enoch: Aramaic Fragments of Qumran Cave 4.* Oxford: Clarendon, 1976.

Molenberg, C. "A Study of the Role of Shemihaza and Asael in I Enoch 6–11." *JJS* 35 (1984): 136-46.

Momigliano, Arnaldo. *Alien Wisdom: The Limits of Hellenization.* Cambridge: Cambridge University Press, 1975.

Moore, Carey A. *Tobit.* AB 40A. New York: Doubleday, 1996.

Moore, George Foot. *Judaism in the First Centuries of the Christian Era: The Age of the Tannaim.* 3 vols. Cambridge, Mass.: Harvard University Press, 1927-1930.

Murphy, Frederick J. *The Religious World of Jesus: An Introduction to Second Temple Palestinian Judaism.* Nashville: Abingdon, 1991.

Murphy, Roland E. *The Tree of Life: An Exploration of Biblical Wisdom Literature.* 2nd ed. Grand Rapids: Wm. B. Eerdmans, 1996.

———. "Introduction to Wisdom Literature." In *The New Jerome Biblical Commentary,* ed. Raymond E. Brown, Joseph A. Fitzmyer, and Murphy. Englewood Cliffs: Prentice-Hall, 1990, 447-52.

———. *Wisdom Literature.* FOTL 13. Grand Rapids: Wm. B. Eerdmans, 1981.

———. *Introduction to the Wisdom Literature of the Old Testament.* Collegeville: Liturgical, 1965.

Neusner, Jacob. *The Four Stages of Rabbinic Judaism.* London: Routledge, 1999.

———, ed. *Judaism in Late Antiquity.* 4 vols. Leiden: Brill, 1995.

———. *The Judaism the Rabbis Take for Granted.* Atlanta: Scholars, 1994.

———. *Studying Classical Judaism: A Primer.* Louisville: Westminster John Knox, 1991.

———. *Wrong Ways and Right Ways in the Study of Formative Judaism: Critical Method and Literature, History, and the History of Religion.* BJS 145. Atlanta: Scholars, 1988.

———. *The Systemic Analysis of Religion.* BJS 137. Atlanta: Scholars, 1988.

———. *From Politics to Piety: The Emergence of Rabbinic Judaism.* 2nd ed. New York: Ktav, 1979.

———. *The Idea of Purity in Ancient Judaism.* Leiden: Brill, 1973.

Newsome, James D. *By the Waters of Babylon: An Introduction to the History and Theology of the Exile.* Atlanta: John Knox, 1979.

Nickelsburg, George W. E. "Enoch, First Book of." *ABD* 2 (1992): 508-16.

———. *Jewish Literature between the Bible and the Mishnah: A Historical and Literary Introduction.* Philadelphia: Fortress, 1981.

———. "Enoch, Levi, and Peter: Recipients of Revelation in Upper Galilee." *JBL* 100 (1981): 575-600.

———. "Apocalyptic and Myth in 1 Enoch 6–11." *JBL* 96 (1977): 383-405.

———. *Resurrection, Immortality and Eternal Life in Intertestamental Judaism.* HSM 26. Cambridge: Harvard University Press, 1972.

Nodet, Eugene. *A Search for the Origins of Judaism: From Joshua to the Mishnah.* JSOTSup 248. Sheffield: Sheffield Academic, 1997.

Noth, Martin. *The History of Israel.* 2nd ed. New York: Harper & Row, 1960.

Olyan, Saul M. "Ben Sira's Relationship to the Priesthood." *HTR* 80 (1987): 261-86.

Peters, Francis E. *The Harvest of Hellenism: A History of the Near East from Alexander the Great to the Triumph of Christianity.* New York: Simon and Schuster, 1970.

Peterson, David L. *Haggai and Zechariah 1–8.* OTL. Philadelphia: Westminster, 1984.

Pfeiffer, Robert H. *A History of New Testament Times with an Introduction to the Apocrypha.* New York: Harper, 1949.

Pomykala, Kenneth E. *The Davidic Dynasty Tradition in Early Judaism: Its History and Significance for Messianism.* Atlanta: Scholars, 1995.

Porten, Bezalel. *Archives from Elephantine: The Life of an Ancient Jewish Military Colony.* Berkeley: University of California Press, 1968.

Prato, Gian Luigi. *Il problema della teodicea in Ben Sira.* AnBib 65. Rome: Biblical Institute, 1975.

Prideaux, Humphrey. *The Old and New Testament Connected in the History of the Jews, and Neighbouring Nations; from the Declension of the Kingdoms of Israel and Judah to the Time of Christ.* 2 vols. London: R. Knaplock & Tonson, 1716-18.

von Rad, Gerhard. *Wisdom in Israel.* Nashville: Abingdon, 1972.

———. *Old Testament Theology.* 2 vols. New York: Harper, 1962-65.

Raphall, Morris J. *Post-Biblical History of the Jews, from the Close of the Old Testament, about the Year 420 B.C.E., till the Destruction of the Second Temple in the Year 70 C.E.* Philadelphia: Moss and Brother, 1855.

Reicke, Bo. *The New Testament Era: The World of the Bible from 500 B.C.* TO A.D. 100. Philadelphia: Fortress, 1968.

Reid, Stephen Breck. *Enoch and Daniel: A Form Critical and Sociological Study of Historical Apocalypses.* Berkeley: BIBAL, 1989.

Rémond, Johannes. *Versuch einer Geschichte der Ausbreitung des Judenthums von Cyrus bis auf den gänzlichen Untergang des jüdischen Staats.* Leipzig, 1789.

Renan, Ernest. *History of the People of Israel.* 5 vols. Boston: Roberts Brothers, 1888-1896.

Ricciotti, Giuseppe. *The History of Israel.* 2 vols. Milwaukee: Bruce, 1958.

Riley, William. *King and Cultus in Chronicles: Worship and the Reinterpretation of History.* JSOTSup 160. Sheffield: JSOT, 1993.

Rivkin, Ellis. *A Hidden Revolution: The Pharisees' Search for the Kingdom Within.* Nashville: Abingdon, 1978.

———. *The Shaping of Jewish History: A Radical New Interpretation.* New York: Scribner, 1971.

Rosso-Ubigli, Liliana. "La fortuna di Enoc nel giudaismo antico: valenze e problemi." *ASE* 1 (1984): 153-63.

———. "Qohelet di fronte all'apocalitica." *Hen* 5 (1983): 31-58.

Rowland, Christopher. *The Open Heaven: A Study of Apocalyptic in Judaism and Christianity.* New York: Crossroad, 1982.

Russell, D. S. *The Method and Message of Jewish Apocalyptic, 200 BC–AD 100.* OTL. Philadelphia: Westminster, 1964.

———. *Between the Testaments.* Philadelphia: Muhlenberg, 1960.

Sacchi, Paolo. *The History of the Second Temple Period.* JSOTSup 285. Sheffield: Sheffield Academic, 2000.

———. *Jewish Apocalyptic and Its History.* JSPSup 20. Sheffield: Sheffield Academic, 1990.

———. *L'apocalittica giudaica e la sua storia.* Brescia: Paideia, 1990.

———. "Giobbe e il Patto (Giobbe 9,32-33)." *Hen* 4 (1982): 175-84.

———, ed. *Apocrifi dell'Antico Testamento.* 5 vols. Turin: UTET, 1981-89; Brescia: Paideia, 1987-2000.

———. *Storia del mondo giudaico.* Turin: SEI, 1976.

———. *Ecclesiaste.* Rome: Paoline, 1971.

Sanders, E. P. *Judaism: Practice and Belief, 63 B.C.E.–66 C.E.* Philadelphia: Trinity, 1992.

———. *Jewish Law from Jesus to the Mishnah.* Philadelphia: Trinity, 1990.

———. *Jesus and Judaism.* Philadelphia: Fortress, 1985.

———. *Paul and Palestinian Judaism.* Philadelphia: Fortress, 1977.

Sanders, Jack T. *Ben Sira and Demotic Wisdom.* SBLMS 28. Chico: Scholars, 1983.

Schäfer, Peter. *The History of the Jews in Antiquity: The Jews of Palestine from Alexander the Great to the Arab Conquest.* Australia: Harwood Academic, 1995.

Schiffman, Lawrence H. *Texts and Traditions: A Source Reader for the Study of Second Temple and Rabbinic Judaism.* Hoboken: Ktav, 1998.

———. *From Text to Tradition: A History of Second Temple and Rabbinic Judaism.* Hoboken: Ktav, 1991.

Schnabel, Eckhard J. *Law and Wisdom from Ben Sira to Paul.* WUNT, 2/16. Tübingen: Mohr, 1985.

Schürer, Emil. *The History of the Jewish People in the Age of Jesus Christ (175 B.C.–A.D.*

135). Ed. Geza Vermes and Fergus Millar. 3 vols. Edinburgh: T. & T. Clark, 1973-1987.

———. *A History of the Jewish People in the Time of Jesus Christ.* 5 vols. Edinburgh: T. & T. Clark, 1885-1890.

———. *Lehrbuch des Neutestamentlichen Zeitgeschichte.* Leipzig: J. C. Hinrichs, 1874.

Shanks, Hershel, ed. *Ancient Israel: From Abraham to the Roman Destruction of the Temple.* Rev. ed. Washington: Biblical Archaeological Society, 1999.

———, ed. *Ancient Israel: A Short History from Abraham to the Roman Destruction of the Temple.* Washington: Biblical Archaeological Society, 1988.

Sievers, Joseph. *The Hasmoneans and Their Supporters: From Mattathias to the Death of John Hyrcanus I.* Atlanta: Scholars, 1990.

Skehan, Patrick W., and Alexander A. Di Lella. *The Wisdom of Ben Sira.* AB 39. Garden City: Doubleday, 1987.

Smith, Jonathan Z. "Wisdom and Apocalyptic." In *Religious Syncretism in Antiquity,* ed. Birger A. Pearson. Missoula: Scholars, 1975, 131-56.

Smith, Morton. *Palestinian Parties and Politics That Shaped the Old Testament.* New York: Columbia University Press, 1971.

Snaith, John G. *Ecclesiasticus, or the Wisdom of Jesus Son of Sirach.* Cambridge Bible Commentary. Cambridge: Cambridge University Press, 1974.

Soggin, J. Alberto. *An Introduction to the History of Israel and Judah.* 2nd ed. Valley Forge: Trinity, 1993.

Stade, Bernhard, ed. *Geschichte des Volkes Israel.* 2 vols. Berlin: G. Grote, 1887-88.

Stadelmann, Helga. *Ben Sira als Schriftgelehrter.* WUNT 6. Tübingen: Mohr, 1980.

Stone, Michael E. "Enoch, Aramaic Levi and Sectarian Origins." *JSJ* 19 (1988): 159-70.

——— and David Satran, eds. *Emerging Judaism: Studies on the Fourth & Third Centuries* B.C.E. Philadelphia: Fortress, 1988.

———, ed. *Jewish Writings of the Second Temple Period.* CRINT 2/2. Philadelphia: Fortress, 1984.

———. *Scriptures, Sects and Visions: A Profile of Judaism from Ezra to the Jewish Revolt.* Philadelphia: Fortress, 1980.

———. "The Book of Enoch and Judaism in the Third Century B.C.E." *CBQ* 40 (1978): 479-92.

Suter, David W. "Fallen Angel, Fallen Priest: The Problem of Family Purity in 1 Enoch 6–16." *HUCA* 50 (1979): 115-35.

Tcherikover, Victor. *Hellenistic Civilization and the Jews.* 1959; repr. Peabody: Hendrickson, 1999.

Tigchelaar, Eibert J. C. *Prophets of Old and the Day of the End: Zechariah, the Book of the Watchers, and Apocalyptic.* OtSt 35. Leiden: Brill, 1996.

Tiller, Patrick A. *A Commentary on the Animal Apocalypse of 1 Enoch.* Atlanta: Scholars, 1993.

Toy, Crawford H. *Judaism and Christianity: A Sketch of the Progress of Thought from Old Testament to New Testament.* Boston: Little & Brown, 1891.

VanderKam, James C. *From Revelation to Canon: Studies in the Hebrew Bible and Second Temple Literature.* JSJSup 62. Leiden: Brill, 2000.

———. *Calendars in the Dead Sea Scrolls: Measuring Time.* London: Routledge, 1998.

———. *Enoch, A Man for All Generations.* Columbia: University of South Carolina Press, 1995.

———. *Enoch and the Growth of an Apocalyptic Tradition.* CBQMS 16. Washington: Catholic Biblical Association of America, 1984.

de Vaux, Roland. *Ancient Israel: Its Life and Institutions.* 1965; repr. Grand Rapids: Wm. B. Eerdmans, 1997.

Vawter, Bruce. *Job and Jonah: Questioning the Hidden God.* New York: Paulist, 1983.

Weingreen, Jacob. *From Bible to Mishna: The Continuity of Tradition.* New York: Holmes & Meier, 1976.

Wellhausen, Julius. *Prolegomena to the History of Ancient Israel.* 1885; repr. Atlanta: Scholars, 1994.

Williamson, H. G. M. *Ezra and Nehemiah.* Sheffield: JSOT, 1987.

Wills, Lawrence M. *The Jew in the Court of the Foreign King: Ancient Jewish Court Legends.* HDR 26. Minneapolis: Fortress, 1990.

Wise, Isaac M. *History of the Hebrews' Second Commonwealth with Special Reference to Its Literature, Culture, and the Origin of Rabbinism and Christianity.* Cincinnati: Bloch & Co., 1880.

Wright, Benjamin G., III. "Fear the Lord and Honor the Priest: Ben Sira as Defender of the Jerusalem Priesthood." In *The Book of Ben Sira in Modern Research,* ed. Pancratius C. Beentjes, 189-222.

Zadok, Ron. *The Jews in Babylonia during the Chaldean and Achaemenian Periods according to the Babylonian Sources.* Haifa: University of Haifa Press, 1979.

Zeitlin, Solomon. *The Rise and Fall of the Judaean State: A Political, Social, and Religious History of the Second Commonwealth.* 3 vols. Philadelphia: Jewish Publication Society of America, 1962-1978.

———. *The History of the Second Jewish Commonwealth: Prolegomenon.* Philadelphia: Jewish Publication Society of America, 1933.

INDEX